Street by Stree

CW00349298

WIGAN
ASHTON-IN-MAKERFIELD,
LEIGH, SKELMERSDALE
Abram, Aspull, Atherton, Billinge, Golborne, Hindley, Ince-in-Makerfield, Orrell, Rainford, Standish, Tyldesley, Westhoughton

2nd edition June 2005
© Automobile Association Developments Limited 2005

Original edition printed May 2002

Ordnance Survey® This product includes map data licensed from Ordnance Survey® with the permission of the Controller of Her Majesty's Stationery Office. © Crown copyright 2005. All rights reserved. Licence number 399221.

Published by AA Publishing, a trading name of Automobile Association Developments Limited, whose registered office (from 1st October 2005) will be Fanum House, Basing View, Basingstoke, Hampshire RG21 4EA.
Registered number 1878835.

Mapping produced by the Cartography Department of The Automobile Association. (A02417)

A CIP Catalogue record for this book is available from the British Library.

Printed by Oriental Press in Dubai

The contents of this atlas are believed to be correct at the time of the latest revision. However, the publishers cannot be held responsible or liable for any loss or damage occasioned to any person acting or refraining from action as a result of any use or reliance on any material in this atlas, nor for any errors, omissions or changes in such material. This does not affect your statutory rights. The publishers would welcome information to correct any errors or omissions and to keep this atlas up to date. Please write to Publishing, The Automobile Association, Fanum House (FH17), Basing View, Basingstoke, Hampshire, RG21 4EA.

Ref: ML201z

Key to map pages	ii-iii
Key to map symbols	iv-1
Enlarged map pages	2-3
Main map pages	4-77
Index – towns & villages	78
Index – streets	79-91
Index – featured places	91-93
Acknowledgements	93

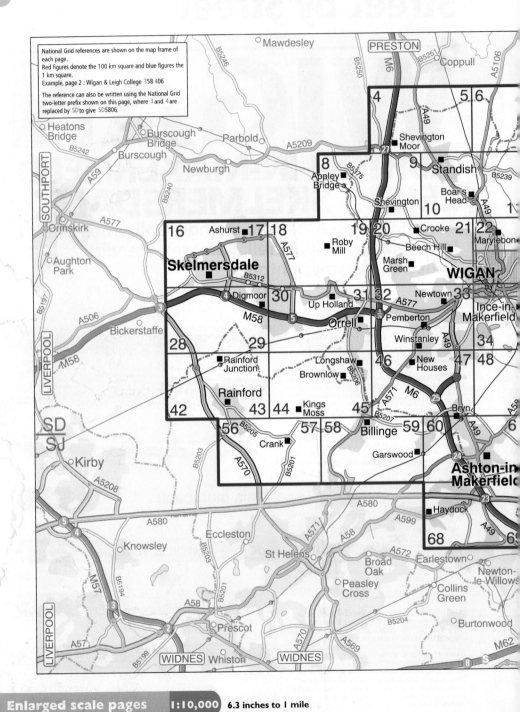

ii

National Grid references are shown on the map frame of each page.
Red figures denote the 100 km square and blue figures the 1 km square.
Example, page 2 : Wigan & Leigh College 358 406

The reference can also be written using the National Grid two-letter prefix shown on this page, where 3 and 4 are replaced by SD to give SD5806.

Mawdesley

PRESTON
Coppull

Heatons Bridge
Burscough Bridge
Burscough
Parbold
Newburgh

SOUTHPORT

Shevington Moor

Appley Bridge
Shevington
Standish
Boar's Head
10

Ormskirk

Aughton Park

16   Ashurst 17 18
Skelmersdale

Roby Mill
Crooke
Beech Hill
Marsh Green

19 20 21 22
Marylebon

WIGAN

Bickerstaffe

Digmoor 30
M58

Up Holland
Orrell
31 32 Newtown 33
Pemberton
Winstanley

Ince-in-Makerfield

34

LIVERPOOL

28   29
Rainford Junction
Longshaw
Brownlow
46   New Houses
47 48

Rainford
42   43 44 Kings Moss
45
Billinge 59 60
Bryn

SD
SJ

Kirby
56   Crank 57 58
Garswood
Ashton-in Makerfield

Knowsley
Eccleston
Haydock
68   69

LIVERPOOL

A580
St Helens
Broad Oak
Peasley Cross
Collins Green
Earlestown
Newton-le-Willows
Burtonwood

Prescot
WIDNES Whiston
WIDNES

Enlarged scale pages   1:10,000   6.3 inches to 1 mile

0 — 1/4 — miles — 1/2
0 — 1/4 — 1/2 — kilometres — 3/4 — 1

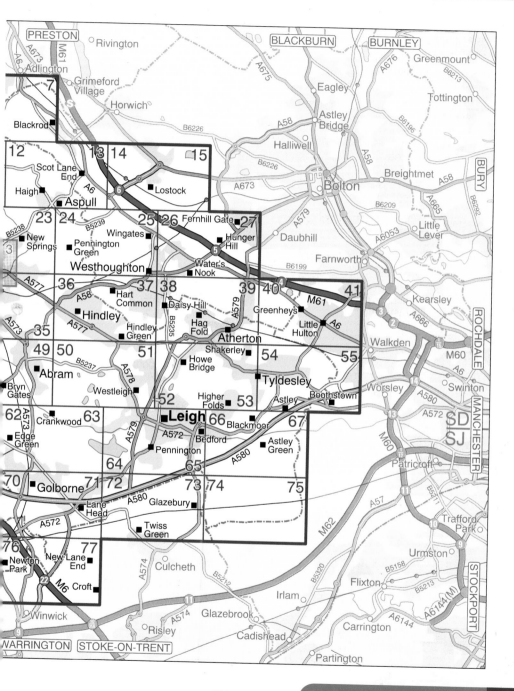

PRESTON
Rivington
BLACKBURN
BURNLEY
Greenmount
A673
M61
A676
Adlington
Grimeford Village
B6213
Tottington
Horwich
Eagley
7
Blackrod
B6226
Astley Bridge
A58
B6196
Halliwell
A58
12
13
14
15
Scot Lane End
A673
Breightmet
A58
BURY
Bolton
B6226
Haigh
A6
6
Lostock
B6209
A665
B6292
Aspull
A6053
Little Lever
23
24
25
26
Fernhill Gate
27
A579
B5239
Wingates
Hunger Hill
Daubhill
New Springs
Pennington Green
5
Farnworth
B5238
3
Water's Nook
B6199
Westhoughton
36
37
38
39
40
4
Kearsley
A577
Hart Common
Daisy Hill
Greenheys
M61
A6
Hindley
A58
A579
Little Hulton
A666
ROCHDALE
A573
35
A577
Hindley Green
Hag Fold
3
2
A6
Walkden
M60
49
50
51
Shakerley
54
55
Swinton
M60
Abram
B5237
Howe Bridge
Tyldesley
Worsley
A580
A572
Bryn Gates
A578
Westleigh
52
Higher Folds
53
Astley
Boothstown
14
MANCHESTER
62
63
Crankwood
Leigh
66
Blackmoor
67
13
A572
SD
Edge Green
A573
A579
Bedford
Astley Green
A572
SJ
Pennington
A580
64
65
Patricroft
M60
70
71
72
73
74
75
11
Golborne
Lane Head
A580
Glazebury
A57
B5211
Trafford Park
10
76
77
Twiss Green
A574
Urmston
9
Newton Park
New Lane End
Culcheth
B5320
B5158
STOCKPORT
22
M6
Croft
A574
B5212
Flixton
B5213
A6144 (M)
Winwick
M62
Irlam
Glazebrook
A6144
9
Risley
A574
Cadishead
Carrington
WARRINGTON
STOKE-ON-TRENT
Glazebrook
Partington

4.2 inches to 1 mile
Scale of main map pages 1:15,000

0   1/4   miles   1/2   3/4
0   1/4   1/2   kilometres   3/4

Junction 9	Motorway & junction
Services	Motorway service area
	Primary road single/dual carriageway
Services	Primary road service area
	A road single/dual carriageway
	B road single/dual carriageway
	Other road single/dual carriageway
	Minor/private road, access may be restricted
←	One-way street
	Pedestrian area
============	Track or footpath
	Road under construction
⊧- - - - ⊣	Road tunnel
P	Parking
P+	Park & Ride
	Bus/coach station
	Railway & main railway station
	Railway & minor railway station
⊖	Underground station

⊖	Light railway & station
++++++++++	Preserved private railway
LC	Level crossing
•—•—•—•—•	Tramway
- - - - - -	Ferry route
....	Airport runway
— · — · — · —	County, administrative boundary
ʌʌʌʌʌʌʌʌ	Mounds
17	Page continuation 1:15,000
3	Page continuation to enlarged scale 1:10,000
	River/canal, lake, pier
	Aqueduct, lock, weir
465 ▲ Winter Hill	Peak (with height in metres)
	Beach
	Woodland
	Park
	Cemetery
	Built-up area
	Featured building

City wall		Castle	
A&E	Hospital with 24-hour A&E department		Historic house or building
PO	Post Office	Wakehurst Place NT	National Trust property
	Public library	M	Museum or art gallery
i	Tourist Information Centre		Roman antiquity
i	Seasonal Tourist Information Centre		Ancient site, battlefield or monument
	Petrol station, 24 hour Major suppliers only		Industrial interest
†	Church/chapel		Garden
	Public toilets		Garden Centre Garden Centre Association Member
	Toilet with disabled facilities		Garden Centre Wyevale Garden Centre
PH	Public house AA recommended		Arboretum
	Restaurant AA inspected		Farm or animal centre
Madeira Hotel	Hotel AA inspected		Zoological or wildlife collection
	Theatre or performing arts centre		Bird collection
	Cinema		Nature reserve
	Golf course		Aquarium
▲	Camping AA inspected	V	Visitor or heritage centre
	Caravan site AA inspected		Country park
	Camping & caravan site AA inspected		Cave
	Theme park		Windmill
	Abbey, cathedral or priory		Distillery, brewery or vineyard

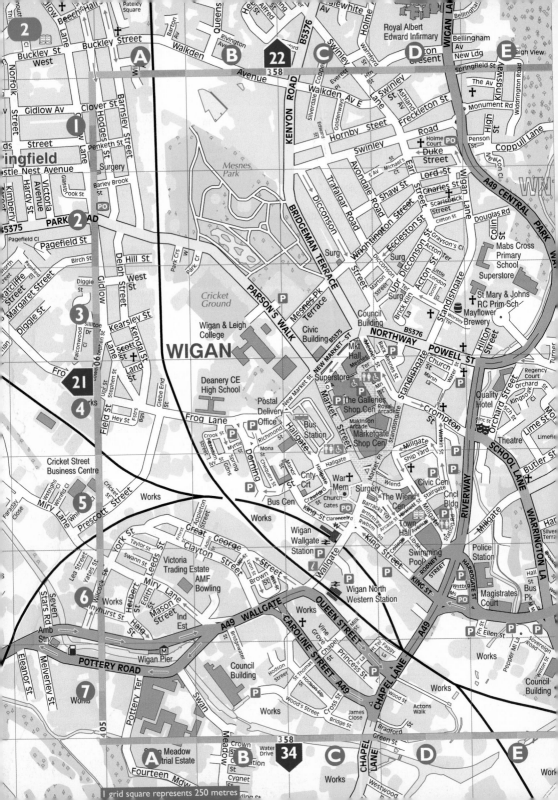

I grid square represents 250 metres

E F G H

Glover
Rd
St Johns
CE Primary
School
Belmont
Pl
Rivington
Pl

Coppull Moor

Coppull Moor Lane

A49

crane
St

Bogburn La

Hic-blb
Lane

Bogburn La

56 57

Lancashire Count
Wigan

I

Talbot
House

2

3

6

Gorse
Hall

Platt

Bradley Lane

Hutton
Street

4

PRESTON ROAD

Fairhurst
Av

Langtree Lane

PO

udlow
St

Langtree
Hall

Bradley Hall
Trading
Estate

5

Kenyon

Primrose La

Ingleby
Cl

Marwick
Cl

Moores La

James Sq

James
Pl

Foxglove
Cl

Langley
Dr

Woodland

Sheldon Avenue

Sterndale
Av

St Maries
RC Primary
School

Littleton
Rd

Edale Dr

Richard
Av

Doveдale Dr

Avondale
Street

Bradley Lane

Bentham
Pl

Copeland Drive

Churchlands

Belfry
Crs

Canon
Close

Sprdi

A49

Greenwood Road

Adelphi
St

Broomfield
Rd

Langton Av

Collingwood

Smalley St

Market St

PO

Woodhurst

Simfield
Works

Langham Rd

Wheatsheaf Wk

HampScd

rst Dr

Cranborne

E F G **STANDISH** H

10

LANE

B5239

RECTORY

St Wilfrids
CE Primary
School

Standish Court
Golf Club

Wilfrid's
Pl

56 57

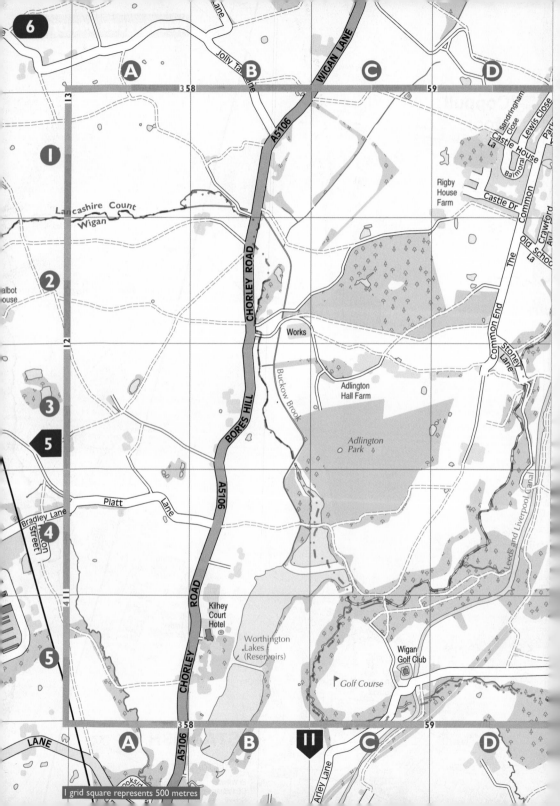

6

A   B   WIGAN LANE   C   D

13   358   59

I

Lancashire Count
Wigan

12

2

albot
ouse

3

5

BORES HILL   Buckow Brook   Adlington
Hall Farm   Adlington
Park

CHORLEY ROAD   A5106

Platt   Lane
Bradley Lane
Preston Street

4

4   11

5   Kilhey
Court
Hotel   Worthington
Lakes
(Reservoirs)   Wigan
Golf Club

Golf Course

LANE   A   II   C   D

358   59

Arley Lane

Jolly Tar Lane   A5106

Wigan Lane

Castle House   Sandringham
Close
Lewis Close
Castle
Balmoral   La
Rigby
House
Farm   Castle Dr   Common
The   Crawford
Old Scho   La   Av
Common End   Stoney
Lane   Leeds and Liverpool Canal
Works

I grid square represents 500 metres

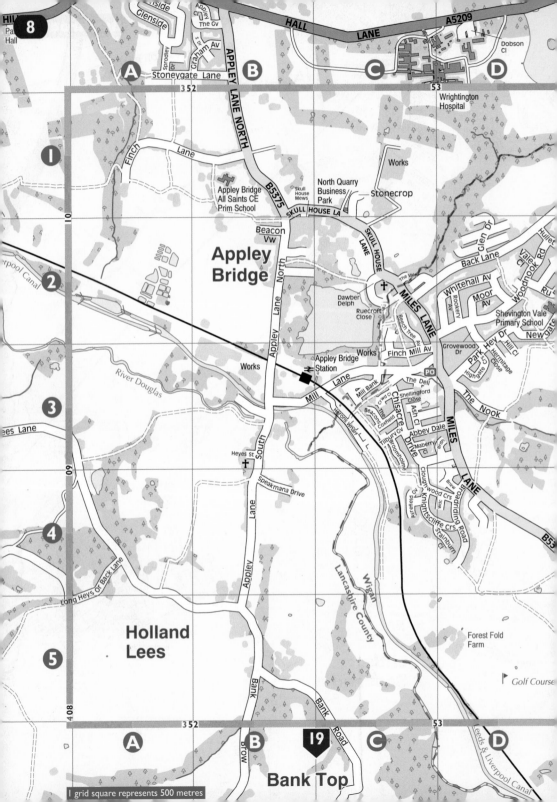

Worthington Lakes (Reservoirs)

Wigan Golf Club

E CHORLEY **F** **6** Golf Course **G** **H** Bolton / Wigan

58 59

Brookside Road

A5106

Bt Cl

C Crs

Sud Rd

Sussex

Devon Dr

WC

Essex Rd

PO

Works

Works

Worthington Lakes Business Park

Arley Lane

I

Pennington La

Pennington Lane

RED ROCK LANE B5239 SCHOOL LANE

Red Rock

2

Rowton Rd

A5106

Winstanleys

Water

Lordy Cl

Lurdin La

Ridge Av

Richmond Cl

Hawthorn Av

Works

Te Breeze

Copperbeech Drive

Limes Av

3

12

Pendlebury Lane

Lane

Sennicar

School Lane

4

CHORLEY RD

PO

Haigh Hall Golf Complex

Golf Course

Leeds & Liverpool Canal

Sennicar Lane

Lane

Mere Oaks School

5

Elmfield Rd

Scott Av

Penbury Rd

Bethersden Road

Newlandwell

Ashford

Larkfield Av

Cranbrook Way

Elkwood Rd

Hazelwood Rd

Willow Tree

Galwey Gv

Woodfield

WIGAN LANE

A49

Broomhey Avenue

Terrace

Brock

Mill Lane

Wingates

Works

Douglas Valley Business Park

Wigan RUFC

WN1

Hall Lane

E **F** **22** **G** **H**

58 59

Works

Blackrod Station

E

PO

F

Cemetery

G

Lane

63

H

Road

Vicarage

Castlecroft Av

MANCHESTER ROAD

Greenbarn

Lymbridge Drive

Vauze House

Highfield Grove

Shawbury Grove

Thursford Grove

Vauze Av

Corston Grove

STATION ROAD

Way

Hillside Avenue

Highfield Rd

Highfield Meadow

B5408

I

Red Moss

2

Greenbarn Way

Blackrod Primary School

MANCHESTER ROAD

Hope Street

BLACKROD BY-PASS ROAD

Park Hall Farm

Mi

Scot Lane End CE Prim Sch

The Cheethams

3

Eskdale Av

Newlands Drive

Dorning Street

B5408

14

M61

Scot Lane End

A6

Scot Lane Industrial Estate

SCOT

LANE

Bolton Wigan

CHORLEY ROAD

Hilton House

4

Brinsop Hall Lane

A60

Eden Fld

Duncan Av

Corfe Cl

Renfrew Cl

Lincoln Dr

Restormel

Brinsop Hall

5

B5238

Harold Street

Lincoln Dr

Exeter Dr

Crs

Devon

Criccieth Av

Old Fold

Road

Restormel

Cooper Turning

B5239

Road

ASPULL

Conway Drive

E

62

F

24

G

63

H

408

BOLTON

DICCONSON

LANE

Dicconson Lane

B527

Code

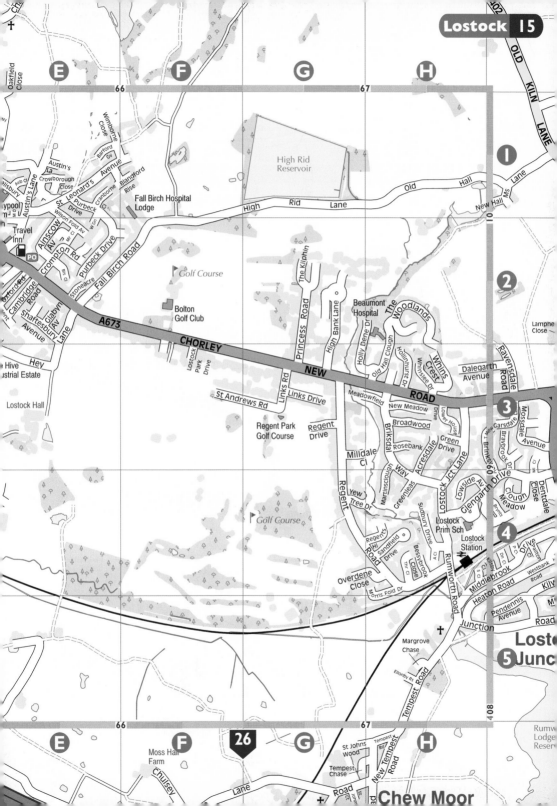

E   F   G   H

66   67

I

Oakfield Close

High Rid Reservoir

2

Old Kiln Lane

New Hall Ms

Old Hall Road

High Rid Lane

Wimborne Close
Barford Gv
Austin's La
Crowborough Close
Austin's Lane
St Leonard's Drive
Purbeck Av
Blandford Rise
Canborne
Avenue
Fall Birch Hospital Lodge

Salisbury
Claypool
Travel Inn
PO
Anscow Av
Crompton Rd
Wilson Fold Av
Purbeck Drive
Fall Birch Road
Stoneacre
Golf Course
Lamphe Close

Oxford Rd
Cambridge Road
Clabyn Av
Shaftesbury Avenue
Bolton Golf Club
A673
Lostock Park Drive
CHORLEY
NEW
ROAD

The Kilphin
Princess Road
High Bank Lane
Beaumont Hospital
The Woodlands
Holly Dene Dr
Old Hall Clough
Hollinhurst Dr
Whitsted Dr
Whins Crest
Dalegarth Avenue
Ravensdale Road
Mossdale Avenue

3

Hey
Hive
Industrial Estate
Lostock Hall

St Andrews Rd
Links Rd
Links Drive
Regent Park Golf Course
Regent Drive
Meadowfield
New Meadow
Broadwood
Rosebank
Briksdal
Acresdale
Green Drive
Lower House
Carsdale
Braybrook Dr
A6099
Glengarth Drive
Dentdale Close
Clough Meadow

Golf Course
Regent Road
Millidale Cl
Yew Tree Dr
Martinsclough
Greenleas Way
Sudbury Drive
Lostock Ind Lane
Lowside Av
Lostock Prim Sch

4

Regents
Sandfield Drive
Besstbrook Close
Overdene Close
Morris Fold Dr
Lostock Station
Middlebrook
Heaton Road
Pendennis Avenue
Ballton Dr
Westbank Rd
Kilv
Road

Rumworth Road
Junction

Lost

5 Junc

Margrove Chase
Ellonby Rd
Tempest Road

408

66   67

E   F   26   G   H

Moss Hall Farm
St Johns Wood
Tempest Road
New Tempest Road
Tempest Chase
Chulsey Lane
Road

Rumw Lodge Reser

Chew Moor

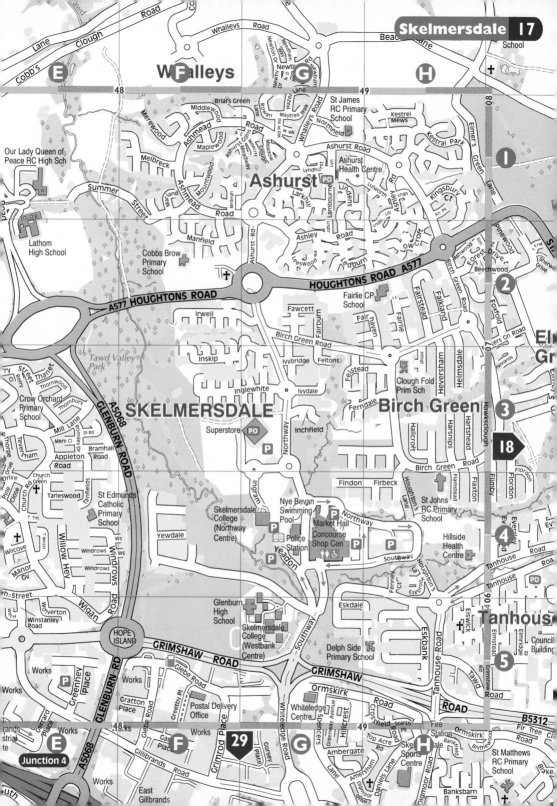

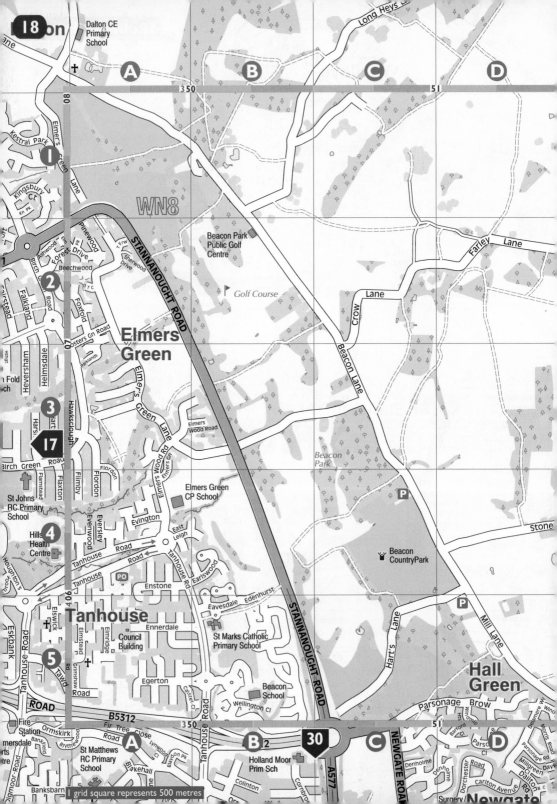

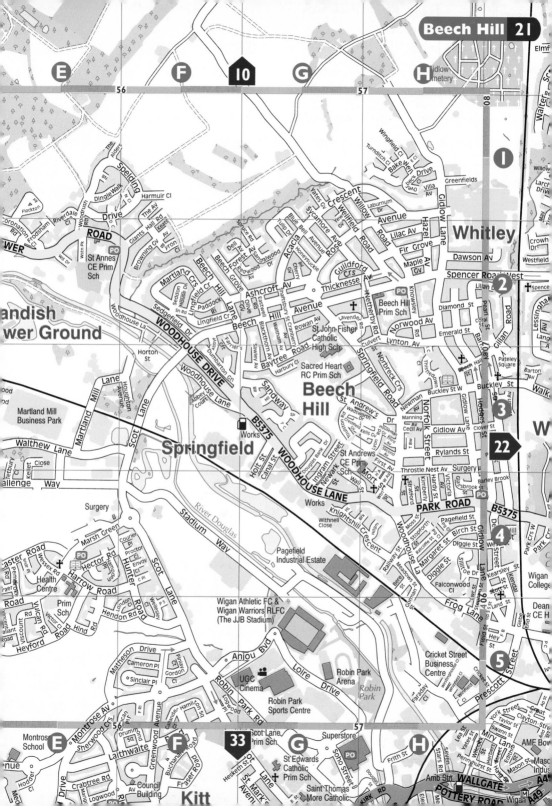

2000

1 mile

500

1000

500

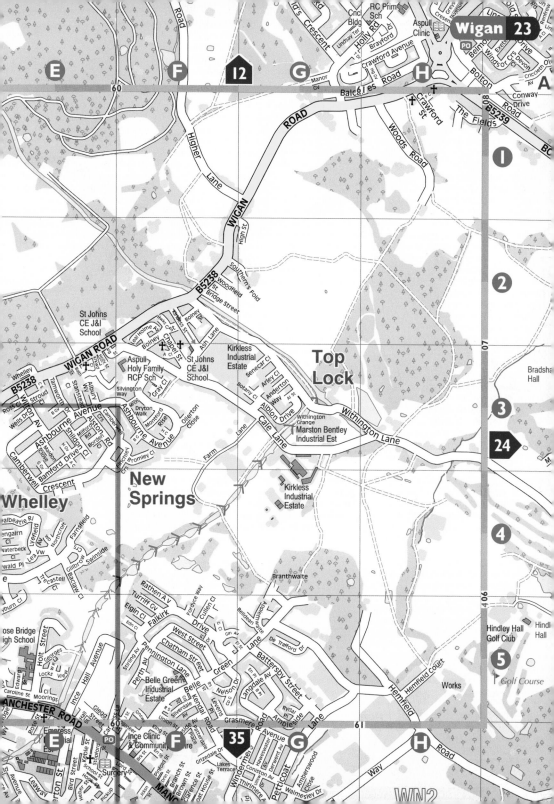

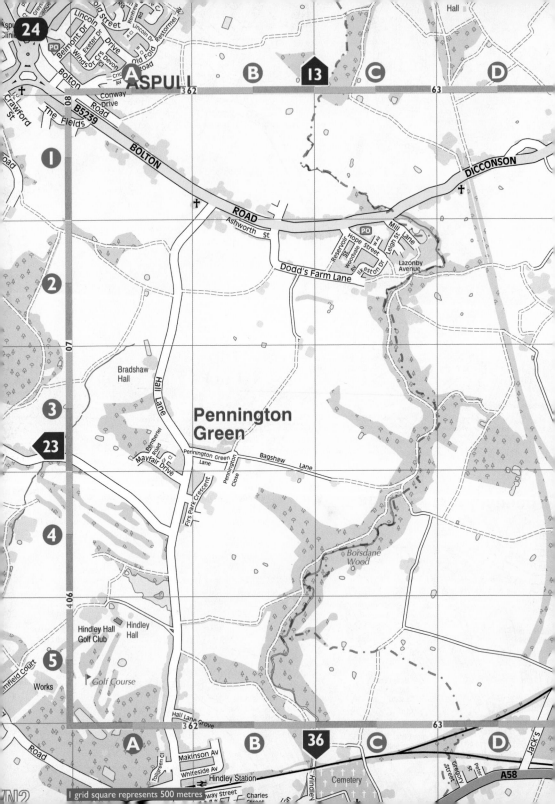

26

A   B   15   C   D

3 66   67

Margrove Chase

Ellonby Rd

New Tempest Road

Tempest Road

Lane

Lane

Wingates Lane

1

08

Moss Hall Farm

Chulsey Gate Lane

St Johns Wood

Tempest Chase

St Johns Road

Haylsham Cl

Copperfields

Tempest Road

Oakbarton

Lock Lane

Chew Moor

Church Lane

Fawcetts Fold

Lever St

Gensmyth Way

Lea

Comtech Bus Park

Seddon Street

2

Dixon St

Albion St

Wingates Sq

Works

Slack Lane

Brook Cnr Cl

Bramble Cl

Chew Moor Lane

CR

Meadowbrook Close

Pocket Nook Rd

Winslow

White

M61

STREET

Part street

Wellington street

Bristle Hall Way

The Gates Primary School

Glazebury Dr

Ingleby Cl

Metal Box

Works

Heatons Grove

Snydale Cl

Calver Hey Close

Herbert Street

3

Westhoughton Station

MANCHESTER

Aspen Cl

Wattsundale

Wayfaring

Wharfedale

Broom Way

Fanleigh Close

Bolton Road

White Horse Gv

A6

A58 · SNYDALE WAY

25

Wesley St

CHURCH

Amber Gv

Churnett Cl

Cherwell Road

Chelmer Close

B5235

Hall Lee Dr

Hall Lee Dr

Upper Lees

Aylesbury Cl

Greta Cl

Lodge

Manley Crs

Manchester Rd

Cheq

Chequerbent Works

Surgery

Bligh St

Grundy street

4

Central Glebe St

Windrush Dr

Sacred Heart RC Prim Sch

Westhoughton Prim Sch

Derby Street

Cow Lees

Winterton Close

Selbourne Cl

Lees Road

Allerton

Bro Cl

Fellbridge Cl

Molyneux

Singleton Rd

St Thomas CE Prim Sch

Beehive Gn

A58

Branker Street

Clinic PO

Market Street

King street

Dams Head Fold

Town Hall

Westhoughton High School

Dale Lee

Captain Lees Gdns

Barnfield Dr

Park Meadow

Falhaven Av

Alexandria Dr

Surg

Water's Nook

Police Station

A58

5

CRICKETERS WAY

Victoria Rd

MILL ST

Alma Road

Park Road

George Street

BOLTON ROAD

PARK ROAD

Lee Bank

Bailey Fold

Forest Drive

Westhoughton CC

Medical Centre

Rosebery St

B5235

Dalton Fold

Bank Side

Wade Rd

BL5

Sunny Garth

Ryelands

Clough Ave

Hollin Acre

LEIGH RD

Landedmans

Stanley Cl

Washacre Prim Sch

A   B   38   C   D

3 66   67

Hooper Green

The Crescent

Green Fold Lane

Southfield Drive

Drive

1 grid square represents 500 metres

A

B 16 C D

LIVERPOOL RD

Kerfoot's Lane

Derby Rd

Old Town

ILWAY RD

RAILWAY ROAD

B5312

B5312

Wheatacre

Works

Gladden Place

Gardiners Place

street

estgate

Road

Old Town Cl
Old Town Wy

sdale
C/
CC

3 46

47

M58

White Moss Road

White Moss Road

W
G
In
Es

I

SKELMERSDALE ROAD B5312

Stanley Farm

05

2

Rainford Road

A570

3

04

4

5

03

RAINFORD ROAD

Coal Pit Lane

Holly Lane

Holly Fold

Holly Fold Farm

A

B

42

C

D

Ben Lane Farm

Ben Lane Court

3 46

47

Orm

Park

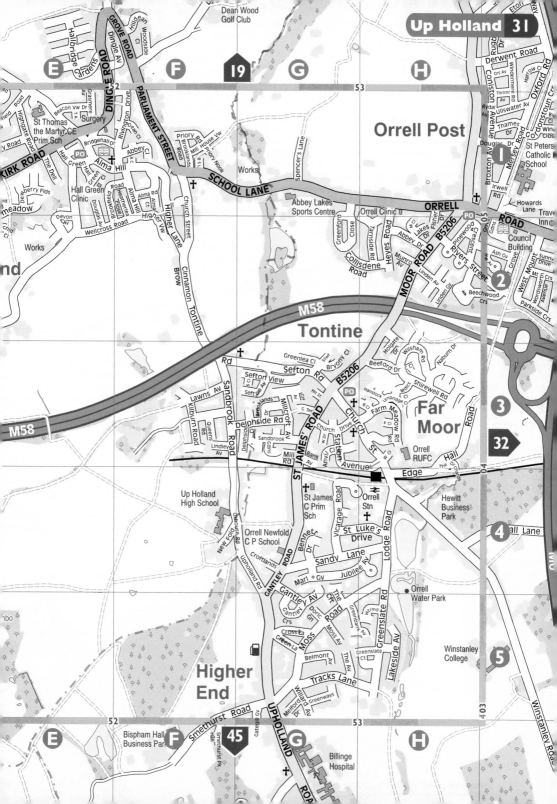

Dean Wood Golf Club

E   F   **19**   G   H

Hallbridge Gardens

Hilldean
Woodside

GROVE ROAD

Dingle Av

Grasmere Av

Beacon Vw Dr

PARLIAMENT STREET

DINGLE ROAD

Rivington Dr

St Thomas the Martyr CE Prim Sch

Surgery

Orrell Post

Priory Rd
Brooklands
Mill House Vw
Priory Nook
B S L

Derwent Road

Windermere Rd

Coniston Avenue

Rydal Av

Ullswater Av

Thrimr Rd

Thames Dr

Winc Clos

Oxford Cr

Eton Av

Bridgehall Dr

PO

Abbey Cl

Alma Hill

Hall Green

The Dell

Hall Green

Heathgate

Draysnook

Douglas Av

Alma Rd

Alma Hill

Alma Dr

Church Street

SCHOOL LANE

Spencer's Lane

Works

ORRELL

Broxton Cl

Melser Rd

Douglas Av

Irwell Rd

I

St Peters Catholic School

Howards Lane

Trav Inn

KIRK ROAD

y Road

Highgate Road

Highfield

sberry Flds

meadow

Devon Av

Higher Vw

Higher Lane

Wellcross Road

Cinnamon Brow

Tontine Road

Abbey Lakes Sports Centre

Orrell Clinic

Greenford Close

Tarnside Rd

Heyes Dr

Lakes Dr

Abbey Dr

Fisher Rd

B5206

Munro Av

Linden Av

Linden Gv

MOOR ROAD

Rivers Street

Crescens St

PO

Council Building

West Mount

Ash Gv

Grs Av

Sunny Drive

Wordsworth Av

Mt Parkside Av

Beechwood Crs

2

Collisdene Road

Works

nd

M58

Tontine

Greenlea Cl

Sefton Rd

Street

Bryony Cl

B5206

Holgate Dr

Wilsnam Rd

Beeford Dr

Shirewell Rd

Natum Dr

Sefton View

Rd

Lawns Av

Sandbrook Road

Kilburn Rd

Queens Rd

Sandbrook Road

Delphside Rd

Delphside Rd

Millcroft Av

Seftlands

G Ter

Sandbrook Gdns

Lindley Av

Mill Rd

ST JAMES' ROAD

Church

Church Drive

Hl St

Hanstock

Molet

Unbridge Cl

Farm Meadow Rd

F Cl

PO

Far Moor

Hall Road

3

M58

Up Holland High School

Oldfold Rd

New Fold

Orrell Newfold C P School

Croftlands

Upholland Rd

GANTLEY ROAD

Bennett Dr

Vicarage Road

St James C Prim Sch

St Luke's Drive

Sandy Lane

Marl Gv

Jubilee Av

Orrell Stn

Bank

Anvil

St

Avenue

Orrell RUFC

Edge

The Orchards

04

Hewitt Business Park

4

all Lane

32

GANTLEY ROAD

Gantley Av

Gantley Crs

Doric St

Road

MOSS

Cross La

Green La

Belmont Rd

Moss Av

The Av

Greenfield Av

Greenslate Rd

Lodge Road

Greenslate Road

Lakeside Av

Greenslate Rd

Orrell Water Park

Winstanley College

5

Higher End

Tracks Lane

Belmont Rd

Melford Dr

Wm

Greenways

Gategill Gv

SMETHURST ROAD

UPHOLLAND ROAD

Smethurst Pk Hall

UPHOLLAND ROAD

E   **52**   F   **45**   G   H   **53**

Bispham Hall Business Park

Billinge Hospital

403

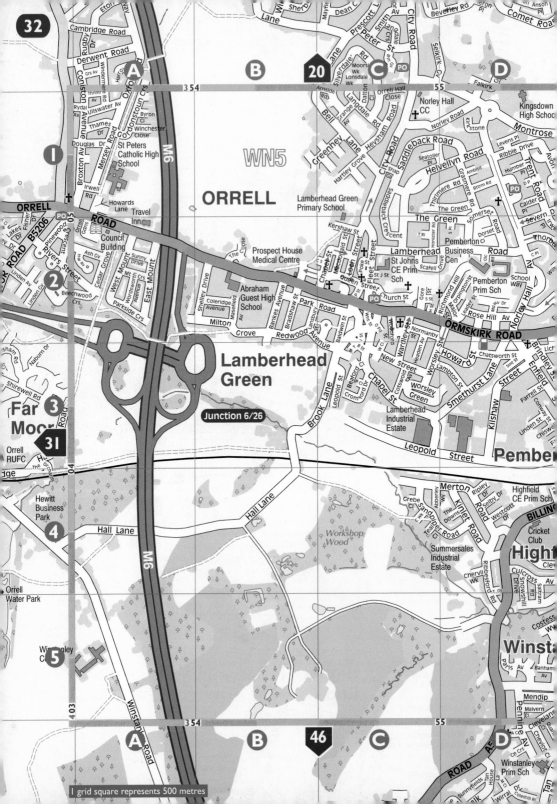

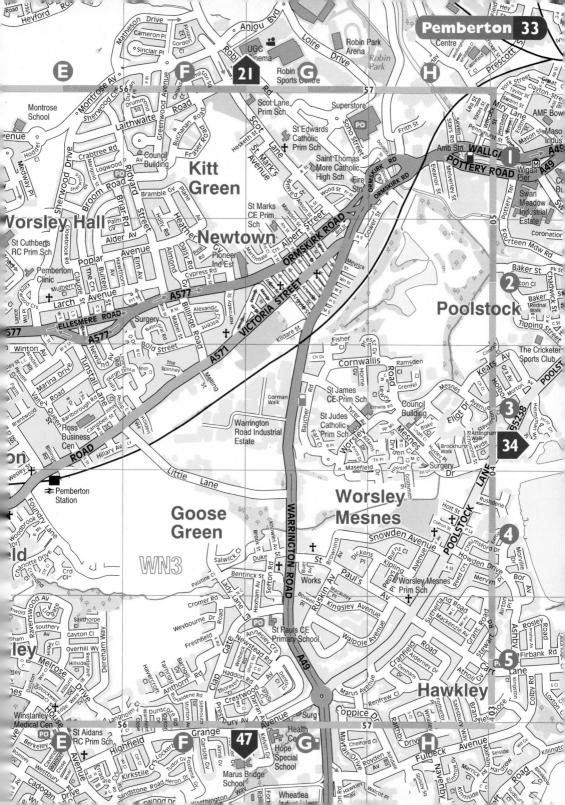

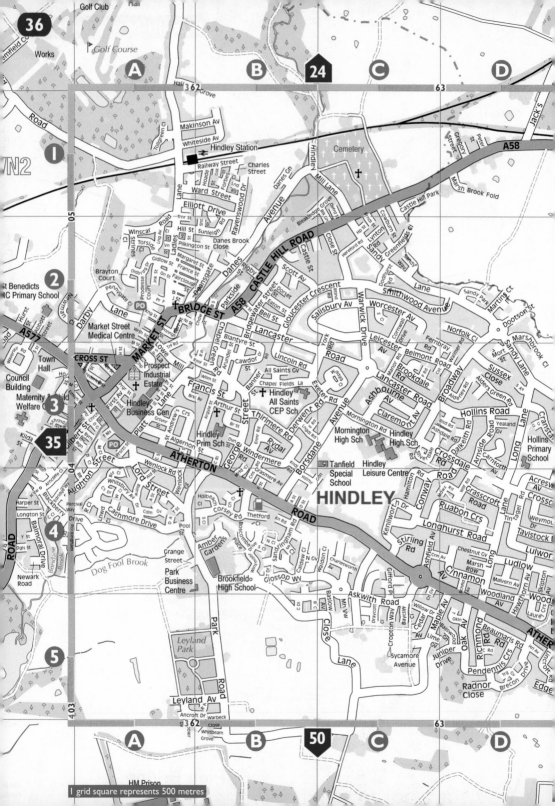

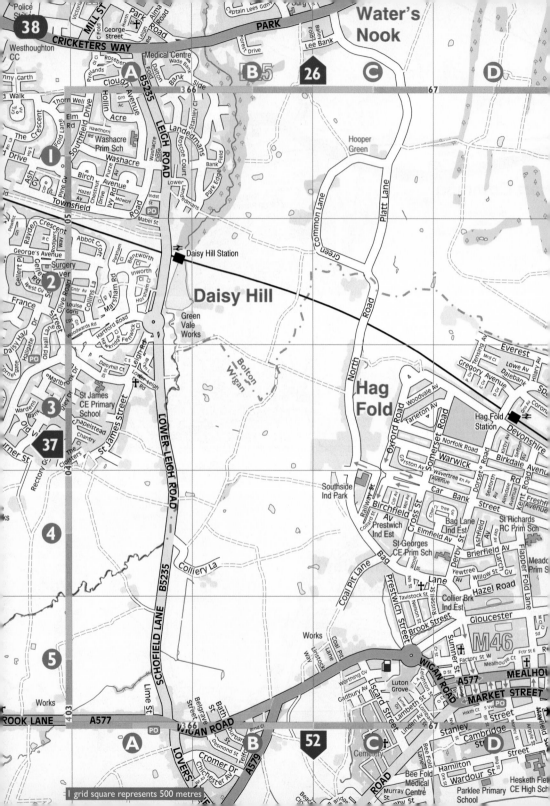

44

LC

Duke's W

Long Lane

Crawford Village
Primary School

Manor
House
Dr

A 350 **B** **30** **C** ets **D**

03 51

Lane

Works

Crawford

Crawford Road

Oakleigh

Holland
Court

Lancashire County
St. Helens

I

2

Langwood

Lane

02

Maddocks

Robin's
Lane

3

◀ **43**

*Holiday
Moss*

Pimbo Road

Kings Moss

4

401

King's
Moss La

Fir Tree
Cl

Brook
La

Crank Road

5

Fire Clay
Farm

350 51

A **B** **57** **C** CK LANE **D**

Red Cat Lane

Gores Lane

GORES L

205

E **F** **31** **G** **H**

52 53 03

Cross La
Green La
MOSS
Cross Av
Cree
Greenslate
Ct
Lakeside Av
Winstanley Rd

Belmont
Av
The Av
Greenways
Well
Dr
Av

Tracks Lane

Higher
End

Bispham Hall
Business Park

Smethurst Road

Smethurst Pk
Hall

Categill Gr

UPHOLLAND

ROAD

Billinge
Hospital

I

Park Road

Crank Road

Coppice Dr

Banbu
Cheltenham Rd
Winchester
Rd
Bophm

Coleridge Rd

Keats
Av

Tennyson

Milton
Gv

Wordsworth

Burns
Close

Cd Mr

Drive

B5206

Cob Moor Rd

PO

Longshaw

Longshaw
Rd

Rd
BV Av

Park Av

Norfolk Rd
LCl

Longshaw

Longshaw
Avenue

2 Rd

Park

Rd

Brownlow La

Trevelyan Dr

Wellbrook Av

Dalecrest

Longshaw
Common

Hunters Cha

Paignton
Cl

Tl
Ol

Longshaw
Common

02

Brownlow

3

Houghwood
Golf Club

46

⏺ Golf Course

4

WIG

Houghwood

Red

Barn

Oakley
Av

Beacon

Road

A571

St Aidan's
Cl

Coutishead
Av
401

M
Fa

5

STREET

NEWTON

Red

Road

E **F** **58** **G** **H**

Crookhurst
Av
Wells
Norbury
Av

Ash Gv
Ross
Crs

Stuart
Cl

53
Crs

MAIN

Maple
Cl

Larch Close

Elm Drive

Well Wy

Robin
St

Gorsey Brow

Garswood
Fold Dr

Cherry Brow

School Brow

Pin
Brow

Council
Building

St Aidans
CE Prim
Sch

Health
Cen

Lordon Flds

Conway
Crs

Royden Av

Greenhill
Crs

Conway Dr

Andrew
St

Royden Road

Blackleyhu

Windsor Road

BILLIN

52

48

Hawkley

34

61

Stubshaw Cross

A B C D

Hawkley Hall High School

Firbank

Fulbeck Avenue

Navenby Road

Whitecroft Road

Stanedge Gv

Sandwith Cl

Bankside Av

47

Wasdale Rd

Road

Gate Lane

Three Sisters
Racing Circuit

Park House
Farm

Bryn Gates Lane

Leeds & Liverpool Canal

Bam

Three Sisters Rd

South
Lancashire
Industrial
Estate

Kingfisher
Ct

Lockett Rd

Antler
Ct

Redgate Rd

Lockett Road

Kestrel Dr

Beaver Ct

Ashton Grange
Industrial Estate

BRYN

Nicol Mere
School

Highwoods Cl

Nicol Mere
Drive

Lockett Business
Park

BOLTON ROAD

A58

Bolton Road

Severn Road

Avon Rd

Welland Road

Conway Rd

Willow Grove School

1 grid square represents 500 metres

02 401 358 59

50

A   **B**   **36**   **C**   **D**

Leyland Park

Leyland Av

Warbeck Close
Whitbeam Grove

Sycamore Avenue

Juniper Drive

Pendennis Crs

Radnor Close

Brecon Drive

I

HM Prison Hindley

Works

Gibson St

2

BICKERSHAW LANE

Barracks Rd

Victoria Avenue

Elizabeth Av

Chapel St

Brown St

Close Lane

Belmont Avenue

Rivington Drive

St James Crs

Church

Beacon Rd

Avenue

SMI

Station Av

Turner Av

Johnson Av

Grange Road

PO

B5237

Chelburn Close

Forresters Close

Atherton St

BICKERSHAW LANE

Works

Bickershaw

Works

Bickershaw CE Primary School

Bolton House Road

Victoria Ter

3

49

Works

4

Thornvale

Beech Grove

Maypole Industrial Estate

Shuttle Hillock Road

Lane

401

5

Park Lane

A   **B**   **63**   **C**   **D**

Crankwood

1 grid square represents 500 metres

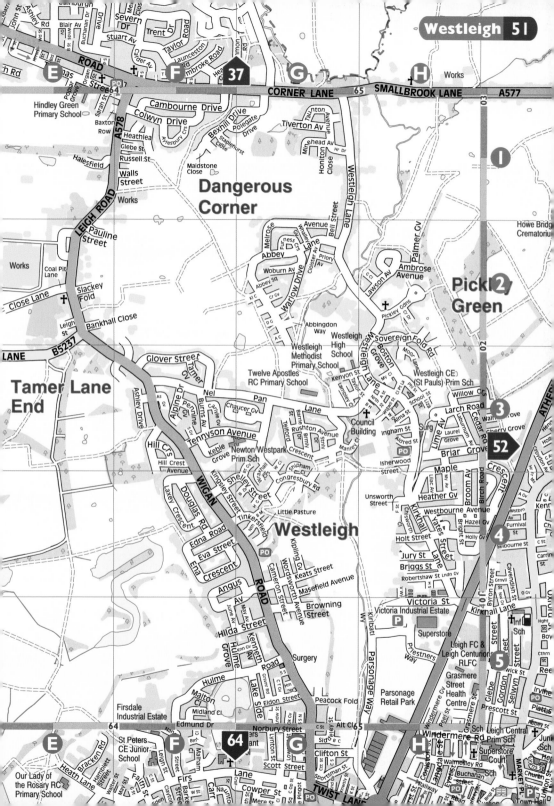

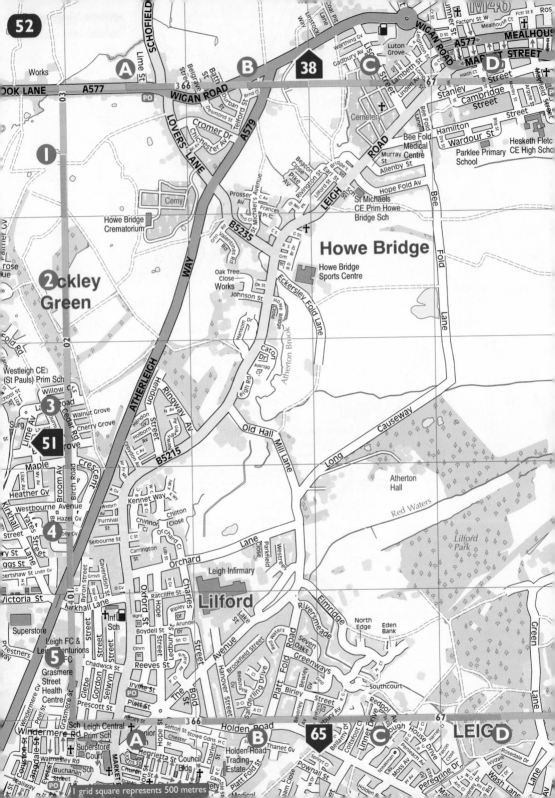

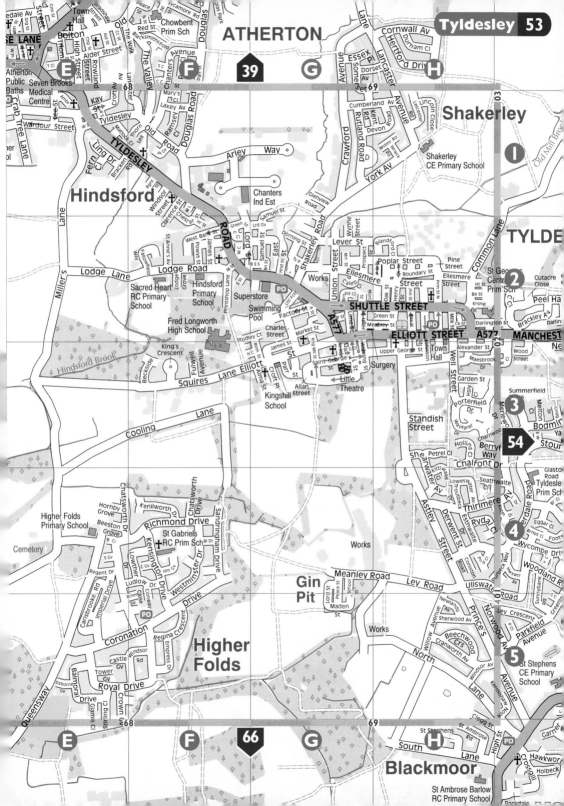

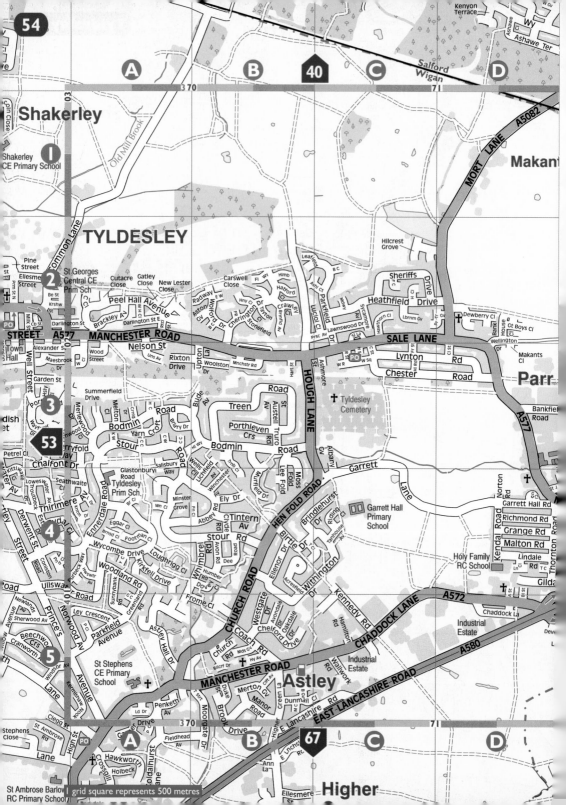

E **F** **46** **G** **H**

St. Helens

NEWTON ROAD 54 55

BILLINGE

B5207

BILLINGE ROAD

Simm's Lane End

Conway Dr
Greenhill Cfs
Greenhill Rd
Windsor Road

Blackley Hurst Hall

Garswood United FC

Leyland Green Road

Downall Green

Hawthorn Av
Poplar Av
Palm Av
Lilac Av
Birch
Elm
Cedar Gv
Poplar
Grove

I

Stirling Drive

Garswood Road

Peebles Close
Selkirk Avenue
Thornhill Road
Smock Lane
Fakland Dr
Oban Drive
Argyll Close
Dunbarne Close
Girvan

Langholm Road

Darver Av
Kinross Avenue

Forres Gv

Hamilton

Manor Close

2

Victoria

Coldstone
Drive
Nwbr Cl

Mlr Crs

Garswood Prim Sch

Station Road

Old Colliery Yard

School Lane

Surgery
PO

Garswood

Works

Arch Lane

Garswood Road

◆ Garswood Station **3**

60

Tithebarn

4

Garswood Old Road

Old Garswood Hall Farm

5

Liverpool Road

A58 LIVERPOOL ROAD

Yew Tradi

Way Grove

Hayd

E 54 **F** **G** 55 **H**

Stubshaw Cross

Town Green

ASHTON-IN-MAKERFIELD

Ashton Grange Industrial Estate

Lockett Business Park

Willow Grove School

Ashton Town AFC

St John Southworth RC J & I Sch.

Jameson's Farm

St Thomas CE.Prim.Sch

Police Station

Oswalds J&I Sch

Premier Lodge

Haydock Park Racecourse

Wigan St Helens

Haydock Park Gardens

Chelwood Park

Haydock Park

A 360 B **49** C Crankwood Road 61 D

Chadwick's
Farm

Riding Lane

ement
Rd

Avon Rd Welland
Road

1

w Grove School

Moorland Rd

AYE BRIDGE ROAD

Aye Bridge
Farm

400

Green Road

Lck La

A573

Lightshaw
Hall Farm

2

Lightshaw
Lane

ROAD

Edge

**Edge
Green**

Dam Lane

3

WIGAN

61

66

ASHTON ROAD

B5207

Manley Av

Farefield
Avenue

Millingford

Cf Av

Bardsley

Bn Cl

H Cl

Justene
Cl

Sandling
Dr

Dove
St

Rock

Ash
Street

4

Edge

Helen

Green

Lane

Gln

Walter's Gn

Linton Avenue

Burn Av

Walter's Gn Crs

Walter's Gn Crs

Swnfld
Walk

Park Avenue

Halewood
Av

Dawish
Wy

PO

St

Sycamore Av

Forster
St

L
St

Willow
Gv

P St

Fold

ASHTON

ROAD

May St

Pplr

Golborne
Clinic

Elliott
Av

Heywood Av

Rothwell Road

CHURCH STREET

Golborne
High School

Belmont Av

Pendle Rd

Pennine
La

LOWTON ROAD

5

Hell Nook

Mansfield St

St

Oakfield Rd

Moorison
Close

Watson
Avenue

Ringley Avenue

Gawsworth
Road

Whitlow Avenue

Duke
Street

York St

Elm Av

Bank Street

Grimshaw
St

Clarence
st

Beech
Rd

Kid Glove Rd

Mnr St

West Av

Derby

Langley

Ulswater Rd

Rivington
Av

Thirlmere Rd

ADA

Gebin Cl

398 360

A

Harvey Lane

Cif Mdw

B

PO

Turton St

Worsley St

John St

Heath St

Charles St

70

St Thomas
CE Prim
School

Gloucester
Rd

Cottesmore
Wy

Primary
School

C

Hazel Av

Naylor Av

Kingsley Avenue

East
Cl

Oak Av

Windsor Road

B5207

D

GOLBO

Golborne CP
School

John Street
Medical Cen

Mill St

Tanner's Lane

Barrowdale Rd

Briar Road

Manor Avenue

Lancaster Rd

Rd

Rosedale

Cl

Twist

E

F

50

G

H

62

63

rankwood

I

Our Lady of
e Rosary RC
Primary School

**Plank
Lane**

Park Lane

400

Crankwood Road

Leeds and Liverpool Canal

Horrocks
St

Cunliffe
Ct

Plank Lane

Norley

2

The C

Johns
Close

3

64

The
Flash

Mossley
Hall

99

Byrom
Hall

Byrom Lane

Green Lane

4

Slag Lane

**Aspull
Commo**

Moss
In   ial
E

5

Sandy Lane

Brook St

Haddon Road

Scott
Road

Ivanhoe
Av

Balmoral Av

Carlton Road

Marmion
Ct

Woodvale
Drive

Rokeby Av

Ryecroft
AV

Linbeck
Grove

Bodden
St

St Nicholas

Kane

398

Alfred Rd

PO

Ashwell
AV

Sawley
AV

Waverley
Rd

Hilary Avenue

Crow Wd
Av

Lincoln

Surgery

The

Unsworth

Merchants
Cfs

Garton
Drive

Stone Pt

Pond St

Green

Lowton St Marys
CE Primary School

Cleveland
Dr

Crampton

Sarsfield
AV

Braithwaite
Av

Beardsmore
Dr

Thornham

Spawell
Cl

Westhead

Brook Lynn
Avenue

Wh Ct

Bridge Av

Lowt
High

Laurel
CV

Chester AV

Rostherne
AV

Norle
Field

Mullen
Cl

Primula
Drive

Clifton
AV

Redman
Allerton

Surgery

Garton

Lane

Durrel

Clarton Rd

Edgerton Rd

Stein

Fl

The Pipers

Bn Av

Reeve

Barford Dr

Adwell

Slisgen

E

F

71

G

**Lowton
Common**

H

Council
Building

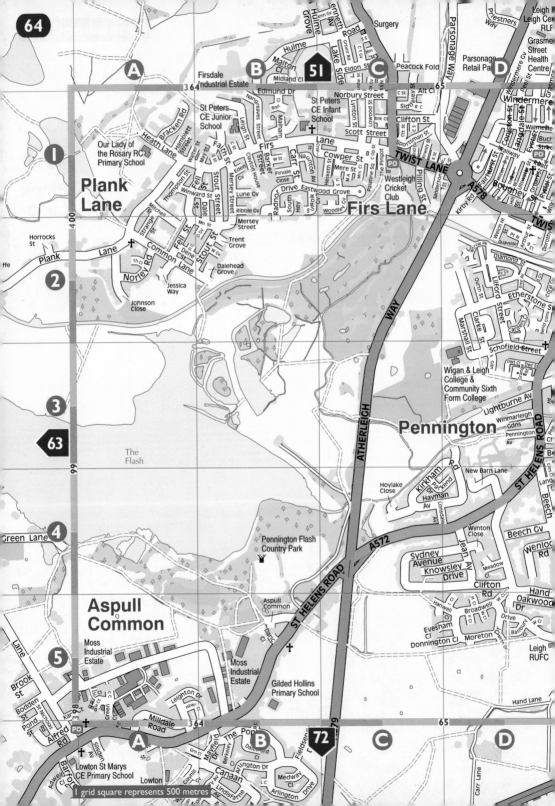

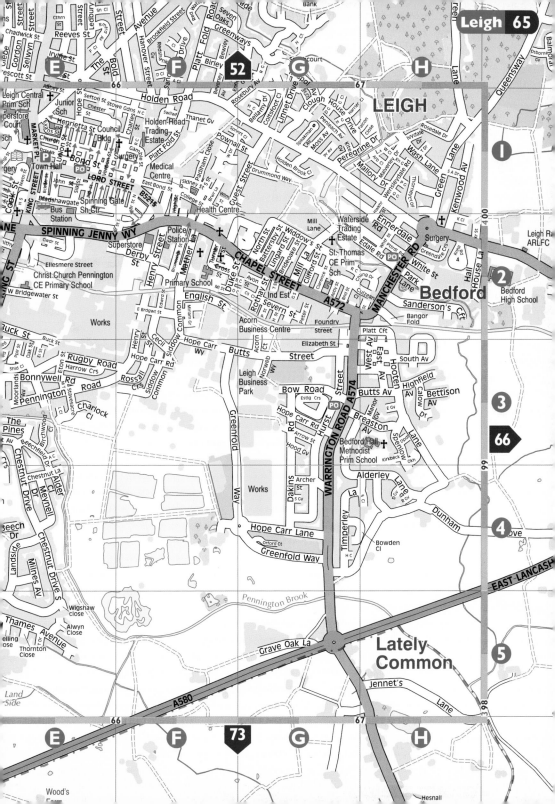

LEIGH

Bedford

Lately Common

St Stephens
CE Primary
School

E

PO

Hawkworth
Holbeck
Crossgill

Parkdale

M29

Town Lane

Peel Lane

Coldalhurst
Lane

Blackmoor
Avenue

Caldwell
Close

Well
Av

Garner
Drive

Penketh
Av

Fieldhead
Av

Moorgate Dr

Brook Drive

Second
Av
Third
Av

First Av

Scott
St

Higher Green Lane

Cleworth
Cl

**Astley
Green**

**Lower
Green**

Green Lane

Moss Side

Sandy La

Great
Moss Rd

llwood
Farm

Town Lane

Astley

Church
Rd

Bllcrf Dr

Hy Av

Mds Gv

Duke
St

Merton Gv

Dunr
Rd

Ann La

E Lancashire Rd

E Lnchshr
Rd

Ellesmere
St

Grundy's
Cl

Boatmans
Row

**Higher
Green**

MANCHESTER ROAD

CHAP

EAST LANCASHIRE ROAD

A580

A580

Industrial
Estate

Wallwork
Rd

54

F

G

H

70

71

Nook Lane

Stirrup
Brook Gv

Linkheld
Dr

Halle

Grove HI

Vic

Vicars

I

Vicars Hall Lane

00

99

98

2

3

4

5

Moss Bank
Farm

Salf
W

E

F

75

G

H

70

71

E **F** 61 **G** **H**

58 59 98

Racecourse

Haydock Park Gardens

Parks

Park

LODGE LANE

Pye Close

A49

M6

Harvey

Mansfield St

Ringley Av

Gawsw

Watts

I

Haydock Park

Sandy Lane

A580

A580 EAST LANCASHIRE ROAD

Junction 23

2

A49 LODGE LANE

Old BOSTON

Haydock Park Farm

Newton Lane

97

Woodlands Industrial Estate

3 Golf Course

70

ASHTON ROAD

Billington Avenue

Newton Lane

Haydock Golf Clu

Johnson Avenue

Martin Av

Queens

Porter Av

Urmston Rd

Elston Av

Williams Av

Dixon Av

Billington Avenue

Horridge Av

Walsh Av

ROAD

M6

4

A12

Weedon Av

Cuniliffe Av

Speakman Av

Frawley Av

Crown Fields

Borron Rd

Crown Gardens

Durham Av

Wheatley Av

Cheltenham Dr

Kershaw

Latham Av

Davies Av

Ruskin

Drive

A49

NEWTON- LE- WILLOWS

Kempton Cl

The Parchments

Rob Lane

396

Belvedere Road

Huskisson Av

Selwyn Cl

Stainer Cl

Bleasdale Rd

Borron Road Industrial Est

Newton-le-Willows Sports Club

Newton-le-Willows Community High School

Dale VW

Castle Hill

Newton Bank Preparatory School

5

Silverdale Rd

Rushton

Cole Avenue

Beechwood Gardens

Manse Gardens

Mercer St

Birley St

HIGH STREET

Surgery

PO

A49 CHURCH

Mere Road

Newton Health Clinic

PO

CROW LANE EAST

Newton-le-Willows Sports Club

SOUTHWORTH

A572

St Helens Community College

St Marys Catholic Sch

Queens Drive

Avocet Cl

St Aelreds RC Technology College

St Peter's CE Prim School

Kirkfield Hotel

Willow Rd

A572

Superstore

Patterson

Barn Way

Cross

St Marys Catholic Jun Sch

Victoria Road

58

Milton Av

Whimbrel Av

Harrison Way

Tutor Bank

Bursar close

59

Willow Av

Park Road North

St Newton-le-Willows Station

Holford Way

Rosemary Dr

Warren

E **F** **G** **H**

PO

Bridge St

King Street

Hope St

Surgery

Fairclough

Brookfield St

Siskin Cl

Serin Av

Pipit Av

Newton Le Willows Primary School

Acorn

Street

Mill St

Alfred Street

Mill Green Special Sch

Waverley Rd
Sawley Birley
Bain
Rd
Hilary Avenue
Crow Lincoln
Av
N Rd
The
Unsworth
Merchants Crs

Linbeck
Grove
Ryecroft RC
Garton Drive

E **F** **63** Brook Lyn Avenue **G** Brook **H**

Brandt St
Bodden
St Nicholas

Alfred Rd

Lowton St Marys
CE Primary School

I

Lowton Common

Surgery
The

Cleveland
Dr

62

Sarsfield
Fieldfare Cl
Mullein
Drive

Redmain
Aldford

Garton
Durrell Wy

The Pipers

Lane Head Av

Council
Building

Norwich

Chester Av
Bourne Av
Rostherne

Laurel Gv

Surgery

Meadway

Durrell Wy
Amis Gv

Clayton Rd
Stein Av
Chandler

Edgerton Rd
Fir Tree Av
Alder Rd Burnsall
Elm Tree Rd

Hesketh
Meadow
Lane

Lowton
Business
Park

Stradbroke
Cl

Pocket
Moorfield
Crs

Nook

Lowton

Ashwood

Woodford Av

St Catherines
RC Primary
School

Elm Tree
Rd

Laburnum
Oaklands Road

The
Elms

Carr La

2

Garside

Rutland Av

CHURCH

Mirfield
Cl
Broughton Av

Tarnway
Ridgeway

Lowton J&I
School

Brancaster
Drive

Bromley
Avenue
Alderley Av

St Lukes
CE Prim
Sch

Cranham
Av
Malton
Elcombe Av
Ranworth

Crannog
Norwood
Av
Osborne

Kings Av
Cedar Av
Beech
Rowan Av

**Lowton
St Mary's**

LANE
Martland

Bradwell Road
Wensley Road

A572

Kenilworth Rd
Funwell

Mulberry
Cl
Larch
Spruce

Maple
Av

PO

A580

E **F**

Heathmoor
AV
Heath

Cotswold Av
Lynwood
Lime Grove
The Limes

Innkeeper's
Lodge

Mather
Av

B5207

**Lane
Head**

3

Lynwood
Av
Headland
Cl

Winton Rd
Delamere
Avenue

72

Heath
Lane

Meadows
on

KENYON LANE

WILTON

4

Wigan
Warrington

5

A579

Kenyon

E **F** Morris's
Farm **77** Lane **G** **H**

Main

74

Netherbarrow Farm

A   B   **66**   C   D

Turf Nest Farm

Lane

3 68   69

I

Hesnall Close

Hurst MI La

Warrington Wigan

Acreville Grove

Sandfield Crescent

2

Queen's AV

Whlly AV

Monk Ct

Duke AV

Crn AV

Windy Bank Farm

Bedford Moss

97

3

Light Oaks Road

73

Old Moss Lane

Light Oaks Moss Farm

WARRINGTON ROAD

Millbrook Cl

4

Hey Shoot Lane

Wigan
Salford

Hawthorne AV

Moss   Lane

3 96

Moss House Farm

5

Works

Holm Leigh Farm

A   B   C   D

3 68   69

I grid square represents 500 metres

E   F   67   G   H

70   71   98

I

Moss Bank Farm

Rindle Road

Salford Wigan

2

LC

97

3

Olive Mount Farm

Astley Road

Chat Moss

4   Twelve Yard

Moss Farm

Cutnook Lan

96

5   Raspberry Lan

Little Woolden Moss

Twelve Yards Road

70   71

E   F   G   Larkhill   H

Newton-le-Willows Station

Newton Park

Mill Green Special Sch

Newton Park Drive

Parkside Farm

Warrington St. Helens

Wood Head

PARKSIDE ROAD

M6

A573

Junction 22

Red Bank Avenue

Red Bank

Hermitage Green Lane

Hermitage Green

Cop Holt Farm

NEWTON ROAD

COLBORNE ROAD

Colborne Rd

Gerosa Av

A573

Old School House Lane

Green La

Green Lane

The Priory

Spires Gdns

Winwick

Waterworks

Lane

LINK ROAD

Highfield Lane

Myddleton Rd

Arbury

Maple Rd

Ash

Ilex Av

Lineside Av

Hollins Lane

Ballantyne Pl

Marryat Cl

Church Walk

Cem

Hornby La

PO

Premier Lodge

Winwick CE Primary School

Winwick Parish Leisure Centre

Hollins Lane

Hollins

'f Course

Bungalow Road

A49

Cholmley

Crnt Dr

Wayfarers Dr

Pennington

Banastre Dr

Rosemary Dr

Holford Way

Mere Road

SOUTHWOR **ROAD**

A572 CHURCH ST

A49

MILL LANE

WINNICK ROAD

Mill Green

Warren EA

1 **2** **3** **4** **5**

A **B** **70** **C** **D**

A **B** **C** **D**

I grid square represents 500 metres

Calderburn Cl HOR/BR BL6 ....14 C2
Calder Dr WALK M28 ....55 F1
WGNE/HIN WN2..........................49 F1
Calder Pl WGNW/BIL/O WN5 ....32 D1
Caldew Cl WGNE/HIN WN2 ....36 B4
Caldford Cl WGNE/HIN WN2 ....12 D4
Caldwell Av TYLD M29 ....66 D2
Caldwell Cl TYLD M29 ....36 D3
Caldwell St WHTN BL5 ....38 A5
Caleb Cl TYLD M29 ....57 H5
Cale La WGNE/HIN WN2 ....23 G3
Calico Wood Av
WGNE/HIN WN2.............................9 E4
Callander Ct
WGNW/BIL/O WN5 ....33 F1
Calow Dr LEIGH WN7 ....65 H3
Calton Cl WGNS/IIMK WN5 ....53 E4
Calveley Wk WGNNW/ST WN6 ......19 H2
Calverhall Wy AIMK WN4 ....60 D3
Calver Hey Cl WHTN BL5 ....26 D3
Calverleigh Cl BOLS/LL BL3 ....27 H5
Camberwell Crs
WGNE/HIN WN2..............................3 J1
Cambourne Dr
WGNE/HIN WN2 ....3 F6
Cambrian Crs WGNS/IIMK WN3 ....46 D1
Cambridge Rd HOR/BR BL6 ....15 E2
SKEL WN8 ....16 D4
WGNW/BIL/O WN5 ....19 H5
Cambridge St ATH M46 ....52 D1
WGN WN1.......................................3 F6
Camdale Cl WGN WN1 ....3 F6
Camelot Cl NEWLW WA12 ....68 C5
Cameron Pl WGNW/BIL/O WN5 ....21 F5
Cameron St LEIGH WN7 ....51 G4
Camm St WGNE/HIN WN2 ....49 F3
Campbell Rd BOLS/LL BL3 ....27 H1
Campbell St
WGNW/BIL/O WN5 ....33 E3
Campbell Wy LHULT M38 ....41 H5
Campion Av AIMK WN4 ....60 C2
Camp Rd AIMK WN4 ....54 A3
Canaan GOL/RIS/CU WA3 ....72 B1
Canal St CHLY/EC PR7 ....7 F1
WGNE/HIN WN2 ....21 E2
WGNNW/ST WN6 ....3 G4
Canal Ter WGNE/HIN WN2 ....3 H6
Canberra Rd
WGNW/BIL/O WN5 ....20 D4
Canmore Cl BOLS/LL BL3 ....27 H2
Cannel Fold WALK M28 ....55 E4
Cannon St ATH M46 ....39 E5
Canon Cl WGNNW/ST WN6 ....5 G5
Canon Wilson Cl
RNFD/HAY WA11 ....68 A3
Cansfield Gv AIMK WN4 ....60 B3
Canterbury Av
GOL/RIS/CU WA3 ....63 E5
Canterbury Cl ATH M46 ....39 F4
Capps St WHTN BL5 ....37 H4
Captain Fold Rd LHULT M38 ....41 E3
Captain Lees Gdns WHTN BL5 ....26 B5
Captain Lees Rd WHTN BL5 ....26 B5
Captain's La AIMK WN4 ....61 F3
Carawood Cl WGNNW/ST WN6 ....6 E5
Car Bank Av ATH M46 ....39 F4
Car Bank Sq ATH M46 ....39 E4
Car Bank St ATH M46 ....38 C4
Carders Cl LEIGH WN7 ....64 C4
Cardiff St SKEL WN8 ....16 C4
Careless La WGNE/HIN WN2 ....3 F6
Carey Cl WGNS/IIMK WN3 ....47 E1
Carfield SKEL WN8 ....30 B2
Carisbrooke Rd LEIGH WN7 ....53 E5
Carlisle St WHTN BL5 ....2 A4 *
WGNNW/ST WN6 ....5 F5
Carlton Av BOLS/LL BL3 ....27 H1
SKEL WN8 ....30 D1
Carlton Cl WALK M28 ....55 H2
Carlton Gv LEIGH WN7 ....51 F3
WGNE/HIN WN2 ....36 C5
Carlton Rd GOL/RIS/CU WA3 ....62 B5
WALK M28 ....55 H2
Carlton St WGNS/IIMK WN3 ....34 A2
Carlyle Gv LEIGH WN7 ....51 F3
Carnegie Dr AIMK WN4 ....60 D1
Carnforth Av WGNE/HIN WN2 ....36 C5
Carnoustie Dr BOLS/LL BL3 ....27 H2
Caroline St WGN WN1 ....J5
WGNS/IIMK WN3 ....2 B6
Carradon Dr WGNNW/ST WN6 ......10 D1
Carr Brook Dr ATH M46 ....39 F4
Carr Common Rd
WGNE/HIN WN2 ....37 G5
Carrfield Av LHULT M38 ....40 D4
Carrfield Gv LHULT M38 ....40 D4
Carrington Gv LEIGH WN7 * 52 A4
Carrington St LEIGH WN7 ....52 A4
Carr La GOL/RIS/CU WA3 ....72 D1
LEIGH WN7 ....71 G1
WGNS/IIMK WN3 ....45 F1
Carr Mill Crs
WGNW/BIL/O WN5 ....58 D2
Carr Mill Rd WGNW/BIL/O WN5 ....58 D3
Carr St LEIGH WN7 ....64 B1
WGNE/HIN WN2 ....36 A2
Car St WGNE/HIN WN2 ....49 F2
Carswell Cl TYLD M29 ....53 F2
Carter Av RNFD/HAY WA11 ....56 B1
Carter St WGNS/IIMK WN3 ....36 D2
Cartleach Gv WALK M28 ....55 E1
Cartleach La WALK M28 ....55 E1
Cartmel Av WGN WN1 ....22 A2
Cartmel Cl BOLS/LL BL3 ....27 E3
Cartwright Gv LEIGH WN7 ....51 F4
Carville Gv HOR/BR BL6 ....14 C4
Carwood Gv HOR/BR BL6 ....14 C1
Cascades SKEL WN8 * 31 G5
Case Rd RNFD/HAY WA11 ....68 A3
Cashmore Dr WGNE/HIN WN2 ....36 A4
Castle Dr CHLY/EC PR7 ....6 F1
Castle Fold LEIGH WN7 ....53 E5
Castle Hey Cl WGNE/HIN WN2 ....36 C1
Castle Hill Pk WGNE/HIN WN2 ......36 C1

Castle Hill Rd WGNE/HIN WN2 ......36 B2
Castle House La CHLY/EC PR7 ....6 D1
Castlemere Cl WGNS/IIMK WN3 ....47 E2
Castle Ri WGNE/HIN WN2 ....53 C2
Castle St TYLD M29 ....53 C2
WGNE/HIN WN2 ....36 B2
Castleton Wy WGNS/IIMK WN3 .....46 D1
Castleway WGNE/HIN WN2 ....36 C3
Caterham Av BOLS/LL BL3 ....27 F1
Catherine St LEIGH WN7 ....52 A5
Catherine Ter WGN WN1 ....3 H2
Caton Dr ATH M46 ....52 B3
Caunce Av GOL/RIS/CU WA3 ....70 B2
Caunce Rd WGN WN1 ....3 G1
Cavendish Dr WGNS/IIMK WN3 .....47 E1
Cavendish St LEIGH WN7 ....52 A4
Cawdor St LEIGH WN7 ....65 E2
WGNE/HIN WN2 ....36 B3
WGNW/BIL/O WN5 ....33 G2
Cawley Av GOL/RIS/CU WA3 ....72 D5
Caxton Cl WGNS/IIMK WN3 ....44 A4
C' Ct AIMK WN4 ....61 E4
Cecil Av WGNNW/ST WN6 ....21 H5
Cecil St LEIGH WN7 ....51 F1
WGN WN1.......................................3 H5
WGNS/IIMK WN3 ....34 B4
Cedar Av ATH M46 ....38 C4
GOL/RIS/CU WA3 ....71 G2
HOR/BR BL6 ....14 D1
WGNE/HIN WN2 ....36 C5
WGNNW/ST WN6 ....10 C2
Cedar Dr WGN WN1 ....22 C3
Cedar Gv AIMK WN4 ....60 A1
RNFD/HAY WA11 ....68 B2
SKEL WN8 ....16 D4
WGNS/IIMK WN3 ....32 A2
WHTN BL5 ....37 H1
Cedar Rd LEIGH WN7 ....51 G5
Celandine Wk WGNS/IIMK WN3 ....32 C4
Cemetery Rd WGNS/IIMK WN3 .....54 D4
Cemetery St WHTN BL5 ....25 H4
Cemetery Vw CHLY/EC PR7 ....7 E1
Central Av ATH M46 ....39 F4
WGN WN1.......................................3 J7
WALK M28 ....55 E4
Central Dr RNFD/HAY WA11 ....43 E4
WGNE/HIN WN2 ....9 G4
WHTN BL5 ....25 H4
Central Park Wy WGN WN1 ....2 E2
Centre Ct LEIGH WN7 ....64 A5
Chadbury Cl HOR/BR BL6 ....26 D2
Chaddock La TYLD M29 ....54 D5
Chadwick St LEIGH WN7 ....52 A5
WGNE/HIN WN2 ....36 B2
WGNS/IIMK WN3 ....34 A2
Chalbury Cl WGNE/HIN WN2 * 36 A4
Chalfont Dr TYLD M29 ....53 H4
Challenge Wy
WGNW/BIL/O WN5 ....20 D4
Chancery Cl TYLD M29 ....54 A3
Chandler Wy GOL/RIS/CU WA3 ......71 G1
Chanters Av ATH M46 ....39 F5
The Chanters WALK M28 ....55 H4
Chantry Cl WHTN BL5 ....38 A3
Chantry Wk AIMK WN4 ....60 C1
Chapel Cl WGNS/IIMK WN3 ....34 C2
Chapelfield Dr WALK M28 ....41 G5
Chapel Fields La
WGNE/HIN WN2 ....36 B3
Chapel Green Rd
WGNE/HIN WN2 ....36 B2
Chapel La WGNS/IIMK WN3 ....33 C3
Chapel Meadow WALK M28 ....55 G4
Chapel Pl AIMK WN4 ....61 E3
Chapelstead WHTN BL5 ....38 A3
Chapel St AIMK WN4 ....39 E5
ATH M46 ....39 E5
CHLY/EC PR7 ....7 E1
LEIGH WN7 ....65 F2
RNFD/HAY WA11 ....68 B3
TYLD M29 ....53 H5
WALK M28 ....55 E5
WGN WN1.......................................2 C6
WGNE/HIN WN2 ....36 A3
WGNE/HIN WN2 ....49 F1
WGNNW/ST WN6 ....50 B2
WGNS/IIMK WN3 ....34 C4
WGNW/BIL/O WN5 ....32 C5
Chapel Vw RNFD/HAY WA11 ....57 G2
Charity St LEIGH WN7 ....64 B1
Charles St GOL/RIS/CU WA3 ....62 B5
LEIGH WN7 ....52 A4
TYLD M29 ....53 G2
WGN WN1..3 G6
WGNE/HIN WN2 ....36 B1
WHTN BL5 ....35 F1
Charlesworth Av
WGNE/HIN WN2 ....36 C4
Charlock Av WHTN BL5 ....37 G2
Charlock Cl LEIGH WN7 ....53 G4
Charlotte Dr WGNS/IIMK WN3 ......33 E4
Charlton Cl AIMK WN4 ....60 D1
Charnock St WGNE/HIN WN2 ....49 G2
Charnwood Cl TYLD M29 ....53 H5
Charnwood Gv WGN WN1 ....55 H1
WHTN BL5 ....25 H2
Charterhouse Rd
WGNS/IIMK WN3 ....34 C2
Chatburn Av GOL/RIS/CU WA3 ......62 D5
Chatham St LEIGH WN7 ....52 A4
WGN WN1..3 G6
WGNE/HIN WN2 ....23 F5
Chatsworth Av
GOL/RIS/CU WA3 ....73 E5
WHTN BL5 ....35 E4
Chatsworth Cl AIMK WN4 ....60 C2
Chatsworth Dr LEIGH WN7 ....53 F4
Chatsworth St
WGNW/BIL/O WN5 ....32 D3
Chatteris Cl WGNE/HIN WN2 ....36 B4
Chaucer Gv LEIGH WN7 ....51 F3
Chaucer Pl WGN WN1 ....22 B2
Chedworth Crs LHULT M38 ....41 F2
Cheetham Gv WGNE/HIN WN2 ......35 G3

The Cheethams HOR/BR BL6.........13 F3
Chelburn Cl WGNE/HIN WN2 ....50 D2
Chelford Av GOL/RIS/CU WA3 ....35 E2
Chelford Cl WGNE/HIN WN3 ....47 G1
Chelford Dr TYLD M29 ....54 B5
Chelmarsh Av AIMK WN4 ....61 F3
Chelmer Av WHTN BL5 ....26 A4
Chelmsford Gv
WGNS/IIMK WN3 ....46 D1
Chelmsford Dr 33 H4
Chelmsford Ms WGN WN1 ....22 B3
Chelsea Ct WHTN BL5 * 37 G3
Cheltenham Av
WGNE/HIN WN2 ....34 C2
Cheltenham Dr NEWLW WA12 ....69 H4
WGNW/BIL/O WN5 ....45 G1
Cheltenham St
WGNE/HIN WN2 ....23 E3
Chelwood Ms HOR/BR BL6 * 15 G3
Chelwood Pk RNFD/HAY WA11 ......81 E5
Chepstow Gv LEIGH WN7 ....53 E4
Chequer Av ATH M46 ....30 C3
Chequer La SKEL WN8 ....30 C4
Chequers St WGN WN1 ....2 B5
Cherington Dr TYLD M29 ....54 B2
Cherrybrook Dr
WGNS/IIMK WN3 ....47 E2
Cherry Cl LEIGH WN7 ....65 E3
Cherrycroft SKEL WN8 ....30 B2
Cherry Gv LEIGH WN7 ....52 A3
WGNE/HIN WN2 ....21 G2
Cherry Tree Gv LEIGH WN7 ....51 G5
ATH M46 ....39 E3
Cherry Tree La
RNFD/HAY WA11 ....57 H4
Cherry Tree Rd
GOL/RIS/CU WA3 ....71 G1
Cherry Tree Wy HOR/BR BL6 * 50 D1
Cherrywood Av WHTN BL5 ....39 H1
Cherrywood Cl WHTN BL5 ....39 H1
Chervil Wk WGNS/IIMK WN3 ....32 D4
Cherwell Cl WGNE/HIN WN2 ....12 D4
Cherwell Rd WHTN BL5 ....26 A3
Chester Av WGNS/IIMK WN3 ....71 E1
Chester Dr AIMK WN4 ....60 A1
Chester Rd TYLD M29 ....54 C5
Chester St ATH M46 ....53 F1
LEIGH WN7 ....65 E1
Chesterton Cl WGNS/IIMK WN3 ....33 H5
Chestnut Av ATH M46 * 38 D4
WHTN BL5 ....35 E4
Chestnut Dr LEIGH WN7 ....65 E5
WHTN BL5 ....38 A1
Chestnut Dr South LEIGH WN7 .....65 E4
Chestnut Gv AIMK WN4 ....61 G2
GOL/RIS/CU WA3 ....71 G1
WGNE/HIN WN2 ....36 C4
Chestnut La LEIGH WN7 ....65 E4
Chestnut Rd WGN WN1 ....3 F1
Chetwode Av AIMK WN4 ....46 D1
Cheviot Av WGNS/IIMK WN3 ....34 B3
Chew Moor La WHTN BL5 ....26 B3
Chichester Av ATH M46 ....52 B1
Chilgrove Av HOR/BR BL6 ....13 E1
Chilham St WGNW/BIL/O WN5 ......32 B2
Chillingham Dr LEIGH WN7 ....65 G2
Chiltern Av AIMK WN4 ....61 F4
Chiltern Cl AIMK WN4 ....61 F4
Chiltern Dr WGNS/IIMK WN3 ....32 D5
Chiltern Rd GOL/RIS/CU WA3 ....72 D5
Chiltern Wy TYLD M29 ....54 A5
Chilton Cl LEIGH WN7 ....52 A4
Chimes Rd AIMK WN4 ....47 G5
Chinnor Cl LEIGH WN7 ....52 A4
Chip Hill Rd BOLS/LL BL3 ....27 G1
Chirton Cl RNFD/HAY WA11 ....68 A2
Chisacre Dr WGNNW/ST WN6 ....8 C3
Chisholm Cl WGNNW/ST WN6 ....4 C1
Chisledon Cl RNFD/HAY WA11 ....68 A2
Chisnall Av WGNNW/ST WN6 ....4 A2
Chisnall La CHLY/EC PR7 ....42 A1
Chiswell St WGNW/BIL/O WN5 ......32 D3
Chisworth Cl LEIGH WN7 ....51 H4
Chorley New Rd HOR/BR BL6 ....14 C1
Chorley Rd CHLY/EC PR7 ....7 F2
WGN WN1..11 E1
WGNNW/ST WN6 ....5 H4
WHTN BL5 ....13 G4
Chorley St WGNS/IIMK WN3 ....34 D2
Chowbent Cl ATH M46 ....39 F5
Christleton Av WGNNW/ST WN6 .....9 G4
Christopher St
WGNS/IIMK WN3 ....35 E2
Chulsey Gate La HOR/BR BL6 ....26 B1
Church Av WGNE/HIN WN2 ....50 C3
Church Dr WGNW/BIL/O WN5 ....31 G3
Churchfield WGNNW/ST WN6 ....9 F4
Church Gates WGN WN1 ....2 C5
Church Gn SKEL WN8 ....17 E4
Church Gv WGN WN1 * 21 G1
Churchill Av GOL/RIS/CU WA3 ....73 G5
Churchlands La
WGNNW/ST WN6 ....10 C1
Church La GOL/RIS/CU WA3 ....71 E2
WGNE/HIN WN2 ....13 E2
WHTN BL5 ....25 H2
Church Rd RNFD/HAY WA11 ....43 E5
RNFD/HAY WA11 ....68 B3
SKEL WN8 ....17 E4
TYLD M29 ....54 B5
WGNE/HIN WN2 ....36 B2
WGNE/HIN WN2 ....12 C4
WGNW/BIL/O WN5 ....30 B1
WHTN BL5 ....35 H2
Churchside FWTH BL4 ....40 D1
Church St AIMK WN4 ....61 E3
HOR/BR BL6 ....7 H5
LEIGH WN7 ....65 E1
NEWLW WA12 ....69 G4
SKEL WN8 ....31 F1
WGN WN1.......................................2 D4
WGNE/HIN WN2 ....12 C4
WGNE/HIN WN2 ....36 B2
WGNNW/ST WN6 ....35 B1
WGNNW/ST WN6 ....10 C2
WGNW/BIL/O WN5 ....31 G3

WGNW/BIL/O WN5 ....32 C2
WHTN BL5 ....25 H4
Churnett Cl WHTN BL5 ....26 A4
Churton Gv WGNNW/ST WN6 ....4 C5
Cinnamon Av WGNE/HIN WN2 ......36 D4
Cinnamon Brow SKEL WN8 ....31 F2
Cirencester Cl LHULT M38 ....41 F2
City Rd WALK M28 ....55 F5
Clanwood Cl WGNS/IIMK WN3 ......47 F1
Clap Gate La WGNS/IIMK WN3 ......33 F5
Claremont Av WGNE/HIN WN2 ......36 D4
Claremont Dr LHULT M38...............41 G5
Claremont Rd
GOL/RIS/CU WA3 ....72 C5
WGNW/BIL/O WN5 ....58 D1
Clarence St AIMK WN4 ....60 C2
ATH M46 ....53 F2
GOL/RIS/CU WA3 ....62 B5
LEIGH WN7 ....65 E2
NEWLW WA12 ....11 F4
WGNE/HIN WN2 ....55 F1
Clarence Yd WGN WN1 ....2 C5
Clarington Gv WGN WN1 ....3 G6
Clarke Av GOL/RIS/CU WA3 ....35 E2
Clarke Crs LHULT M38 ....40 C2
Clarke St LEIGH WN7 ....52 A4
Claude St WGNW/BIL/O WN5 ....33 E2
Claughton Av WALK M28 ....55 G4
Claybridge Cl
WGNW/BIL/O WN5 ....20 C4
Clay Brow Rd SKEL WN8 ....30 B2
Claydon Dr WGNS/IIMK WN3 ....46 D1
Clayhill Gv GOL/RIS/CU WA3 ....72 A1
Claypool Rd HOR/BR BL6 ....14 C1
Clayton Av GOL/RIS/CU WA3 ....71 F1
Clayton House LEIGH WN7 ....64 A4
Clayton Ms SKEL WN8 ....16 C4
Clayton St SKEL WN8 ....16 C4
Clegg's La LHULT M38 ....41 F5
Clegg St SKEL WN8 ....30 D1
TYLD M29 ....53 H5
Clement Av GOL/RIS/CU WA3 ....63 E1
Clevedon Dr WGNS/IIMK WN3 ......32 D4
Cleveland Av WGNS/IIMK WN3 ......46 D1
Cleveland Dr AIMK WN4 ....60 A1
GOL/RIS/CU WA3 ....71 E1
Cleworth Cl TYLD M29 ....54 A5
Clifford Rd BOLS/LL BL3 * 27 H3
Clifton Av TYLD M29 ....53 H4
Clifton Cl TYLD M29 ....54 B5
Clifton Crs WGN WN1 ....22 B3
Clifton Dr HOR/BR BL6 ....7 G4
Cliftonmill Mdw
WGNW/BIL/O WN5 ....70 A1
Clifton Rd AIMK WN4 ....47 E5
LEIGH WN7 ....51 F4
WGNW/BIL/O WN5 ....58 C2
Clifton St LEIGH WN7 ....53 G4
TYLD M29 ....54 B5
WGN WN1.......................................2 D2
WHTN BL5 ....33 H4
Clive Rd WHTN BL5 ....37 H2
Clock Tower Cl WALK M28 ....41 E5
Cloister Av LEIGH WN7 ....64 C5
The Cloisters WHTN BL5 ....37 H3
Closebrook Rd
WGNW/BIL/O WN5 ....33 E2
Close La WGNE/HIN WN2 ....55 G5
Close St WGNE/HIN WN2 ....36 A2
The Close ATH M46 ....39 G3
Cloudstock Gv LHULT M38 ....40 C5
Clough Av WHTN BL5 ....26 A5
Clough Fold WHTN BL5 ....26 A5
Clough Gv AIMK WN4 ....60 A2
Clough House Dr LEIGH WN7 ....65 G1
The Clough AIMK WN4 ....60 A2
Cloughwood Crs
WGNNW/ST WN6 ....8 C5
Clovelly Av LEIGH WN7 ....52 A3
Cloverdale Dr AIMK WN4 ....61 F4
Clover St WGNNW/ST WN6 ....21 H5
Club St RNFD/HAY WA11 ....68 A2
Clyde Rd TYLD M29 ....53 F2
Clyde St LEIGH WN7 * 65 G2
Coach House Dr
WGNW/BIL/O WN5 ....20 C4
Coach Rd TYLD M29 ....54 B5
Coal Pit La ATH M46 ....38 C5
LEIGH WN7 ....38 B4
ORM L39 ....28 B4
Cobden St NEWLW WA12 ....69 G5
TYLD M29 ....53 G2
Cob Moor Av
WGNW/BIL/O WN5 ....45 G2
Cob Moor Rd
WGNW/BIL/O WN5 ....45 G2
Cocker St LHULT M38 ....41 F4
Code La WHTN BL5 ....25 F1
Colburn Cl WGNS/IIMK WN3 ....47 H1
Colby Rd WGNE/HIN WN2 ....54 A5
Coldalhurst La TYLD M29 ....67 E1
Colebourne Dr AIMK WN4 ....60 A1
Cole Av NEWLW WA12 ....69 F5
Coleclough Pl
GOL/RIS/CU WA3 ....73 E5
Coleridge Av
WGNW/BIL/O WN5 ....32 D2
Coleridge Rd
GOL/RIS/CU WA3 ....45 G2
Colerne Wy WGNS/IIMK WN3 ....32 C4
Colesbourne Dr LHULT M38 ....41 F2
Coleshill Ri WGNS/IIMK WN3 ....46 D1
Colin St WGN WN1 ....2 C6
Colinton SKEL WN8 ....30 B1
Collard St ATH M46 ....38 C4
College Av WGN WN1 ....2 C6
College Rd SKEL WN8 ....19 E4
College St LEIGH WN7 ....65 E2
Collett Cl WGN WN1 ....3 J5
Colliers Cl WGNS/IIMK WN3 ....64 D3
Collier St WGNE/HIN WN2 ....36 A2

Colliery La ATH M46 ....38 A4
Collinge St WGNE/HIN WN2 ....49 F1
Collingwood St ....
WGN WN1......................................10 B1
Collingwood Av WHTN BL5 ....25 H4
Collins La WHTN BL5 ....38 A2
Collisdene Rd
WGNW/BIL/O WN5 ....31 G2
Colnbrook WGNNW/ST WN6 ....9 C1
Coltsfoot Cl LEIGH WN7 ....52 B1
Colwyn Dr WGNE/HIN WN2 ....51 F1
Colwyn Gv ATH M46 ....38 D5
Combermere Cl TYLD M29 ....54 A2
Comet Rd WGNW/BIL/O WN5 ....20 D5
Commodore Pl
WGNW/BIL/O WN5 ....21 F4
Common End CHLY/EC PR7 ....6 C5
Common La GOL/RIS/CU WA3 ....72 C5
LEIGH WN7 ....64 A2
TYLD M29 ....53 H2
Common Nook
WGNE/HIN WN2 ....35 F2
Common Side Rd WALK M28 ....55 E4
Common St WHTN BL5 ....37 E1
The Common CHLY/EC PR7 ....6 D2
Concord Av WGNS/IIMK WN3 ....34 A5
Congresbury Rd LEIGH WN7 ....51 G4
Coniston Av ATH M46 ....39 E3
FWTH BL4 ....40 D1
LHULT M38 ....41 F4
WGN WN1......................................22 A2
WGNE/HIN WN2 ....35 G1
Coniston Dr WGNE/HIN WN2 ....49 G5
Coniston Gv LHULT M38 ....41 F4
Coniston Park Dr
WGNNW/ST WN6 ....10 D5
Coniston Rd TYLD M29 ....53 H4
WGNE/HIN WN2 ....36 B4
Coniston St LEIGH WN7 * 64 C1
Coniston Wy
RNFD/HAY WA11 ....43 E1
Conrad Cl WGNS/IIMK WN3 ....35 E5
Constantia St WGNS/IIMK WN3 .....33 H5
Conway Av WGNE/HIN WN2 ....24 A1
Conway Crs WGNW/BIL/O WN5 .....45 H5
Conway Dr WGNE/HIN WN2 ....24 A1
WGNS/IIMK WN3 ....59 E1
Conway Rd AIMK WN4 ....61 H1
WGNE/HIN WN2 ....36 C4
Conway St WGNW/BIL/O WN5 ....32 D3
Cook Av RNFD/HAY WA11 ....68 B2
Cooke St LEIGH WN7 ....47 G5
LEIGH WN7 ....65 E1
WGNNW/ST WN6 ....49 F2
Cooling La TYLD M29 ....53 E3
Coombe Cl TYLD M29 ....54 A5
Co-operative St LEIGH WN7 ....64 C1
LHULT M38 * 40 D3
Coopers Gln WGNE/HIN WN2 ....23 F5
Coop St WGN WN1 ....3 F5
Copeland Dr WGNE/HIN WN2 ....5 G5
Copesthorne Cl
WGNE/HIN WN2 ....12 D4
Coplow Dl WGNE/HIN WN2 ....36 B5
Copperas St WGNNW/ST WN6 ....9 F3
Copperas La HOR/BR BL6 ....12 C1
WGNE/HIN WN2 ....12 B4
Copperbeech Dr
WGNNW/ST WN6 ....11 E1
Copperfield WGN WN1 ....1 C5
Copperfields HOR/BR BL6 ....26 C2
Coppice Dr WGNS/IIMK WN3 ....33 G5
Coppice La WGNS/IIMK WN3 ....33 G1
Coppull Moor La CHLY/EC PR7 ....5 E1
The Copse NEWLW WA12 ....68 D5
WGNE/HIN WN2 ....32 B2
Coral Gv WGN WN1 ....64 D2
Coralin Wy AIMK WN4 ....47 G4
Corfe Cl WGNE/HIN WN2 ....21 H2
Corfe Cl WGNE/HIN WN2 * 3 K5
Corhampton Crs ATH M46 ....39 F5
Cornbrook SKEL WN8 ....30 B1
Cornbrook Cl WHTN BL5 ....26 A4
Cornelian Gv AIMK WN4 ....60 C1
Cornergate WHTN BL5 ....37 H3
Corner La WGNE/HIN WN2 ....51 H4
Cornlea Dr WALK M28 ....55 H4
Cornmill Ct GOL/RIS/CU WA3 * 77 F4
Corn St LEIGH WN7 ....64 C1
Cornwall Av TYLD M29 ....39 H5
WHTN BL5 ....25 C5
Cornwall Crs WGN WN1 ....11 G1
Cornwall Dr WGNE/HIN WN2 ....36 C2
Cornwallis Rd WGNS/IIMK WN3 ....33 H3
Cornwall Pl WGNW/BIL/O WN5 .....32 D2
Coronation Av ATH M46 ....38 D5
GOL/RIS/CU WA3 ....73 H2
Coronation Dr LEIGH WN7 ....68 D2
RNFD/HAY WA11 ....68 D2
Coronation Rd
WGNNW/ST WN6 ....21 E2
Coronation St AIMK WN4 ....47 E5
WGNS/IIMK WN3 ....34 A2
Coronation Wk
WGNW/BIL/O WN5 ....58 C2
Corporation St
WGNS/IIMK WN3 ....34 A2
Corrie St LHULT M38 ....41 F4
Corsey Rd WGNE/HIN WN2 ....34 H2
Corston Gv WGNE/HIN WN2 ....36 C5
Cosgate Cl WGNE/HIN WN2 ....31 H3
Costessey Wy
WGNS/IIMK WN3 ....32 D5
Cosworth Cl LEIGH WN7 ....65 G2
Cotswold Av GOL/RIS/CU WA3 ......71 E3
Cottage Cft WGN WN1 ....22 B3
Cottesmore Wy
GOL/RIS/CU WA3 ....62 C5
Cotton St LEIGH WN7 ....64 C1
Coultshead Av
WGNW/BIL/O WN5 ....45 H5

Council Av *AIMK* WN4 ....61 E3
County Police St
WGNE/HIN WN2 ....3 K6
County Rd *WALK* M28 ....41 F4
Coupes Gn *WHTN* BL5 ....37 H3
Coupland Rd *WGNW/BIL/O* WN5 ......37 E4
Courier Pl *WGNW/BIL/O* WN5 ....21 F4
Courtyard Dr *ATH* M46 ....41 E5
Coverdale Rd *WHTN* BL5 ....25 C5
The Coverts *WGNNW/ST* WN6 ......10 D3
Cowburn St *LEIGH* WN7 ....64 C5
WGNE/HIN WN2 ....36 C1
Cowdals Rd *HOR/BR* BL6 ....26 C1
Cow Lees *WHTN* BL5 ....26 B4
Cowling St *WGNS/IIMK* WN3 ....34 A2
Cowper St *LEIGH* WN7 ....64 C5
Coxfield *WGNNW/ST* WN6 ....8 C3
Cox Wy *ATH* M46 ....53 E1
Crab Tree La *ATH* M46 ....53 E1
Crabtree Rd
WGNW/BIL/O WN5 ....33 E1
Crag Gv *RNFD/HAY* WA11 ....58 B2
Cramond Cl *WGNS/IIMK* WN3 ....33 G4
Cranberry Av *WGNNW/ST* WN6 ......21 C2
Cranberry Dr *BOLS/LL* BL3 ....27 C1
Cranborne Cl *HOR/BR* BL6 ....15 E1
WGNNW/ST WN6 ....10 A1
Cranbrook Av *AIMK* WN4 ....60 D2
Cranbrook Wk *WGNE/HIN* WN2 ....22 A1
Cranby St *WGNE/HIN* WN2 ....36 A3
Crane St *CHLY/EC* PR7 ....5 E1
Cranfield Rd *HOR/BR* BL6 ....14 C1
WGNS/IIMK WN3 ....33 H5
Cranham Av *GOL/RIS/CU* WA3 ......71 F2
Cranham Close Crs
LHULT M58 * 41 F2
Crank Hl *RNFD/HAY* WA11 ....57 C2
Crank Rd *RNFD/HAY* WA11 ....44 C4
Crankwood Rd
WGNE/HIN WN2 ....49 G5
Cranleigh *WGNNW/ST* WN6 ....10 C2
Cranleigh Cl *HOR/BR* BL6 ....13 E1
Cranleigh Dr *TYLD* M29 ....54 A3
Cranshaw St *TYLD* M29 ....54 C3
Cranstal Dr *WGNE/HIN* WN2 ....36 D3
Cranwell Av *GOL/RIS/CU* WA3 ......71 F2
Cranworth Av *TYLD* M29 ....53 H5
Craven Av *GOL/RIS/CU* WA3 ....71 F2
TYLD M29 ....54 A3
WGNE/HIN WN2 ....12 D5
Crawford Pl *WGN* WN1 * 22 C2
Crawford Rd *SKEL* WN8 ....44 A1
Crawford St *WGN* WN1 ....2 F3
WGNE/HIN WN2 ....23 H1
Crawley Cl *TYLD* M29 ....54 B2
Crediton Dr *WGNE/HIN* WN2 ....49 F2
Crescent Av *AIMK* WN4 ....60 D2
FWTH BL4 ....41 H2
Crescent Cl *LHULT* M58 ....41 G3
Crescent Rd *HOR/BR* BL6 ....14 C4
The Crescent *HOR/BR* BL6 ....14 C1
WGNE/HIN WN2 * 36 A3
WGNW/BIL/O WN5 ....33 E2
WHTN BL5 ....26 B5
Cressell Rd *WGNNW/ST* WN6 ......9 H1
Cressingham Rd *BOLS/LL* BL3 ......27 G2
Crestfield Gv *WGNNW/ST* WN6 ....21 G3
Crestfold *WALK* M28 ....41 F4
Crestwood Av
WGNS/IIMK WN3 ....33 H4
Creswick Cl *WGNE/HIN* WN2 ....35 H4
Criccleth Av *WGNE/HIN* WN2 ......13 E5
Cricketers Wy *WHTN* BL5 ....37 H1
Cricketfield La *WALK* M28 ....41 H5
Cricket St *WGNNW/ST* WN6 ....33 E5
Cringle Cl *BOLS/LL* BL3 ....27 F1
Crippen St *ATH* M46 ....52 B2
Cripple Ga *WGNNW/ST* WN6 ....10 D3
Croal Av *WGNE/HIN* WN2 ....49 F2
Croft Av *ATH* M46 ....53 E1
GOL/RIS/CU WA3 ....62 A4
WGNW/BIL/O WN5 ....31 G3
Croft Gv *LHULT* M58 ....41 E5
Croft Heath Gdns
GOL/RIS/CU WA3 ....77 H4
Croft Pl *TYLD* M29 ....53 G3
Croft St *GOL/RIS/CU* WA3 * 70 D1
LHULT M58 ....41 E3
WHTN BL5 ....35 H2
The Croft *WGNW/BIL/O* WN5 ......31 G4
Croftwood Sq
WGNW/BIL/O WN5 ....20 D3
Crombouke Dr *LEIGH* WN7 ....51 H2
Crombouke Fold *WALK* M28 ....55 G4
Cromedale Crs
WGNNW/ST WN6 ....10 D3
Cromer Dr *ATH* M46 ....52 B1
Cromer Rd *WGNS/IIMK* WN3 ......33 F5
Cromford Dr
WGNW/BIL/O WN5 ....21 G3
Crompton Rd *HOR/BR* BL6 ....15 E2
Crompton St *WGN* WN1 ....2 D2
WGNS/IIMK WN3 ....35 E5
Cromwell Av *WGNW/BIL/O* WN5 ....39 F1
Crookall St *AIMK* WN4 ....61 F2
Crook Gv *WGNNW/ST* WN6 ....10 C3
Crookhurst Av
WGNNW/ST WN6 ....45 C5
Crook St *WGN* WN1 ....2 D4
WGNE/HIN WN2 ....36 A4
Cropton Wy *WGNE/HIN* WN2 ......36 C5
Crosby St *ATH* M46 ....39 F4
Crossdale Rd *WGNE/HIN* WN2 ....36 C5
Crossdale Wy *RNFD/HAY* WA11 ....58 A3
Crossfield Rd *SKEL* WN8 ....17 H5
Crossford Cl *WGNE/HIN* WN2 ......23 E4
Crossgill *TYLD* M29 ....67 E1
Crosslands Rd *WALK* M28 ....55 H5
Cross La *WGNE/HIN* WN2 ....36 C5
Cross Pit La *RNFD/HAY* WA11 ......43 E5
Cross St *ATH* M46 ....38 C4
GOL/RIS/CU WA3 ....70 B2
LEIGH WN7 ....65 F2

TYLD M29 * 53 G3
WGNE/HIN WN2 ....36 A3
Croston St *WGNE/HIN* WN2 ....35 H2
Crowborough Cl *HOR/BR* BL6 ......15 E1
Crowhurst Dr *WGNE/HIN* WN2 ....22 A2
Crow La *SKEL* WN8 ....19 E5
Crow La East *NEWLW* WA12 ....69 F5
Crow La West *NEWLW* WA12 ......68 D5
Crown Fields Cl *NEWLW* WA12 ....69 E4
Crown Gdns *NEWLW* WA12 ....69 E5
Crown La *WGNE/HIN* WN2 ....36 C5
Crown Park Dr *NEWLW* WA12 ......69 E5
Crown St *ATH* M46 ....38 D5
WGNE/HIN WN2 ....35 H2
WGNS/IIMK WN3 ....34 A2
Crow Orchard Rd
WGNNW/ST WN6 ....4 B5
Crowther Dr *WGNS/IIMK* WN3 ....47 F2
Crow Wood Rd
GOL/RIS/CU WA3 ....63 E5
Croxteth Dr *RNFD/HAY* WA11 ......43 E4
Croydon Av *LEIGH* WN7 ....52 A3
Crummock Dr
WGNS/IIMK WN3 ....33 G5
Crummock Rd *FWTH* BL4 ....40 D1
Culcheth Av *WGNE/HIN* WN2 ......49 G2
Culcheth Hall Dr
WA3 ....73 E5
Culcross Av *WGNS/IIMK* WN3 ......32 D4
Cullen Cl *WGNE/HIN* WN2 ....75 F5
Culraven *WGNE/HIN* WN2 * 12 C3
Culvert St *WGNE/HIN* WN2 ....21 H5
Culzean Cl *LEIGH* WN7 ....65 G2
Cumberbatch Pl
WGNS/IIMK WN3 ....35 E4
Cumberland Av *TYLD* M29 ....53 G1
Cumberland Rd *ATH* M46 ....39 F4
Cumberland St *WGN* WN1 ....3 G2
Cumbrian Cl *WGNE/HIN* WN2 ......49 G1
Cunliffe Av *NEWLW* WA12 ....69 E4
Cunliffe Cl *LEIGH* WN7 ....63 H2
Cunliffe St *LEIGH* WN7 ....64 C5
Cunningham Rd *WHTN* BL5 ....37 F1
Curlew Cl *GOL/RIS/CU* WA3 ....71 E1
Curtis St *WGNE/HIN* WN2 ....33 E2
Cutacre Cl *TYLD* M29 ....54 A2
Cuthbert St *BOLS/LL* BL3 ....27 H3
Cygnet St *WGNS/IIMK* WN3 ....34 A2
Cypress Rd *WGNW/BIL/O* WN5 ....33 F2

D

Dagmar St *WALK* M28 ....41 H4
Dailton Rd *SKEL* WN8 ....30 D1
Dairy Farm Rd
RNFD/HAY WA11 ....42 C4
Daisybank Cl *WGNE/HIN* WN2 ....36 A3
Daisyfield *HOR/BR* BL6 * 14 C1
Daisy Hall Dr *WHTN* BL5 ....37 H3
Daisyhill Ct *WHTN* BL5 ....38 A3
Daisy Rd *WGNW/BIL/O* WN5 ......33 F2
Dakins Rd *LEIGH* WN7 ....65 G4
Dalbeatie Ri *WGN* WN1 ....3 J2
Dalby Rd *WGNE/HIN* WN2 ....37 E3
Dalebank *ATH* M46 ....38 D3
Dalecrest *WGNW/BIL/O* WN5 ......45 G2
Dalegarth Av *HOR/BR* BL6 ....15 H3
Dale Gv *LEIGH* WN7 ....64 B2
Dalehead Gv *LEIGH* WN7 ....64 B2
Dalehead Pl *RNFD/HAY* WA11 ......58 A5
Dale Lee *WHTN* BL5 ....26 B5
Dale Rd *GOL/RIS/CU* WA3 ....70 B2
Dalesford Cl *LEIGH* WN7 ....72 B1
Daleside Av *AIMK* WN4 ....47 H3
Dale St *LEIGH* WN7 ....64 B1
WGNS/IIMK WN3 ....35 E5
WHTN BL5 ....38 A3
Dale St East *HOR/BR* BL6 ....14 C1
Dale Vw *NEWLW* WA12 ....69 H5
Dalkeith Rd *WGNE/HIN* WN2 ......23 E2
Dalston Dr *RNFD/HAY* WA11 ....58 A5
Dalston Gv *WGNS/IIMK* WN3 ......33 E5
Dalton Cl *WGNW/BIL/O* WN5 ......32 C1
Dalton Dr *WGNS/IIMK* WN3 ....33 F5
Dalton Fold *WHTN* BL5 ....26 A5
Dalton Gv *AIMK* WN4 ....60 D2
Dalton Fold *NEWLW* WA12 ....68 A5
Dam La *GOL/RIS/CU* WA3 ....62 A3
GOL/RIS/CU WA3 ....77 G5
Dams Head Fold *WHTN* BL5 ....26 A4
Danbers *SKEL* WN8 ....30 C2
Dandy St *WGNE/HIN* WN2 * 36 A4
Danes Av *WGNE/HIN* WN2 ....36 B2
Danes Brook Cl
WGNE/HIN WN2 ....36 B2
Danesbury Cl
WGNW/BIL/O WN5 ....38 D2
Danes Gn *WGNE/HIN* WN2 ....36 B1
Danesway *WGN* WN1 ....22 C2
Daniels La *SKEL* WN8 ....29 H1
Darby La *WGNE/HIN* WN2 ....36 A2
Darfield *SKEL* WN8 ....30 C1
Daric Cl *LEIGH* WN7 ....64 B5
Dark La *HOR/BR* BL6 ....14 C1
Darley Rd *WGNS/IIMK* WN3 ....34 A3
Darlington St *TYLD* M29 ....53 H2
WGNE/HIN WN2 ....36 A4
Darlington St East *TYLD* M29 ......54 A2
Darnhall St *WGNS/IIMK* WN3 * 35 E4
Darnley Av *WALK* M28 ....55 H5
Darran Av *WGNS/IIMK* WN3 ....33 G5
Darvel Av *AIMK* WN4 ....59 H2
David Brow *BOLS/LL* BL3 ....27 H3
Davies Av *NEWLW* WA12 ....69 F5
Davies St *WGNE/HIN* WN2 ....49 F1

Dawber Delph *WGNNW/ST* WN6 ....8 C2
Dawber St *AIMK* WN4 ....61 G2
Dawley Cl *AIMK* WN4 ....60 D3
Dawlish Wy *GOL/RIS/CU* WA3 ......62 A5
Dawnwood Sq
WGNW/BIL/O WN5 ....20 D3
Dawson Av *WGNNW/ST* WN6 ......21 H2
Dawson St *ATH* M46 * 38 D5
Daybrook *SKEL* WN8 ....30 C2
Dayfield *SKEL* WN8 ....30 C2
Deacon Cl *GOL/RIS/CU* WA3 ....77 H4
Deakin St *WGNE/HIN* WN2 * 34 D3
Dealey Rd *BOLS/LL* BL3 ....27 H1
Dean Cl *SKEL* WN8 ....31 F1
WGNS/IIMK WN3 ....58 C3
Dean Ct *GOL/RIS/CU* WA3 ....70 A1
Dean Crs *WGNW/BIL/O* WN5 ......20 C5
Dean Meadow *NEWLW* WA12 ......69 F5
Dean Rd *GOL/RIS/CU* WA3 ....70 A1
Deansgate *WGNE/HIN* WN2 ....36 D5
Dean Wood Av
WGNW/BIL/O WN5 ....19 H4
Dearden Av *LHULT* M58 ....55 H1
Debdale La *TYLD* M29 ....66 C2
Deben Cl *WGNNW/ST* WN6 ....10 D3
Deepdale *LEIGH* WN7 ....65 H3
Deepdale Av
WGNE/HIN WN2 * 58 B5
Dee Rd *TYLD* M29 ....54 B4
Defiance St *ATH* M46 ....38 D5
Delamere Av *GOL/RIS/CU* WA3 ....71 F3
Delamere Rd *SKEL* WN8 ....17 E3
Delamere Wy *SKEL* WN8 ....30 D1
Delegate St *WGNS/IIMK* WN3 ......34 D2
Delfhaven Ct *WGNNW/ST* WN6 ....10 C5
Dell Av *WGNNW/ST* WN6 ....21 F2
Dellside Cl *AIMK* WN4 ....47 H3
Denholme *SKEL* WN8 ....30 C1
Denton Gv *WGNW/BIL/O* WN5 ....20 C5
Derby Dr *RNFD/HAY* WA11 ....56 B1
Derby Rd *GOL/RIS/CU* WA3 ....62 D5
SKEL WN8 ....16 B5
Derbyshire Rd
WGNS/IIMK WN3 ....47 E2
Derby St *ATH* M46 ....14 C1
HOR/BR BL6 ....14 C1
LEIGH WN7 ....65 F2
WGNS/IIMK WN3 ....35 E4
Dereham Wy *WGNS/IIMK* WN3 ....33 C5
Derngate Dr *WGNNW/ST* WN6 ....10 D3
Derwent Av *GOL/RIS/CU* WA3 ......62 D5
WGNE/HIN WN2 ....35 G1
Derwent Cl *LEIGH* WN7 ....64 D3
SKEL WN8 ....16 D5
Derwent Pl *WGNW/BIL/O* WN5 ....32 D1
Derwent Rd *AIMK* WN4 ....61 H1
FWTH BL4 ....41 E1
WGNE/HIN WN2 ....36 D5
WGNW/BIL/O WN5 ....20 A5
Derwent St *LEIGH* WN7 ....64 D3
WGNE/HIN WN2 ....36 D5
TYLD M29 ....53 H4
Desmond St *ATH* M46 ....52 B1
De Trafford Dr
WGNE/HIN WN2 ....23 G3
Devoke Av *RNFD/HAY* WA11 ....57 H5
Devon Av *SKEL* WN8 ....31 F2
Devon Cl *WGNE/HIN* WN2 ....13 E5
Devon Dr *WGN* WN1 ....11 E1
Devon Rd *TYLD* M29 ....53 G2
Devonshire Dr *WALK* M28 ....54 D5
Devonshire Rd *ATH* M46 ....38 D3
WALK M28 ....41 H2
Devon St *LEIGH* WN7 ....65 G4
Dewberry Cl *TYLD* M29 ....54 D2
Dewberry Flds *SKEL* WN8 ....31 E1
Diamond St *LEIGH* WN7 ....64 B5
WGNNW/ST WN6 ....21 H2
Diane Rd *AIMK* WN4 ....61 H2
Dicconson Crs *WGN* WN1 ....2 D3
Dicconson La *WHTN* BL5 ....24 D1
Dicconson St *WGN* WN1 ....2 C2
Dursley Ct *AIMK* WN4 ....47 H3
Dickens Dr *WGNE/HIN* WN2 ....49 G3
Dickenson St *WGNE/HIN* WN2 ....36 B4
Dickens Pl *WGNS/IIMK* WN3 ....33 G4
Didsbury Gv *WGNE/HIN* WN2 ......36 A3
Diggle St *WGNNW/ST* WN6 ....21 H4
Digmoor Dr *SKEL* WN8 ....30 B1
Digmoor Rd *SKEL* WN8 ....29 G1
Dingle Av *SKEL* WN8 ....19 E5
Dingle Dr *SKEL* WN8 ....31 E1
Dingle Wk *WGNNW/ST* WN6 ....21 H4
Dixon Av *NEWLW* WA12 ....69 F4
Dixon Cl *RNFD/HAY* WA11 ....68 D1
Dixon Dr *WGNW/BIL/O* WN5 ....9 F5
Dixon St *WHTN* BL5 ....25 H2
Dobb Brow Rd *WHTN* BL5 ....37 G1
Dobson Pkwy *WGNE/HIN* WN2 ....36 C4
Doctor's Nook *LEIGH* WN7 ....65 E1
Dodd's Farm La
WGNE/HIN WN2 ....24 B2
Dodhurst Rd *WGNE/HIN* WN2 ......35 H2
Doefield Av *WALK* M28 ....55 H3
Doeford Cl *GOL/RIS/CU* WA3 ......72 A3

Donnington Cl *LEIGH* WN7 ....64 C5
Dootson St *WGNE/HIN* WN2 ....36 D2
WGNE/HIN WN2 ....49 F2
Dorchester Rd *SKEL* WN8 ....30 D1
Doric Gn *WGNW/BIL/O* WN5 ....20 D3
Dorket Gv *WHTN* BL5 ....37 G2
Dorning Rd *ATH* M46 ....53 G2
HOR/BR BL6 ....13 F3
LEIGH WN7 ....64 D1
Dorning St *LEIGH* WN7 ....64 D1
WGN WN1 ....2 C2
Dorney Av *WGNNW/ST* WN6 ......39 G5
Dorset Av *WGNE/HIN* WN2 ....13 H5
Dorset Cl *WGNW/BIL/O* WN5 ......32 D2
Dorset Rd *ATH* M46 ....38 D4
WGN WN1 ....11 E1
Dorset St *LEIGH* WN7 ....66 A2
WGNE/HIN WN2 ....35 H1
Douglas Av *WGNE/HIN* WN2 ....58 C3
Douglas Bank Dr
WGNW/BIL/O WN5 ....21 G4
Douglas Dr *WGNNW/ST* WN6 ....9 E5
WGNW/BIL/O WN5 ....31 H1
Douglas Pk *ATH* M46 ....39 F5
Douglas Rd *ATH* M46 ....53 F1
LEIGH WN7 ....51 F4
WGNE/HIN WN2 ....37 E5
WGNW/BIL/O WN5 ....4 C5
Douglas St *ATH* M46 ....39 F5
WGNE/HIN WN2 ....35 H4
WGNW/BIL/O WN5 ....33 H1
Dovecote La *LHULT* M58 ....40 D5
Dovedale Crs *AIMK* WN4 ....47 H3
Dovedale Dr *WGNNW/ST* WN6 ......9 H1
Dovedale Rd *AIMK* WN4 ....47 H3
Dovey Cl *TYLD* M29 ....54 B4
Dover St *WGNE/HIN* WN2 ....35 F5
Dowling Cl *WGNE/HIN* WN2 ....35 H4
Downall Green Rd *AIMK* WN4 ......47 F5
Downing Cl *WGNE/HIN* WN2 ....35 H4
Downing St *LEIGH* WN7 ....65 E1
WGN WN1 ....3 G5
The Downs *WGNS/IIMK* WN3 ......32 D4
Downton Av *WGNW/BIL/O* WN5 ..36 A4
Doyle Rd *BOLS/LL* BL3 ....27 H2
Drake Hall *WHTN* BL5 ....37 G3
Drake St *ATH* M46 ....52 D1
Draycott Cl *WGNE/HIN* WN2 ......36 C5
The Drive *LEIGH* WN7 ....64 C5
WHTN BL5 * 38 D2
Droxford Gv *ATH* M46 ....39 F3
Druid St *AIMK* WN4 ....61 H4
Drummer's La *AIMK* WN4 ....47 H4
Drummond Sq
WGNE/HIN WN2 ....33 F1
Dryburgh Av *AIMK* WN4 ....47 G4
Dryden Cl *WGNS/IIMK* WN3 ....33 H3
Dryton Wk *WGNE/HIN* WN2 ....23 F3
Duchy Av *WHTN* BL5 ....27 G1
Duddon St *WGNW/BIL/O* WN5 ....10 C3
Dudley St *AIMK* WN4 ....60 D2
Duerden St *BOLS/LL* BL3 * 27 H3
Duke Av *GOL/RIS/CU* WA3 ....73 G2
Duke St *AIMK* WN4 ....61 F3
GOL/RIS/CU WA3 ....62 B5
LEIGH WN7 ....65 F2
LHULT M58 ....55 G1
TYLD M29 ....54 B5
WGN WN1 ....2 C3
WGN WN1 ....3 J5
WGNE/HIN WN2 ....35 F5
Duke's Wood Gv *SKEL* WN8 ....30 A5
Dukinfield St *LEIGH* WN7 * 65 F2
Dumbarton Gn
WGNNW/ST WN6 ....21 F3
Dunblane Cl *AIMK* WN4 ....59 H2
Duncan Av *NEWLW* WA12 ....69 F4
Duncan Pl *WGNW/BIL/O* WN5 ......3 H4
Dunham Cl *GOL/RIS/CU* WA3 ......62 A3
Dunham St *WHTN* BL5 ....37 G3
Dunlin Av *NEWLW* WA12 ....69 F5
Dunlin Gv *LEIGH* WN7 ....65 H3
Dunmail Av *RNFD/HAY* WA11 ......58 B5
Dunnock Cl *WGNE/HIN* WN2 ......37 E4
Dunscore Rd *WGNS/IIMK* WN3 ....34 D2
Dunsdale Dr *AIMK* WN4 ....47 H3
Dunster Cl *WGNE/HIN* WN2 ....49 F2
Dunster Pl *WALK* M28 ....55 E4
Dunster Rd *WALK* M28 ....55 E4
Durant St *WGNNW/ST* WN6 ....52 B1
Durham Cl *TYLD* M29 ....53 G2
Durham Rd *WGNE/HIN* WN2 ....36 B3
Durham St *ATH* M46 ....38 D5
Durrell Wy *GOL/RIS/CU* WA3 ......71 F1
Durrington Pl *WHTN* BL5 ....26 B5
Dutton Cl *WGNE/HIN* WN2 ....36 B4
Dutton Gv *LEIGH* WN7 ....65 H4
Duxbury Ct *RNFD/HAY* WA11 ......43 E4
Dyer St *GOL/RIS/CU* WA3 ....70 A1

E

Eagle Crs *RNFD/HAY* WA11 ....43 F5
Earl St *ATH* M46 ....52 C1
WGNNW/ST WN6 ....35 F1
Earlswood *SKEL* WN8 ....18 B4
East Av *GOL/RIS/CU* WA3 ....62 D5
LEIGH WN7 ....65 H3
East Bond St *LEIGH* WN7 ....64 C5
East Bridgewater St
LEIGH WN7 ....65 F2
Eastgarth *WGNE/HIN* WN2 ....36 D1
Eastham Wy *LHULT* M58 ....41 G3
East Lancashire Rd
GOL/RIS/CU WA3 ....70 C3
RNFD/HAY WA11 ....56 A1

TYLD M29 ....67 E1
WALK M28 ....55 E4
East Leigh SKEL WN8 ....18 A4
Eastleigh Crs *LEIGH* WN7 ....65 G3
East Moor *WALK* M28 ....55 F4
East Mt *WGNE/HIN* WN2 ....32 A2
Easton Cl *WGNS/IIMK* WN3 ....47 H1
East St *AIMK* WN4 ....61 G2
ATH M46 ....53 G2
WGNE/HIN WN2 ....37 E5
Eastwell Rd *AIMK* WN4 ....60 D5
WGNNW/ST WN6 ....21 G2
Eastwood Av *NEWLW* WA12 ....76 A1
WGNE/HIN WN2 ....41 F5
Eastwood Dr *BOLS/LL* BL3 ....27 H2
Eastwood Gv *LEIGH* WN7 ....64 D3
Eatock St *WGNE/HIN* WN2 ....35 G5
Eatock Wy *WHTN* BL5 ....37 G2
Eaton St *WGNE/HIN* WN2 ....36 B2
Eavesdale *SKEL* WN8 ....18 B5
Eccles Rd *WGNW/BIL/O* WN5 ......20 D2
Eckersley Fold La *ATH* M46 ....52 B2
Eckersley St *WGN* WN1 ....3 G2
Edale Cl *ATH* M46 ....38 D5
Edale Dr *WGNNW/ST* WN6 ....8 F5
Edale Rd *BOLS/LL* BL3 * 27 H1
FWTH BL4 ....41 G1
LEIGH WN7 ....65 G2
Eddisford Dr *GOL/RIS/CU* WA3 ....72 C4
Eddleston St *AIMK* WN4 ....47 G5
Eden Av *GOL/RIS/CU* WA3 ....73 H5
RNFD/HAY WA11 ....42 D4
Eden Bank *LEIGH* WN7 ....57 E5
Eden Gv *LEIGH* WN7 ....64 B1
Edenhurst *SKEL* WN8 ....18 B5
Edensor Cl *WGNNW/ST* WN6 ......21 H1
Edenvale *WALK* M28 ....55 F4
Edge Gn *WALK* M28 * 55 F1
Edge Green La
GOL/RIS/CU WA3 ....62 A4
Edge Green Rd
GOL/RIS/CU WA3 ....62 A3
Edge Green St *AIMK* WN4 ....61 G2
Edge Hall Rd
WGNW/BIL/O WN5 ....31 H4
Edgerley Pl *AIMK* WN4 ....60 D3
Edgerton Rd *GOL/RIS/CU* WA3 ....71 F1
Edge Ware Gv
WGNW/BIL/O WN5 ....33 E5
Edgeway Rd *WGNS/IIMK* WN3 ....47 H2
Edgewood *WGNNW/ST* WN6 ....9 F5
Edgeworth Rd
GOL/RIS/CU WA3 ....62 A5
WGNE/HIN WN2 ....36 D5
Edinburgh Cl *WGNE/HIN* WN2 ....23 F5
Edinburgh Dr *WGNE/HIN* WN2 ....37 E5
WGNS/IIMK WN3 ....33 E5
Edmund St *AIMK* WN4 ....61 B1
Edmund Dr *LEIGH* WN7 ....64 B1
Edna Rd *LEIGH* WN7 ....51 F4
Edridge Wy *WGNE/HIN* WN2 ......35 H4
Edstone Cl *BOLS/LL* BL3 ....27 G1
Edward Dr *AIMK* WN4 ....61 G2
Edward St *LEIGH* WN7 ....65 F2
WGN WN1 ....2 C1
WGN WN1 ....3 J5
WGN WN1 ....25 H5
Edwin St *WGN* WN1 ....3 G6
Egerton SKEL WN8 ....18 A5
Egerton St *WGNE/HIN* WN2 ....36 A2
Eggar Ct *TYLD* M29 ....54 A4
Elaine Cl *AIMK* WN4 ....61 G1
Elcombe Av *GOL/RIS/CU* WA3 ....71 F2
Elderberry Cl *WGN* WN1 ....22 A1
Eldercot Gv *BOLS/LL* BL3 ....27 H1
Eldercot Rd *BOLS/LL* BL3 ....27 H1
Eldon Gdns *AIMK* WN4 ....47 H5
Eldon St *LEIGH* WN7 ....51 G5
Eleanor St *WGNS/IIMK* WN3 ....33 H1
Elgin Av *GOL/RIS/CU* WA3 ....60 A2
Elgin Cl *WGNE/HIN* WN2 ....23 F5
Eliot Dr *WGNS/IIMK* WN3 ....33 H3
Elizabertham Dr
WGNS/IIMK WN3 ....34 D4
Elizabeth Av *WGNE/HIN* WN2 ......50 B2
Elizabeth Rd *RNFD/HAY* WA11 ....38 E2
Elizabeth St *ATH* M46 ....39 E5
WGNE/HIN WN2 ....36 B2
WGNNW/ST WN6 ....23 E5
Elkstone Av *LHULT* M58 ....41 F2
Elkstone Cl *WGNS/IIMK* WN3 ......46 D1
Elkwood Cl *WGN* WN1 ....22 A1
Elland Cl *WHTN* BL5 ....25 G2
Ellenbrook Rd *WALK* M28 ....55 G3
Ellendale Gra *WALK* M28 ....55 C3
Ellenor Dr *TYLD* M29 ....54 B4
Ellen St *WGN* WN1 * 2 E6
Ellerbeck Crs *WALK* M28 ....55 H4
Ellesmere Av *WALK* M28 ....55 H5
Ellesmere Rd *AIMK* WN4 ....60 C1
GOL/RIS/CU WA3 ....72 D5
WGNS/IIMK WN3 ....33 F2
Ellesmere St *LEIGH* WN7 ....65 E2
LHULT M58 ....41 H5
TYLD M29 ....53 H5
Elliott Av *GOL/RIS/CU* WA3..........62 C5
Elliott Dr *WGNE/HIN* WN2 ....36 A1
Elliott St *FWTH* BL4 ....41 H1
TYLD M29 ....53 F3
Ellis Crs *WALK* M28 ....55 G4
Ellis Rd *WGNW/BIL/O* WN5 ....58 C2
Ellis St *WGN* WN1 ....3 G2
Ellonby Ri *HOR/BR* BL6 ....14 D5
Elm Av *AIMK* WN4 ....60 A1
NEWLW WA12 ....68 D5
HOR/BR BL6 ....14 D1
Elm Cft *WGN* WN1 ....22 A1
Elm Dr *WGNW/BIL/O* WN5 ....58 D1
Elmers Gn *SKEL* WN8 ....18 A4
Elmer's Green La *SKEL* WN8 ......17 H1

Elmers Wood Rd SKEL WN8 18 A4
Elmfield WGNNW/ST WN6 9 G4
Elmfield Av ATH M46 38 C4
Elmfield Rd WGN WN1 11 E5
Elm Gdns RNFD/HAY WA11 43 E5
Elm Gv SKEL WN8 * 16 D4
Elmhow Gv WGNS/IIMK WN3 47 H1
Elmridge LEIGH WN7 52 C5
SKEL WN8 18 A5
Elm Rd RNFD/HAY WA11 * 68 B2
WGNE/HIN WN2 49 H4
WHTN BL5 37 H1
Elmsbury St AIMK WN4 60 C1
Elmstead SKEL WN8 18 A5
The Elms GOL/RIS/CU WA3 71 G2
Elm St LEIGH WN7 65 E3
TYLD M29 * 53 H2
WGNE/HIN WN2 49 F1
Elm Tree Rd GOL/RIS/CU WA3 71 G2
Elmwood SKEL WN8 17 H2
Elmwood Av AIMK WN4 60 D4
Elmwood Cl WHTN BL5 39 H2
Elmwood Gv FWTH BL4 41 H2
Elnup Av WGNNW/ST WN6 9 G4
Elsdon Dr ATH M46 39 F4
Elsham Dr WALK M28 41 G5
Elstead Gv AIMK WN4 60 A2
Elston Av NEWLW WA12 69 E4
Elswick SKEL WN8 17 H5
Elterwater Rd FWTH BL4 40 D1
Eltham Cl AIMK WN4 61 G3
Elton Cl GOL/RIS/CU WA3 71 F2
Elvington Cl
WGNW/BIL/O WN5 20 C4
Elvington Crs WALK M28 55 H3
Elway Rd AIMK WN4 61 F3
Elworthy Gv WGN WN1 3 H1
Ely Cl WALK M28 55 G3
Ely Dr TYLD M29 54 B4
Emerald Av LEIGH WN7 64 D2
Emerald St WGNNW/ST WN6 21 H2
Emlyn St WGNE/HIN WN2 35 H3
Empress Dr LEIGH WN7 53 F5
Ena Crs LEIGH WN7 51 F4
Endsley Av WALK M28 55 H2
Enfield Gv LEIGH WN7 65 F1
Enfield St WGNW/BIL/O WN5 32 D3
Engineer St WGNE/HIN WN2 35 F1
Engine Fold Rd WALK M28 41 F5
Engine La TYLD M29 39 H4
English St LEIGH WN7 65 F2
Enid Pl WGNE/HIN WN2 49 E3
Ennerdale SKEL WN8 18 A5
Ennerdale Av AIMK WN4 61 E2
Ennerdale Pl WGNE/HIN WN2 23 G5
Ennerdale Rd LEIGH WN7 65 H2
TYLD M29 54 A4
WGNE/HIN WN2 36 B3
Enstone SKEL WN8 18 A4
Enstone Wy TYLD M29 54 B2
Enterprise Pk HOR/BR BL6 14 B2
Entwistle Gv LEIGH WN7 65 H3
Envoy Cl WGNW/BIL/O WN5 21 F4
Ephraim's Fold
WGNE/HIN WN2 13 E4
Epsom Dr WGNE/HIN WN2 49 E4
Erradale Crs WGNS/IIMK WN3 47 E1
Erskine Pl WGNE/HIN WN2 49 G2
Eskbank SKEL WN8 17 H5
Eskbrook SKEL WN8 17 H4
Eskdale SKEL WN8 17 G5
Eskdale Av HOR/BR BL6 13 F3
WGN WN1 22 A2
Eskdale Rd AIMK WN4 61 E1
WGNE/HIN WN2 36 B3
Essex Pl TYLD M29 39 G5
Essex Rd WGN WN1 11 E2
Essex St HOR/BR BL6 14 C1
WGN WN1 3 G3
Esthwaite Dr TYLD M29 53 H4
Etherstone St LEIGH WN7 64 D2
Eton St LEIGH WN7 65 E3
Eton Ter WGNS/IIMK WN3 34 D3
Eton Wy WGNW/BIL/O WN5 20 A5
Evans Cl RNFD/HAY WA11 68 C2
Evans St LEIGH WN7 65 E1
Eva St LEIGH WN7 51 F4
Evenwood SKEL WN8 18 A4
Evenwood Ct SKEL WN8 * 17 H4
Everard Cl WALK M28 55 G3
Everbrom Rd BOLS/LL BL3 27 H3
Everest Pl WGN WN1 2 C1
Everest Rd ATH M46 38 D3
Eversley SKEL WN8 18 A4
Everton St AIMK WN4 60 A1
Evesham Cl LEIGH WN7 64 C5
Evington SKEL WN8 18 A4
Exeter Dr WGNE/HIN WN2 13 E5
Exeter Rd WGNE/HIN WN2 36 B3
Exford Av WGNS/IIMK WN3 34 A4
Eyet St LEIGH WN7 64 D1

F

Factory Fold WGNE/HIN WN2 * 35 F1
Factory St TYLD M29 53 G2
Factory St East ATH M46 38 D5
Factory St West ATH M46 38 D5
Faggy La WGNS/IIMK WN3 2 D7
Fairacres WGNNW/ST WN6 9 G1
Fairbourne Av
WGNS/IIMK WN3 33 H4
Fairburn SKEL WN8 17 G2
Fairclough St WGN WN1 2 E6
WGNE/HIN WN2 36 A2
Fairfield Av WGNE/HIN WN2 49 F1
WGNW/BIL/O WN5 33 E3
Fairfield Gdns
RNFD/HAY WA11 57 F4
Fairfield Rd FWTH BL4 41 H1
Fairfield St WGNW/BIL/O WN5 32 D3
Fairhaven SKEL WN8 17 G2
Fairhaven Av WHTN BL5 26 C5
Fairholme Av AIMK WN4 61 E2
Fairhurst Av WGNNW/ST WN6 5 E4
Fairhurst Dr WALK M28 55 E1
Fairhurst St LEIGH WN7 64 D1
WGNS/IIMK WN3 2 A5
Fairlie SKEL WN8 17 H2
Fairlyn Cl WHTN BL5 39 H1
Fairlyn Dr WHTN BL5 39 H1
Fairstead SKEL WN8 17 H2
Fairstead Cl WHTN BL5 25 G5
Fair Vw WGNW/BIL/O WN5 58 C1
Fair View Av
WGNW/BIL/O WN5 58 C1
Fairview Cl AIMK WN4 61 E2
The Fairways AIMK WN4 60 A4
SKEL WN8 18 A2
WHTN BL5 25 H5
Faith St LEIGH WN7 64 B1
Falcon Cl LEIGH WN7 65 G1
Falcon Dr LHULT M38 41 F3
Falconers Gn WGNS/IIMK WN3 34 A3
Falconwood Cha WALK M28 55 G5
Falconwood Cl
WGNNW/ST WN6 21 H4
Falkirk Dr WGNE/HIN WN2 23 F5
Falkirk Gv WGNW/BIL/O WN5 20 D5
Falkland SKEL WN8 17 H2
Falkland Dr AIMK WN4 59 H2
Fall Birch Rd HOR/BR BL6 15 E2
Fallow Cl WHTN BL5 25 H3
Fallowfield Wy ATH M46 53 F2
Falstone Cl WGNS/IIMK WN3 47 E1
Faraday Cl WGNNW/ST WN6 21 H5
Fardon Cl WGNS/IIMK WN3 33 G5
Farefield Av GOL/RIS/CU WA3 62 A4
Farley La SKEL WN8 18 D2
Farliegh Cl WHTN BL5 26 B3
Farm La WGNE/HIN WN2 23 F3
Farm Meadow Rd
WGNW/BIL/O WN5 31 H3
Farndale Gv AIMK WN4 61 F4
Farndale Sq LHULT M38 41 H5
Farnham Cl LEIGH WN7 52 A5
Farnsfield WGN WN1 3 K3
Farnworth St LEIGH WN7 * 65 G2
Farr Cl WGNS/IIMK WN3 33 G3
Farrell St WGNW/BIL/O WN5 32 D3
Farrier's Cft WGNNW/ST WN6 21 F2
Fawcett SKEL WN8 17 G2
Fawcetts Fold WHTN BL5 25 H1
Fearnham Cl LEIGH WN7 64 D5
Fellbridge Cl WHTN BL5 26 B4
Fellside WGN WN1 3 F1
Fell St LEIGH WN7 64 B1
Felstead SKEL WN8 17 G3
Feltons SKEL WN8 17 G3
Fenney Ct SKEL WN8 17 H4
Fenwick Cl WHTN BL5 38 A2
Fereday St WALK M28 41 H4
Ferguson Ri
WGNW/BIL/O WN5 21 F5
Fern Bank RNFD/HAY WA11 42 D4
Fernbray Rd WGNE/HIN WN2 36 C2
Fern Cl ATH M46 53 E1
SKEL WN8 16 D4
WGNNW/ST WN6 9 F4
Ferndale SKEL WN8 17 G3
Fernhill Av BOLS/LL BL3 27 H1
Fernhurst Cl WGNS/IIMK WN3 35 E2
Fernlea Gv AIMK WN4 60 A1
Fern Lea Gv LHULT M38 41 E4
Fernleigh HOR/BR BL6 * 14 C1
Fernside Gv WGNS/IIMK WN3 47 E2
Ferny Knoll Rd
RNFD/HAY WA11 29 E4
Ferrer St AIMK WN4 47 G5
Festival Rd RNFD/HAY WA11 56 B1
Fieldfare Cl GOL/RIS/CU WA3 71 E1
Fieldhead Av TYLD M29 67 E1
Fieldsend Dr LEIGH WN7 72 B1
The Fields WGNE/HIN WN2 23 H1
WGNNW/ST WN6 10 C2
Field St WGNE/HIN WN2 36 B4
WGNNW/ST WN6 2 A4
WGNS/IIMK WN3 35 E4
Fieldview SKEL WN8 30 D1
Fieldway WGNE/HIN WN2 49 G1
Finch Av FWTH BL4 41 E1
RNFD/HAY WA11 56 B1
Finchdale Gdns
GOL/RIS/CU WA3 72 A1
Finch La WGNNW/ST WN6 8 A1
Finchley Crs WGNE/HIN WN2 3 K1
Finch Mill Av WGNNW/ST WN6 8 C3
Findon SKEL WN8 17 G4
Finlay Ct WGNW/BIL/O WN5 21 F5
Finney Gv RNFD/HAY WA11 68 B3
Firbank Rd WGNS/IIMK WN3 34 A5
Firbeck SKEL WN8 17 H4
Fircroft WGNNW/ST WN6 4 B5
Firecrest Cl WALK M28 55 G3
Firethorn Cl WHTN BL5 26 A3
Fir Gv WGNNW/ST WN6 21 H2
Firs La LEIGH WN7 64 B1
Firs Park Crs WGNE/HIN WN2 24 A4
Firs Rd WHTN BL5 39 G2
First Av ATH M46 39 E4
TYLD M29 67 F2
WGNE/HIN WN2 36 A3
WGNNW/ST WN6 21 H3
Firswood Rd BRSC L40 16 B1
Fir Tree Av GOL/RIS/CU WA3 71 G1
WALK M28 55 G5
Fir Tree Cl RNFD/HAY WA11 44 C4
SKEL WN8 30 A1
Fir Tree Crs WGNS/IIMK WN3 35 E5
Fir Tree Dr WGNS/IIMK WN3 35 E5
Fir Tree St WGNS/IIMK WN3 * 35 E4
Fir Tree Wy HOR/BR BL6 14 D1
Firvale Cl LEIGH WN7 64 B1
Firwood SKEL WN8 18 A2
Firwood Av FWTH BL4 41 H2
Firwood Gv AIMK WN4 60 C4
Fisher Av WGNE/HIN WN2 49 H4
Fisher Cl WGNS/IIMK WN3 33 G2
Fisher Dr WGNW/BIL/O WN5 31 H2
Fitzadam St WGN WN1 2 B4
Flamstead SKEL WN8 17 H4
Flapper Fold La ATH M46 38 D4
Flaxton SKEL WN8 17 H4
Fleet St WGNW/BIL/O WN5 32 C2
Fleetwood Dr NEWLW WA12 69 E5
Fleetwood Rd WALK M28 41 F5
Fleming Dr AIMK WN4 61 G2
Fletcher Av ATH M46 39 E3
Fletcher St ATH M46 * 38 D5
Flimby SKEL WN8 18 A4
Flockton Av WGNNW/ST WN6 21 E1
Flora St AIMK WN4 61 E4
Flordon SKEL WN8 18 A4
Florence St WGN WN1 3 H4
Fold St GOL/RIS/CU WA3 62 B5
Foley St WGNE/HIN WN2 36 A3
Fontwell Cl WGNNW/ST WN6 10 C1
Footman Cl TYLD M29 54 A4
Forbes Cl WGNE/HIN WN2 36 B1
Fordland Cl GOL/RIS/CU WA3 63 F5
Fordyce Wy WGNE/HIN WN2 23 F5
Forest Av WGNNW/ST WN6 21 F2
Forest Dr SKEL WN8 17 H2
WGNNW/ST WN6 4 B5
WHTN BL5 26 B5
Forge St WGNE/HIN WN2 3 H6
Formby Av ATH M46 39 E4
Forres Gv AIMK WN4 59 H2
Forresters Cl WGNE/HIN WN2 50 B3
Forster St GOL/RIS/CU WA3 62 B5
Forth St LEIGH WN7 65 H2
Forton Rd WGNS/IIMK WN3 47 G1
Foster Av WGNS/IIMK WN3 34 D2
Fosters Buildings
WGNNW/ST WN6 2 A4
Fosters Green Rd SKEL WN8 17 H3
Foster St WGNNW/ST WN6 * 21 H4
Fotherby Pl WGNS/IIMK WN3 33 H5
Foundry La WGNS/IIMK WN3 33 E4
Foundry St LEIGH WN7 65 G2
WGNE/HIN WN2 36 A3
Fountain Pk WHTN BL5 37 F3
Fountains Av RNFD/HAY WA11 68 C2
Fountains Cl TYLD M29 54 B4
Fountains Wk
GOL/RIS/CU WA3 72 A1
Fourmarts Rd
WGNW/BIL/O WN5 20 D3
Fourteen Meadows Rd
WGNS/IIMK WN3 34 A2
Fowler Cl WGN WN1 3 G5
Fowley Common La
GOL/RIS/CU WA3 73 G4
Foxdene Gv WGNS/IIMK WN3 47 F1
Foxfield Gv WGNNW/ST WN6 9 G4
Foxfold SKEL WN8 18 A2
Foxfold Cl WALK M28 55 E4
Foxglove Cl WGNNW/ST WN6 5 E5
Foxwood Cl
WGNW/BIL/O WN5 31 H3
Foy St AIMK WN4 * 61 E3
Frances Pl ATH M46 52 B1
France St WGNE/HIN WN2 36 A2
WGNW/BIL/O WN5 33 G1
WHTN BL5 37 H2
Francis St LEIGH WN7 51 H4
TYLD M29 54 C3
WGNE/HIN WN2 36 A3
Fraser Rd WGNW/BIL/O WN5 33 F1
Frawley Av NEWLW WA12 69 E4
Freckleton St WGN WN1 2 D1
Frederica Gdns
WGNE/HIN WN2 35 F5
Frederick St AIMK WN4 60 D1
WGNE/HIN WN2 36 A3
WGNS/IIMK WN3 34 C2
Frederic St WGN WN1 * 3 H5
Freelands TYLD M29 54 B2
Freesia Av WALK M28 41 E5
Frenchwood Ct
WGNE/HIN WN2 23 H1
Freshfield Av ATH M46 38 D4
Freshfield Rd WGNE/HIN WN2 36 C3
WGNS/IIMK WN3 33 F5
Friars Cl TYLD M29 54 C2
Frith St WGNNW/ST WN6 33 H1
Frodsham Cl WGNNW/ST WN6 21 E2
Frog La WGNNW/ST WN6 21 H5
Frome Cl TYLD M29 54 A5
Fulbeck Av WGNS/IIMK WN3 47 H1
Fulbrook Wy TYLD M29 54 B2
Fulmar Cl WHTN BL5 37 G2
Fulwell Av TYLD M29 53 F3
Fulwood Rd GOL/RIS/CU WA3 71 F3
Furlong Cl WGNE/HIN WN2 49 E4
Furness Crs LEIGH WN7 51 G2
Furnival St LEIGH WN7 52 A4
Furze Av WHTN BL5 38 A1
Futura Pk HOR/BR BL6 14 B2

G

Gadbury Av ATH M46 38 C5
Gainsborough Cl
WGNS/IIMK WN3 33 E5
Galwey Gv WGN WN1 22 B1
Gambleside Cl WALK M28 55 G3
Gamble St LEIGH WN7 65 F1
Gantley Av WGNW/BIL/O WN5 31 G4
Gantley Crs WGNW/BIL/O WN5 31 G5
Gantley Rd WGNW/BIL/O WN5 31 G5
Garden La WALK M28 55 F5
Garden St TYLD M29 53 H3
Gardiners Pl SKEL WN8 16 D5
Garner Dr TYLD M29 67 E1
Garnett Pl SKEL WN8 29 F1
Garrett Hall Rd WALK M28 54 D4
Garrett La TYLD M29 54 C4
Garside Av GOL/RIS/CU WA3 71 E2
Garside Gv WGNS/IIMK WN3 47 F1
Garston Av ATH M46 38 C3
Garston Cl LEIGH WN7 51 H2
Garswood Av RNFD/HAY WA11 43 F4
Garswood Crs
WGNW/BIL/O WN5 58 C2
Garswood Old Rd AIMK WN4 59 E5
Garswood Rd AIMK WN4 59 H3
WGNW/BIL/O WN5 58 D2
Garswood St AIMK WN4 61 E3
Garthmere Rd ATH M46 39 G3
Garton Dr GOL/RIS/CU WA3 63 F5
Gaskell St WGNE/HIN WN2 36 B1
Gas St CHLY/EC PR7 7 E1
WGNE/HIN WN2 49 G1
Gategill Gv WGNW/BIL/O WN5 45 G1
Gatehouse Rd WALK M28 41 F4
Gathurst Hall
WGNNW/ST WN6 * 20 A2
Gathurst La WGNNW/ST WN6 9 E5
Gathurst Rd
WGNW/BIL/O WN5 19 H5
Gatley Cl TYLD M29 54 A2
Gawsworth Rd
GOL/RIS/CU WA3 62 A5
Gaynor Av RNFD/HAY WA11 68 C2
Gayton Cl WGNS/IIMK WN3 33 E5
Gellert Pl WHTN BL5 37 H2
Gellert Rd WHTN BL5 37 H2
Geoffrey St WHTN BL5 27 G5
Georges La WGN WN1 3 J5
George's Ter
WGNW/BIL/O WN5 31 G3
George St AIMK WN4 61 F2
ATH M46 39 E5
FWTH BL4 41 G1
NEWLW WA12 * 68 D5
WGNE/HIN WN2 3 K7
WGNE/HIN WN2 36 B4
WHTN BL5 26 A5
Gerard St AIMK WN4 61 E3
Gerosa Av WARRN/WOL WA2 76 C4
Gerrard Cl WGNE/HIN WN2 24 A3
Gerrard Pl SKEL WN8 29 E1
Gerrard Rd GOL/RIS/CU WA3 77 H5
WGNW/BIL/O WN5 58 D1
Gerrard St LEIGH WN7 * 65 E1
WHTN BL5 25 H4
Ghyll Gv RNFD/HAY WA11 58 A5
Giants Hall Rd
WGNNW/ST WN6 21 F2
Gibbon's Rd AIMK WN4 60 A4
Gibson Gv WALK M28 41 F5
Gibson La WALK M28 41 F5
Gibson St WGNE/HIN WN2 50 A1
Gidlow Av WGNNW/ST WN6 21 H3
Gidlow La WGNNW/ST WN6 21 H1
Gidlow St WGNE/HIN WN2 23 F5
Gifford Pl WGNE/HIN WN2 36 C4
Gilbert St WALK M28 55 H2
WGNE/HIN WN2 35 H3
Gilda Rd WALK M28 54 D4
Gillan Rd WGNNW/ST WN6 22 A3
Gill Av WGNNW/ST WN6 9 G4
Gillbrow Crs WGN WN1 3 K3
Gillers Gn WALK M28 55 H1
Gillibrands Rd SKEL WN8 29 G1
Gilpin Pl WGNE/HIN WN2 49 E1
Gilroy St WGN WN1 3 F5
Girton Av AIMK WN4 60 C2
Girvan Crs AIMK WN4 59 H2
Gisburn Av GOL/RIS/CU WA3 62 A4
Glabyn Av HOR/BR BL6 15 E2
Gladden Hey Dr
WGNS/IIMK WN3 47 E2
Gladden Pl SKEL WN8 16 D5
The Glade WGNNW/ST WN6 9 G4
Gladstone St WHTN BL5 25 H4
Gladstone Wy NEWLW WA12 69 E5
Glaisdale Cl AIMK WN4 61 F3
Glamis Cl LEIGH WN7 53 E5
Glassbrook St
WGNNW/ST WN6 21 H4
Glastonbury Av
GOL/RIS/CU WA3 72 A1
Glastonbury Rd TYLD M29 54 A4
Glazebury Dr WHTN BL5 26 A3
Glebe Av AIMK WN4 61 E4
Glebe Cl WGNNW/ST WN6 10 B1
Glebe End St WGNNW/ST WN6 2 A4
Glebe Rd SKEL WN8 29 F1
WGNNW/ST WN6 10 C2
Glebe St LEIGH WN7 52 A5
WGNE/HIN WN2 51 F1
WHTN BL5 25 H4
Glegg St WGNE/HIN WN2 3 K5
Glemsford Cl WGNS/IIMK WN3 34 A5
Glenbeck Cl HOR/BR BL6 14 C1
Glenbranter Av
WGNE/HIN WN2 23 F5
Glenburn Rd SKEL WN8 16 D1
SKEL WN8 29 E1
Glencar WHTN BL5 37 G1
Glendale Av AIMK WN4 61 F2
Glendale Rd WALK M28 55 E4
Glendevon Cl BOLS/LL BL3 27 F1
WGNE/HIN WN2 23 F5
Glen Dr WGNNW/ST WN6 8 D2
Gleneagles BOLS/LL BL3 27 G2
Glengarth Dr HOR/BR BL6 15 H4
Glenmaye Gv WGNE/HIN WN2 36 D3
Glenpark LEIGH WN7 52 B5
Glenview Rd TYLD M29 53 G1
Glossop Wy WGNE/HIN WN2 36 B4
Gloucester Av
GOL/RIS/CU WA3 62 C5
Gloucester Crs
WGNE/HIN WN2 36 B2
Gloucester Pl ATH M46 39 E4
Gloucester Rd
WGNW/BIL/O WN5 32 D2
Gloucester St ATH M46 38 D5
Glover St LEIGH WN7 51 F3
Golborne Dale Rd
NEWLW WA12 70 B5
Golborne Gallery WGN WN1 * 2 C4
Golborne Pl WGN WN1 * 3 G4
Golborne Rd AIMK WN4 61 G2
GOL/RIS/CU WA3 70 D1
WARRN/WOL WA2 76 C4
Golborne St NEWLW WA12 69 H5
Goldcrest Cl WALK M28 55 G4
Goldenways WGN WN1 2 C1
Goldsmith Pl WGNS/IIMK WN3 33 H4
Goodshaw Rd WALK M28 55 H3
Gordon Av AIMK WN4 60 B2
RNFD/HAY WA11 68 C2
Gordon Cl WGNW/BIL/O WN5 21 F5
Gordonstoun Crs
WGNW/BIL/O WN5 32 A1
Gordon St LEIGH WN7 52 A5
WGN WN1 3 H6
Gores La RNFD/HAY WA11 44 C5
Gore St WGNW/BIL/O WN5 32 C2
Gorman St WGNNW/ST WN6 21 H5
Gorman Wk WGNS/IIMK WN3 33 G3
Gorse Dr LHULT M38 41 E2
Gorses Dr WGNE/HIN WN2 12 D4
Gorsey Brow
WGNW/BIL/O WN5 58 C1
Gorsey Brow Cl
WGNW/BIL/O WN5 58 C1
Gorsey Hey WHTN BL5 37 H1
Gorsey Pl SKEL WN8 29 G1
Gorton Gv WALK M28 41 H3
Gorton St FWTH BL4 41 G1
Gower St WGNW/BIL/O WN5 33 G2
Goyt Hey Av
WGNW/BIL/O WN5 58 D2
Grace St LEIGH WN7 64 B1
Grafton St ATH M46 52 B2
CHLY/EC PR7 7 E1
Graham St WGNE/HIN WN2 49 F2
Grampian Wy
GOL/RIS/CU WA3 63 E5
Grange Av WGNS/IIMK WN3 34 A3
WGNW/BIL/O WN5 32 C1
Grange Cl GOL/RIS/CU WA3 70 D3
Grange Rd AIMK WN4 47 G5
RNFD/HAY WA11 68 A4
WALK M28 54 D4
WGNE/HIN WN2 50 B2
Grange St LEIGH WN7 64 D3
WGNE/HIN WN2 36 A4
The Grange WHTN BL5 25 F5
Grange Va RNFD/HAY WA11 68 A3
Grantham Gv WGNE/HIN WN2 3 J1
Grantley St AIMK WN4 60 D1
Grant Rd WGNS/IIMK WN3 33 H5
Grantwood AIMK WN4 60 D1
Granville St LEIGH WN7 52 A4
WALK M28 41 H5
WGNE/HIN WN2 * 36 B3
Grasmere Av FWTH BL4 41 E1
SKEL WN8 19 E5
WGNE/HIN WN2 35 F1
WGNE/HIN WN2 36 B4
WGNW/BIL/O WN5 20 A5
Grasmere Dr AIMK WN4 61 E1
Grasmere Rd
WGNW/BIL/O WN5 32 D1
Grasmere St LEIGH WN7 64 D1
Grasmere Ter WGNE/HIN WN2 49 G3
Grasscroft Rd WGNE/HIN WN2 36 D4
Gratten Ct WALK M28 41 H4
Gratton Pl SKEL WN8 17 F5
Grave Oak La GOL/RIS/CU WA3 65 G5
Gray Av RNFD/HAY WA11 68 A3
Gray Cl WGNE/HIN WN2 23 F3
Graymar Rd LHULT M38 41 F4
Grayson Rd LHULT M38 41 G4
Grayson's Cl WGN WN1 2 D2
Graysons Rd RNFD/HAY WA11 43 E3
Great Acre WGN WN1 3 F2
Great Bank Rd WHTN BL5 25 G3
Great Boys Cl TYLD M29 54 D2
Great Delph RNFD/HAY WA11 68 A2
Great Fold LEIGH WN7 66 B2
Great George St
WGNS/IIMK WN3 2 A5
Great Moss Rd TYLD M29 67 F4
Greaves Cl WGNNW/ST WN6 9 E2
Grebe Cl WGNS/IIMK WN3 32 C4
Greenacre WGN WN1 3 F2
Green Acre WHTN BL5 38 A1
Greenacres Cl
GOL/RIS/CU WA3 72 A1
Greenall St AIMK WN4 61 E1
Green Av LHULT M38 40 D3
TYLD M29 66 D2
Greenbank WGNE/HIN WN2 36 D5
WGNE/HIN WN2 49 G4
Greenbank Av
WGNW/BIL/O WN5 31 G5
Greenbarn Wy HOR/BR BL6 13 F2
Greenburn Av
RNFD/HAY WA11 58 B5
Green Cl ATH M46 53 F2
Green Common La WHTN BL5 38 C2
Green Ct GOL/RIS/CU WA3 64 A5
Greencourt Dr LHULT M38 41 E4
Greendale ATH M46 39 F4
Greendale Crs LEIGH WN7 65 H2
Green Dr HOR/BR BL6 15 H3
Greenfield Av WGNE/HIN WN2 3 J7
Greenfield Cl WHTN BL5 26 B4
Greenfield Rd ATH M46 39 F3
Greenfields WGNNW/ST WN6 21 H1
Greenfields Cl NEWLW WA12 69 F5
WGNE/HIN WN2 36 C2
Greenfields Crs AIMK WN4 61 E2
Greenfield Vw
WGNW/BIL/O WN5 58 C2
Greenfold Av FWTH BL4 41 G1
Green Fold La WHTN BL5 37 H1
Greenfold Wy LEIGH WN7 65 G4
Greenford Cl
WGNW/BIL/O WN5 31 G2
Green Hall Cl ATH M46 39 G3
Green Hayes Av WGN WN1 22 B2

Greenhey *WGNW/BIL/O* WN5 ......32 B1
Greenheys PI *SKEL* WN8 ....17 E5
Greenheys Rd *LHULT* M38 ....40 D2
Greenhill Av *FWTH* BL4 ....41 H1
Greenhill Crs
   WGNW/BIL/O WN5 ....59 E1
Greenhill Rd
   WGNW/BIL/O WN5 ....58 C1
Greenland Av *WGNNW/ST* WN6...10 B2
Greenland CI *TYLD* M29 ....54 A5
Greenland La *GOL/RIS/CU* WA3 ....63 H4
Green La *GOL/RIS/CU* WA3 ....52 D5
   LEIGH WN7 ....52 D5
   RNFD/HAY WA11 ....56 B1
Green Lane Ct
   WARRN/WOL WA2 ....76 B5
Greenlea CI *WGNW/BIL/O* WN5 ....31 G3
Greenleaf CI *WALK* M28 ....55 E5
Greenleas *HOR/BR* BL6 ....37 C1
Green Mdw *WHTN* BL5 ....37 C1
Greenoak Dr *WALK* M28 ....41 H3
Greenough St *ATH* M46 ....52 B2
   WGN WN1 ....3 F4
Green Pine Rd *HOR/BR* BL6 ....14 C3
Greenrigg CI *WGNNW/ST* WN6 ....10 C3
Greenshank CI *LEIGH* WN7 ....65 G1
Greensward CI
   WGNNW/ST WN6 ....9 C1
The Green *WGNNW/ST* WN6 ....32 C2
Greenvale *WGNNW/ST* WN6 ....20 A1
Greenway AIMK WN4 ....60 D2
Greenway Av *WALK* M28 ....29 C5
Greenway CI *SKEL* WN8 ....18 C5
Greenways *LEIGH* WN7 ....52 B5
   WGNNW/ST WN6 ....10 D4
   WGNW/BIL/O WN5 ....31 G5
Greenwood Av *LHULT* M38 ....33 F1
Greenwood CI *WALK* M28 ....54 D4
Greenwood La *HOR/BR* BL6 ....14 D1
Greenwood Rd
   WGNNW/ST WN6 ....5 F5
Greetby PI *SKEL* WN8 ....17 F5
Gregory Av *ATH* M46 ....38 D3
Gregory St *WGNE/HIN* WN2 * 35 H2
   TYLD M29 ....54 A4
   WGNE/HIN WN2 ....49 G1
   WGNS/IIMK WN3 ....34 B2
Grenaby Av *WGNE/HIN* WN2 ......36 D3
Grenfel CI *WGNS/IIMK* WN3 ....33 H3
Gresley CI WN1 ....3 K4
Gretna Rd *ATH* M46 ....52 B2
Greyfriars AIMK WN4 ....60 C3
Grey Rd *AIMK* WN4 ....60 D3
Greystone Av *WGNE/HIN* WN2 ....12 D5
Grimeford La *HOR/BR* BL6 ....7 H2
Grimrod PI *SKEL* WN8 ....29 F1
Grimshaw Rd *SKEL* WN8 ....17 C5
Grimshaw St *GOL/RIS/CU* WA3 ....62 B5
Grizedale Dr *WGNE/HIN* WN2 ......35 F1
Grosvenor Av
   GOL/RIS/CU WA3 ....71 C1
Grosvenor CI *WALK* M28 ....41 H3
Grosvenor Dr *WALK* M28 ....41 H3
Grosvenor Rd *LEIGH* WN7 ....51 C5
   WALK M28 ....41 H3
Grosvenor St *WGNS/IIMK* WN3 ....36 A3
   WGNW/BIL/O WN5 ....33 C2
Grove HI *WALK* M28 ....55 E5
Grove La *WGNNW/ST* WN6 ....10 C2
Grove PI *WGNNW/ST* WN6 ....10 C2
Grove Rd *SKEL* WN8 ....19 E5
Grove St *AIMK* WN4 ....60 D2
   LEIGH WN7 ....65 C2
The Grove *GOL/RIS/CU* WA3 ......63 E5
   WGNE/HIN WN2 ....3 H7
Grovewood Dr
   WGNNW/ST WN6 ....8 D3
Grundy's CI *TYLD* M29 ....67 F1
Grundy St *GOL/RIS/CU* WA3 ....70 B2
   WHTN BL5 ....25 H4
Guest St *LEIGH* WN7 ....65 F1
Guildford Crs *WGNNW/ST* WN6 ....21 C2
Gunters Av *WHTN* BL5 ....37 H2

H

Habergham CI *WALK* M28 ....55 H4
Hackworth CI *WGN* WN1 ....3 C5
Hadbutt La *TYLD* M29 ....66 C2
Haddon Rd *GOL/RIS/CU* WA3 ......63 E5
   WGNS/IIMK WN3 ....33 F5
Hague Bush CI
   GOL/RIS/CU WA3 * 63 F5
Haigh Rd *WGNE/HIN* WN2 ....12 C4
Haigh Vw WN1 ....22 C3
   WGNS/IIMK WN3 ....34 D2
Haig St *WGNS/IIMK* WN3..............2 A6
Haile Dr *WALK* M28 ....55 E5
Haile CI *LEIGH* WN7 ....64 C1
Hale Gv *AIMK* WN4 ....60 C1
Halesfield *WGNE/HIN* WN2 ....51 E1
Halewood Av *GOL/RIS/CU* WA3 ....62 A5
Half Acre La *HOR/BR* BL6 ....12 D1
Hallbridge Gdns *SKEL* WN8 ....19 E5
Hall CI *WGNNW/ST* WN6 ....17 H3
Hallcroft *SKEL* WN8 ....2 C5
Hallgate *WGN* WN1 ....37 H3
   WHTN BL5 ....37 H3
Hall Gn *SKEL* WN8 ....31 E1

Hall Green CI *SKEL* WN8 ....31 E1
Hall House La *LEIGH* WN7 ....65 H2
Hall La *HOR/BR* BL6 ....14 D3
   WGNE/HIN WN2 ....22 C1
   WGNE/HIN WN2 ....35 C1
   WGNW/BIL/O WN5 ....30 D4
Hall Lane Gv *WGNE/HIN* WN2 ......24 A5
Hall Lee Dr *WHTN* BL5 ....26 B4
Hall Rd *RNFD/HAY* WA11..............68 B2
Hallstead Av *LHULT* M38 ....40 D4
Hallstead CI *LHULT* M38 ....40 D4
Hall St *WGN* WN1 ....2 E6
   WGNE/HIN WN2 ....3 K6
   WGNE/HIN WN2 ....48 D4
Hallview Wy *LHULT* M38 ....41 E5
Hall Wood Av *RNFD/HAY* WA11 ....68 C1
Hallworthy CI *LEIGH* WN7 ....64 A5
Halstead Gv *LEIGH* WN7 ....65 G1
Halton St *RNFD/HAY* WA11 * 68 B3
Hambledon CI *ATH* M46 ....39 F3
Hamblett St *LEIGH* WN7 ....64 A1
Hamilton Rd *AIMK* WN4 ....59 H2
   TYLD M29 ....54 C5
   WGNE/HIN WN2 ....36 C4
Hamilton Sq
   WGNW/BIL/O WN5 ....21 F5
Hamilton St *ATH* M46 ....52 D1
   LEIGH WN7 ....51 G5
Hampden PI
   WGNW/BIL/O WN5 ....21 E4
Hampson CI *AIMK* WN4 ....61 E4
Hampson St *ATH* M46 * 38 D5
Hampstead Rd
   WGNW/BIL/O WN5 ....10 A1
Hampton Cv *LEIGH* WN7 ....53 H4
Hanborough Ct *TYLD* M29 ....53 F3
Hand La *LEIGH* WN7 ....64 D5
Hanmer St *WGNE/HIN* WN2 ....36 A3
Hanover Rd *WGNE/HIN* WN2 ......35 H2
Hanover St *LEIGH* WN7 ....64 D1
Hansom St *ATH* M46 ....52 B5
Hanson St *CHLY/EC* PR7 ....7 F1
Hanstock *WGNW/BIL/O* WN5 ......31 H3
Hanwell CI *LEIGH* WN7 ....64 C5
Harbern Dr *LEIGH* WN7 ....51 G1
Harbourne Av *WALK* M28 ....55 H3
Harbourne CI *WALK* M28 ....55 H3
Harbury CI *BOLS/LL* BL3 ....27 H2
   WGNW/ST WN6 ....21 H3
Hardcare St *WGNS/IIMK* WN3 ......34 C2
Hardie Av *FWTH* BL4 ....41 C1
Hardman St *WGNS/IIMK* WN3 ......34 A2
Hardrow CI *WGNS/IIMK* WN3 ......48 A1
Hardwick Rd *AIMK* WN4 ....60 C5
Hardybutts *WGN* WN1 ....2 E5
Hardy CI *WHTN* BL5 ....25 H2
Hardy St *WGNNW/ST* WN6 ....21 H4
Harebell Av *WALK* M28 * 41 E5
Harewood Rd *WGNE/HIN* WN2 ......3 J5
Harland Dr *AIMK* WN4 ....61 F3
Harlea Av *WGNE/HIN* WN2 ....36 D5
Harlech Av *WGNNW/ST* WN6 ......36 D4
Harlech St *AIMK* WN4 ....60 C1
Harmuir CI *WGNNW/ST* WN6 ......21 F1
Harold Av *AIMK* WN4 ....60 D5
Harold Rd *RNFD/HAY* WA11 ....68 C2
Harold St *WGNE/HIN* WN2 ....13 E5
Harper St *WGN* WN1 ....2 E6
   WGNE/HIN WN2 ....35 H4
Harptree Gv *LEIGH* WN7 ....51 G4
Harrison Crs *HOR/BR* BL6 ....7 H4
Harrison Dr *RNFD/HAY* WA11 ......43 E4
Harrison Rd *CHLY/EC* PR7 ....7 F1
Harrison St *LHULT* M38 ....41 F4
   WGNE/HIN WN2 ....37 E5
Harrison Wy *NEWLW* WA12 ....69 H5
Harris Rd *WGNW/BIL/O* WN5 ......21 E4
Harrogate St *WGN* WN1 ....3 K7
Harrop St *BOLS/LL* BL3 ....27 H1
   WALK M28 ....55 H5
Harrowby Rd *BOLS/LL* BL3 * 27 H2
Harrowby St
   WGNW/BIL/O WN5 ....33 F2
Harrow CI *WGNW/BIL/O* WN5 ......20 A5
Harrow Crs *LEIGH* WN7 ....53 H4
Harrow Rd *WGNS/IIMK* WN3 ......35 E4
Harsnips *SKEL* WN8 ....17 H3
Hartford Rd *WHTN* BL5 ....38 A2
Hartington Dr
   WGNNW/ST WN6 ....10 C3
Hartland Dr *TYLD* M29 ....54 A3
Hartley Av *WGN* WN1 ....3 G6
Hartley Gv *WGNW/BIL/O* WN5 ....32 C1
Hartley St *WGNW/BIL/O* WN5 ......32 C2
Hartley Ter *WGNS/IIMK* WN3 ......2 C7
Harts Farm Ms *LEIGH* WN7 ....52 A3
Hartshead *SKEL* WN8 ....17 H5
Hart's La *LEIGH* WN7 ....18 C5
Hart St *TYLD* M29 ....53 F5
   WHTN BL5 ....37 E1
Hartswell CI *GOL/RIS/CU* WA3 ....62 B5
Harvey CI *GOL/RIS/CU* WA3 ....62 A5
Harvey La *GOL/RIS/CU* WA3 ....62 A5
Harvey St *WGNS/IIMK* WN3 ....34 D2
Haseldine St *LEIGH* WN7 ....43 C1
Haseley CI *TYLD* M29 ....53 H3
Haskoll St *HOR/BR* BL6 ....14 C5
Hassnes CI *WGNS/IIMK* WN3 ......48 A1
Hatford CI *TYLD* M29 ....54 B4
Hathaway CI *LEIGH* WN7 ....52 C5
Hathaway Wk
   WGNS/IIMK WN3 ....35 G4
Hatton Av *ATH* M46 ....39 E3
Hatton St *CHLY/EC* PR7 ....7 E1
Havenwood Rd *WGN* WN1 ....22 A1
Havercroft CI *WGNS/IIMK* WN3 ....35 F5
Havisham Ct *HOR/BR* BL6 ....7 E4
Hawarde CI *NEWLW* WA12 ....68 D5
Hawes Crs *AIMK* WN4 ....61 E1
Haweswater Av *TYLD* M29 ....54 A4
   WGNE/HIN WN2 ....35 C1
Hawkhurst CI *LEIGH* WN7 ....65 H2

Hawkley Av *WGNS/IIMK* WN3 ......47 C1
Hawkridge CI *WHTN* BL5 ....38 A2
Hawkrigg CI *WGNNW/ST* WN6 ......8 D3
Hawksclough *SKEL* WN8 ....17 H5
Hawkshaw CI *WGNE/HIN* WN2 ....23 F2
Hawkshead Dr *BOLS/LL* BL3 ......27 H2
Hawkworth *TYLD* M29 ....67 E1
Haworth St *WGNE/HIN* WN7 * 36 A2
Hawthorn Av *AIMK* WN4 ....61 E5
   WGN WN1 ....11 E4
   WGNE/HIN WN2 ....36 D5
   WGNE/HIN WN2 ....32 A2
   WGNE/HIN WN2 ....33 E2
Hawthorn CI *LEIGH* WN7 ....55 C2
Hawthorn Crs *SKEL* WN8 ....16 D4
Hawthorne Av
   GOL/RIS/CU WA3 ....73 H4
   HOR/BR BL6 ....14 C1
Hawthorne Gv *LEIGH* WN7 * 51 H4
Hawthorn Rd *WHTN* BL5 ....38 A1
Haydock CI *WGN* WN1..................55 C5
Haydock La *RNFD/HAY* WA11 ......68 A1
Haydock Park Gdns
   NEWLW WA12 ....61 E5
Haydock Rd *AIMK* WN4 ....61 E5
   WHTN BL5 ....68 D5
Hayes St *LEIGH* WN7 ....64 C1
Hayfell Rd *WGNS/IIMK* WN3 ......47 H2
Hayfield Av *TYLD* M29 ....54 B5
Hayman Av *LEIGH* WN7 ....64 C4
Haymill Av *LHULT* M38 ....41 F2
Haysbrook Av *LHULT* M38 ....55 E5
Hayward Gv *WGNW/ST* WN6 ......31 G3
Haywood CI *GOL/RIS/CU* WA3 ....63 F5
Hazel Av *LHULT* M38 ....40 D3
   WGNE/HIN WN2 ....21 H1
   WHTN BL5 ....38 A1
Hazeldene *WHTN* BL5 ....37 G3
Hazel Gv *GOL/RIS/CU* WA3 ....70 C1
   LEIGH WN7 ....51 H4
Hazel La *SKEL* WN8 ....17 C1
Hazelmere Gdns
   WGNE/HIN WN2 ....36 B4
Hazel Rd *ATH* M46 ....38 D4
Hazelton CI *LEIGH* WN7 ....64 C5
Hazelwood Rd *WGN* WN1 ....22 A1
Hazlehurst Ct *AIMK* WN4 ....61 F3
Headen Av *WGNW/BIL/O* WN5 ....32 C3
Headland CI *GOL/RIS/CU* WA3 ....71 F3
Heardman Av
   WGNNW/ST WN6 ....21 H4
Heather Brae *NEWLW* WA12 ......68 D5
Heather Gv *AIMK* WN4 ....61 H2
   LEIGH WN7 ....51 H4
   WGN WN1 ....33 F1
Heatherlea CI *SKEL* WN8 ....31 F1
Heathfield Dr *TYLD* M29 ....54 C2
Heath Gdns *WGNE/HIN* WN2 ......3 F3
Heathgate *SKEL* WN8 ....17 H3
Heath La *GOL/RIS/CU* WA3 ....71 E3
   GOL/RIS/CU WA3 ....77 H2
   LEIGH WN7 ....64 A1
Heathlea *WGNE/HIN* WN2 ....51 F1
Heathmoor Av
   GOL/RIS/CU WA3 ....71 E3
Heath Rd *AIMK* WN4 ....61 E4
   GOL/RIS/CU WA3 ....70 B1
Heaton CI *SKEL* WN8 ....30 D1
Heaton Rd *HOR/BR* BL6 ....15 H5
Heatons Gv *WHTN* BL5 ....26 B3
Heaton St *WGN* WN1 ....2 C1
   WGNE/HIN WN2 ....13 E4
   WGNW/ST WN6 ....10 B1
   WGNS/IIMK WN5 ....34 D2
Hebden Av *GOL/RIS/CU* WA3 ......73 C5
Hebdon CI *AIMK* WN4 ....59 H3
Heber St *WGNW/BIL/O* WN5 ......21 E4
Hector Rd *WGNW/BIL/O* WN5 ......21 E4
Heddles Ct *LEIGH* WN7 * 64 D2
Hedgemead *WGNE/HIN* WN2 ......21 H4
The Hedgerows
   RNFD/HAY WA11 ....68 C2
Heeley St *WGN* WN1 ....22 A3
The Heights *HOR/BR* BL6 ....14 C1
Helen Bank Dr
   RNFD/HAY WA11 ....43 E3
Helen CI *LHULT* M38 ....60 D2
Helias CI *LHULT* M38 ....41 E5
Hell Nook *GOL/RIS/CU* WA3 ......61 H5
Helmclough Wy *WALK* M28 ....55 H3
Helmsdale *SKEL* WN8 ....17 H3
Helmsman Wy
   WGNS/IIMK WN3 ....34 A3
Helsby Wy *WGNS/IIMK* WN3 ......46 D1
Helston Wy *TYLD* M29 ....54 B3
Helvellyn Rd
   WGNW/BIL/O WN5 ....32 C1
Hemfield CI *WGNE/HIN* WN2 ......23 H5
Hemfield Rd *WGNE/HIN* WN2 ......23 H5
Hemley CI *WHTN* BL5 ....37 G2
Henderson Dr
   RNFD/HAY WA11 ....43 F3
Hendon Gv *LEIGH* WN7 ....53 H4
Hendon Rd *WGNW/BIL/O* WN5 ....21 E5
Henderson St *LEIGH* WN7 ....52 A3
Hen Fold Rd *TYLD* M29 ....54 B4
Henley Sq *WGNE/HIN* WN2 ....36 A2
Henniker Rd *BOLS/LL* BL3 ....27 H5
Henrietta St *LEIGH* WN7 ....65 F1
Henri Herman St *BOLS/LL* BL3 ....27 H2
Henry Park St *WGN* WN1 ....3 H6
Henry St *LEIGH* WN7 ....53 H2
   TYLD M29 ....53 G5
   WGNE/HIN WN2 ....34 D4
Hepworth CI *GOL/RIS/CU* WA3 ....62 A4
Herbert St *WGNS/IIMK* WN3 ......34 A4
   WHTN BL5 ....25 H3
Hereford Av
   GOL/RIS/CU WA3 * 70 C1
Hereford CI *AIMK* WN4 ....61 F4
Hereford Rd *WGNE/HIN* WN2 ......36 C2

Herevale Gra *WALK* M28 ....55 G4
Hermitage CI *WGNNW/ST* WN6 ....8 D3
Hermitage Green La
   WARRN/WOL WA2 ....75 H1
Heron Av *FWTH* BL4 ....41 E1
Heron Dr *RNFD/HAY* WA11 ....43 E4
Heron Gv *RNFD/HAY* WA11 ....56 C1
Heron PI *WGNW/BIL/O* WN5 ......47 F1
Herons Whf *WGNNW/ST* WN6 ......8 C3
Hertford Dr *TYLD* M29 ....39 E5
Hesketh Ct *ATH* M46 ....38 D5
Hesketh Dr *WGNNW/ST* WN6 ......8 D5
Hesketh Meadow La
   GOL/RIS/CU WA3 ....71 H2
Hesketh St *ATH* M46 ....39 E4
   LEIGH WN7 ....64 C1
   WGNW/BIL/O WN5 ....33 F1
Hesnall CI *GOL/RIS/CU* WA3 ......73 H5
Heversham CI *LEIGH* WN7 ....17 H5
Hewlett St *WGN* WN1 ....33 C5
   WHTN BL5 ....37 E1
Hexham Av *WGNS/IIMK* WN3 ......33 G5
Hexham CI *ATH* M46 ....39 H2
Heyes Av *RNFD/HAY* WA11 ....43 F5
   RNFD/HAY WA11 ....43 F5
Heyes Gv *RNFD/HAY* WA11 ....43 F5
Heyes St *SKEL* WN8 ....8 E5
Heyford Rd *WGNW/BIL/O* WN5 ....21 E5
Heysham Rd
   WGNW/BIL/O WN5 ....32 C1
Hey Shoot La *GOL/RIS/CU* WA3 ..73 H4
Hey St *WGNNW/ST* WN6 ....33 G5
   WGNE/HIN WN2 ....33 F1
Heywood Av *GOL/RIS/CU* WA3 ....62 C5
Hic-Bibi La *CHLY/EC* PR7 ....5 F1
Hieland Rd *WGN* WN1 ....3 G1
High Bank *ATH* M46 ....39 H2
High Bank La *HOR/BR* BL6 ....12 B5
High Beeches Crs *AIMK* WN4 ......47 H5
Highbury CI *WHTN* BL5 ....37 G2
Highcliffe Ct *WGNNW/ST* WN6 ....10 C3
Highcrest Gv *TYLD* M29 ....54 C2
Higher Damshead *WHTN* BL5 ....26 A5
Higher Drake Meadow
   WHTN BL5 ....37 C3
Higher Green La *TYLD* M29 ....67 F2
Higher Highfield Ct
   WGNE/HIN WN2 ....21 F1
Higher La *RNFD/HAY* WA11 ....43 F5
   RNFD/HAY WA11 ....57 E2
   SKEL WN8 ....31 F1
   WGNE/HIN WN2 ....23 F1
Higher Southfield *WHTN* BL5 ......37 H1
Higher Vw *SKEL* WN8 ....17 H1
Highfield Av *ATH* M46 ....39 F3
   GOL/RIS/CU WA3 ....70 A1
   LEIGH WN7 ....65 H3
   WALK M28 ....54 D3
   WGN WN1 ....3 H2
   WGNNW/ST WN6 ....10 C3
Highfield Dr *FWTH* BL4 ....41 F1
   RNFD/HAY WA11 ....57 F5
   WGNNW/ST WN6 ....10 C3
Highfield Grange Av
   WGNS/IIMK WN3 ....47 E1
Highfield Gv *WGNE/HIN* WN2 ......12 D5
Highfield La *GOL/RIS/CU* WA3 ....70 D4
   WARRN/WOL WA2 ....75 H3
Highfield Rd *HOR/BR* BL6 ....13 F1
   LHULT M38 ....41 E3
Highgate *BOLS/LL* BL3 ....26 B3
Highgate Crs *WGNNW/ST* WN6 ....8 D3
Highgate La *LHULT* M38 ....40 D3
Highgate Rd *WGNE/HIN* WN2 ......3 H7
Highland Rd *HOR/BR* BL6 ....14 C1
Highmarsh Crs *NEWLW* WA12 ....68 D5
Highmeadow *SKEL* WN8 ....30 D2
High Pk *WGNNW/ST* WN6 ....9 H4
High Rid La *HOR/BR* BL6 ....15 G1
High St *ATH* M46 ....39 E5
   SKEL WN8 ....30 D1
   LEIGH WN7 ....65 F1
   NEWLW WA12 ....68 D5
   SKEL WN8 ....16 D4
   TYLD M29 ....53 G2
   TYLD M29 ....67 F2
   WALK M28 ....41 H5
   WGN WN1 ....2 E1
   WGNE/HIN WN2 ....35 G2
   WGNNW/ST WN6 ....10 B1
   WGNS/IIMK WN3 ....34 D2
Highwoods CI *AIMK* WN4 ....59 H3
Hilary Av *ATH* M46 ....38 D3
   GOL/RIS/CU WA3 ....63 E5
Hilary Cv *FWTH* BL4 ....41 H1
Hilda St *LEIGH* WN7 ....65 E1
Hilden St *LEIGH* WN7 ....65 E1
Hildyard St *WGNW/BIL/O* WN5 ....33 E5
Higay CI *WGNS/IIMK* WN3 ....33 E5
Hillary Av *WGNE/HIN* WN2 ....36 D5
Hillbank *WGNNW/ST* WN6 ....10 D3
Hillbeck Crs *AIMK* WN4 ....60 A2
Hill CI *WGNNW/ST* WN6 ....8 D3
Hill Crs *LEIGH* WN7 ....51 F3
Hill Crest *SKEL* WN8 ....39 G5
Hillcrest *SKEL* WN8 ....29 G1
   LEIGH WN7 ....49 G1
Hill Crest Av *LEIGH* WN7 ....51 F3
Hillcrest Rd *TYLD* M29 ....54 C5
Hilldean *SKEL* WN8 ....55 F4
Hillfield Dr *WALK* M28 ....55 F4
Hill La *HOR/BR* BL6 ....7 G4
Hillreed *WGNNW/ST* WN6 ....21 G4
Hillside Av *AIMK* WN4 ....41 F3
   ATH M46 ....39 F4
   FWTH BL4 ....41 H4
   WALK M28 ....41 H4
Hillside CI *BOLS/LL* BL3 ....27 E3
   WGNS/IIMK WN3 ....33 E5
   WGNW/ST WN6 ....58 C2
Hill St *LEIGH* WN7 ....64 D1
   WGNE/HIN WN2 ....36 A2

   WGNNW/ST WN6 ....2 A2
Hill Top *RNFD/HAY* WA11 ....39 G3
Hilton CI *AIMK* WN4 ....56 C4
Hilton Ct *LEIGH* WN7 ....65 F1
Hilton Crs *WALK* M28 ....55 G5
Hilton Gv *WALK* M28 ....41 G5
Hilton La *WALK* M28 ....55 G1
Hilton Rd *WGNW/BIL/O* WN5 ......12 D4
Hilton St *AIMK* WN4 ....41 F4
   WGN WN1 ....2 E5
   WGNS/IIMK WN3 ....34 D2
Hinchcombe CI *LHULT* M38 * 41 F2
Hindburn Dr *WALK* M28 ....55 F3
Hindles CI *ATH* M46 ....52 B1
Hindley Mill La
   WGNE/HIN WN2 ....36 B1
Hindley Rd *WHTN* BL5 ....37 G3
Hindley Wk *WGN* WN1 * 2 C4
Hindsford St *ATH* M46 ....53 C2
Hind's Head Av
   WGNNW/ST WN6 ....4 A1
Hirst Av *WALK* M28 ....41 H3
Hoade St *WGNE/HIN* WN2 ....36 B1
Hobby Gv *LEIGH* WN7 ....65 G1
Hob Hey La *GOL/RIS/CU* WA3 ....72 A1
Hockery Vw *WGNE/HIN* WN2 ......35 H4
Hodder Av *WGNE/HIN* WN2 ....49 E1
Hodder CI *WGNW/BIL/O* WN5 ....33 E1
Hodges St *WGNNW/ST* WN6 ......21 H3
Hodnet Dr *AIMK* WN4 ....61 F3
Hodston St *WGNS/IIMK* WN3 ......36 B4
Holbeach CI *WGNE/HIN* WN2 ......36 B4
Holbeck *TYLD* M29 ....67 E1
Holbeck CI *HOR/BR* BL6 ....14 C2
Holborn Av *RNFD/HAY* WA11 ......52 A3
   WGNS/IIMK WN3 ....34 A3
Holbrook Av *LHULT* M38 ....41 F2
Holcombe Av *GOL/RIS/CU* WA3 ..70 D1
Holden Brook CI *LEIGH* WN7 ......65 G1
Holden Lea *WHTN* BL5 ....25 H2
Holden Rd *LEIGH* WN7 ....65 F1
Holden Wk *WGNW/BIL/O* WN5 ....33 F3
Holding St *WGNE/HIN* WN2 ....36 A2
Holford Wy *NEWLW* WA12 ....76 A1
Holgate Dr *WGNW/BIL/O* WN5 ....31 H3
Holland Ct *SKEL* WN8 ....44 A1
Holland Moss *SKEL* WN8 ....44 A1
The Hollies *ATH* M46 ....39 E5
   WGNE/HIN WN2 * 22 C2
   SKEL WN8 ....26 A5
Hollin Acre *WHTN* BL5 ....26 A5
Hollinbrook *WGNNW/ST* WN6 ....21 G3
Hollingwood CI *AIMK* WN4 ....60 D3
Hollin Hey CI
   WGNW/BIL/O WN5 ....58 C3
Hollins CI *HOR/BR* BL6 ....15 H3
Hollins CI *AIMK* WN4 ....60 A2
   TYLD M29 ....53 H3
Hollins Rd *WGNE/HIN* WN2 ....54 C5
Hollinswood Rd *WALK* M28 ....55 G5
Hollinbush Sq *GOL/RIS/CU* WA3 ..43 F5
Holly CI *SKEL* WN8 ....16 D4
Holly Crs *RNFD/HAY* WA11 ....43 F5
Hollydene *WGNE/HIN* WN2 * 12 C5
Holly Dene Dr *HOR/BR* BL6 ....15 G5
Holly Fold La *RNFD/HAY* WA11 ....28 D5
Holly Gv *LEIGH* WN7 ....64 C4
Holly Heath Dr *WGN* WN1 ....22 A1
Holly La *SKEL* WN8 ....28 C4
Holly Rd *GOL/RIS/CU* WA3 ....70 D1
   WGNE/HIN WN2 ....12 C5
Holly St *WGNE/HIN* WN2 ....33 F1
Holmbrook *TYLD* M29 ....54 B2
Holme Av *WGN* WN1 ....22 B3
Holmebrook Dr *HOR/BR* BL6 ......14 C2
Holme Ct *WGN* WN1 ....2 D1
Holmes House Av
   WGNS/IIMK WN3 ....32 D5
Holme Ter *WGN* WN1 ....22 A2
Holmfield Gn *BOLS/LL* BL3 ....27 G2
Holmsfield CI *WGNE/HIN* WN2 ....23 F3
Holmwood CI *AIMK* WN4 ....60 D1
Holt Av *WGNW/BIL/O* WN5 ....58 C2
Holt Crs *WGNW/BIL/O* WN5 ....58 C2
Holton Wy *WGNS/IIMK* WN3 ......47 F2
Holt St *LEIGH* WN7 ....51 H4
   TYLD M29 ....53 H2
   WGN WN1 ....35 H3
   WGN WN1 ....3 J5
   WGNS/IIMK WN3 ....34 H4
   WGNW/BIL/O WN5 ....31 G3
Holtswell CI *GOL/RIS/CU* WA3 ....62 A5
Homestead Av
   RNFD/HAY WA11 ....68 B2
Honeybourne CI *TYLD* M29 ....54 B2
Honister CI *WGNW/BIL/O* WN5 ....32 C2
Honiton CI *LEIGH* WN7 ....54 C1
Hood CI *TYLD* M29 ....54 C2
Hood Gv *LEIGH* WN7 ....64 C4
Hook St *WGNE/HIN* WN2 ....3 K6
Hooten La *LEIGH* WN7 ....65 H3
Hope Av *LHULT* M38 ....41 G4
Hope Carr La *LEIGH* WN7 ....65 G4
Hope Carr Rd *LEIGH* WN7 ....65 G3
Hope Carr Wy *LEIGH* WN7 ....9 G4
Hope Fold Av *ATH* M46 ....52 C1
Hope Hey La *LHULT* M38 ....41 E3
Hope Island *SKEL* WN8 ....17 E5
Hope La *GOL/RIS/CU* WA3 ....66 B4
Hope St *ATH* M46 ....39 E5
   HOR/BR BL6 ....13 F1
   LEIGH WN7 ....52 A5
   LHULT M38 ....41 F4
   TYLD M29 ....67 E1
   WGN WN1 * 2 C4
   WGNE/HIN WN2 ....24 C2
   WGNE/HIN WN2 ....36 A2

WGNS/IIMK WN5 ......34 D4
Hopwood Cl GOL/RIS/CU WA3 ...71 G1
Hopwood Crs RNFD/HAY WA11 ...56 B1
Horkers Nook WHTN BL5 ...37 G1
Hornbeam Crs AIMK WN4 ...61 E3
Hornby Dr BOLS/LL BL3 ...28 A1
Hornby St LEIGH WN7 ...53 E4
Hornby St WGN WN1 ...2 C1
Horncastle Cl GOL/RIS/CU WA3 ...71 G1
Horne Gv WGNS/IIMK WN5 ...33 G3
Hornsey Gv WGNS/IIMK WN5 ...33 H4
Horridge Av NEWLW WA12 ...69 F4
Horridge Fold Av WHTN BL5 ...27 G3
Horrocks St ATH M46 ...55 G2
    LEIGH WN7 ...65 H2
    LEIGH WN7 ...64 D1
Horsefield St BOLS/LL BL3 ...27 H1
Horsham Cl WHTN BL5 ...38 A2
Horsham Gv WGNE/HIN WN2 ...3 K1
Horton St WGNNW/ST WN6 ...21 F5
The Hoskers WHTN BL5 ...37 G1
Hough La TYLD M29 ...54 B3
Hough St BOLS/LL BL3 ...27 H1
    TYLD M29 ...54 C3
Houghton Av
    WGNW/BIL/O WN5 ...21 F3
Houghton La WGNNW/ST WN6 ...17 H4
Houghton's La SKEL WN8 ...17 H4
Houghton Rd SKEL WN8 ...17 F2
Houghton St SKEL WN8 ...31 F5
Houghwood Gra AIMK WN4 ...60 C3
Houseman Gv
    WGNW/BIL/O WN5 ...21 H3
Housley Cl WGNS/IIMK WN5 ...33 H4
Howard Av BOLS/LL BL3 ...27 H1
Howards La WGNW/BIL/O WN5...32 A1
Howard St WGNW/BIL/O WN5...32 D3
Howarth St LEIGH WN7 ...65 G2
    WHTN BL5 ...
Howbridge Cl WALK M28 ...55 H5
Howden Dr WGNS/IIMK WN5 ...33 H4
Howe Bridge Cl ATH M46 ...52 E2
Hoylake Cl LEIGH WN7 ...64 C4
Hullet Cl WGNNW/ST WN6 ...8 D2
Hulme Gv LEIGH WN7 ...65 H1
Hulme Rd LEIGH WN7 ...51 F5
Hulton Av WALK M28 ...41 G5
Hulton Cl BOLS/LL BL3 ...27 H1
Hulton Dr BOLS/LL BL3 ...27 H2
Hulton La BOLS/LL BL3 ...27 H2
Humber Pl WGNW/BIL/O WN5...32 D3
Humber Rd TYLD M29 ...54 D4
Humphrey St WGNE/HIN WN2*...29 F5
Hunger Hill Av BOLS/LL BL3 ...27 F3
Hunter Rd WGNW/BIL/O WN5 ...21 F4
Hunters Cha
    WGNNW/ST WN5 ...45 H2
Hunt Rd RNFD/HAY WA11 ...68 B3
Hunt St ATH M46 ...39 E5
    WGN WN1 ...
Hurlston Av WALK M28 * ...55 E5
Hurst Cl WHTN BL5 ...39 G1
Hurstfield Rd WALK M28 ...55 G3
Hurst La GOL/RIS/CU WA3 ...73 G2
Hurst Mill La GOL/RIS/CU WA3...73 H4
Hurst St LEIGH WN7 ...64 B1
    WALK M28 ...41 H2
    WGNE/HIN WN2 ...
Huskisson Wy NEWLW WA12...69 E5
Hutton Av WALK M28 ...55 E5
Hutton Cl GOL/RIS/CU WA3 ...72 D4
Hutton Cl SKEL WN8 ...16 C4
Hutton St WGN WN1 ...5 H4
Huxley Pl WGNS/IIMK WN5 ...33 H2
Huyton Rd CHLY/EC PR7 ...7 F1
Hyacinth Cl RNFD/HAY WA11...68 C3
Hyatt St WGNNW/ST WN6 ...21 F5
Hyde Cl WGNS/IIMK WN3 ...33 H5
Hyde Dr WALK M28 ...55 H1
Hyde Rd WALK M28 ...55 H1
Hyde's Brow RNFD/HAY WA11...43 F3
Hythe St BOLS/LL BL3 * ...27 H1

Ice House Cl WALK M28 ...41 E5
Ilkeston Dr WGNE/HIN WN2 ...24 C2
Imperial Dr LEIGH WN7 ...53 E5
Ince Green La WGNE/HIN WN2 ...3 G6
    WGNS/IIMK WN3 ...34 D2
Ince Hall Av WGNE/HIN WN2 ...3 K5
Inchfield SKEL WN8 ...17 G4
Industrial St WHTN BL5 ...38 A1
Ingersol Rd HOR/BR BL6 ...14 D2
Ingham Dr LEIGH WN7 ...51 H5
Ingleby Ct WGNNW/ST WN6 ...
    WHTN BL5 ...26 A3
Inglemoss Dr RNFD/HAY WA11...44 B4
Ingles Fold WALK M28...55 G4
Inglesham Cl LEIGH WN7 ...64 D5
Ingleton Dr RNFD/HAY WA11...44 B4
Inglewhite SKEL WN8 ...17 F5
Inglewhite Av WALK WA12* ...
Inglewhite Crs WGN WN1 * ...22 B3
Inglewood Av WGN WN1 ...3 G6
Inglewood Rd
    RNFD/HAY WA11 ...56 C5
Ingram SKEL WN8 ...17 G4
Ingram St WGNE/HIN WN2 ...
    WGNE/HIN WN2 ...21 C4
Inskip SKEL WN8 ...17 F5
Inward Dr WGNNW/ST WN6 ...21 F1
Inworth Cl WHTN BL5 ...38 A2
Iredale Crs WGNNW/ST WN6 ...10 C3
Ironmonger La
    WGNS/IIMK WN3 ...2 C7
Irvine Av WALK M28 ...55 H1
Irvine St LEIGH WN7 ...52 A5
Irwell SKEL WN8 ...17 F2

Irwell Av LHULT M38 ...41 G4
Irwell Cl WGNW/BIL/O WN5 ...32 D2
Irwell Rd WGNW/BIL/O WN5...32 A1
Isabella St WGN WN1 ...3 G4
Isherwood St LEIGH WN7 ...51 H3
Ivanhoe Av GOL/RIS/CU WA3...63 E5
Ivybridge SKEL WN8 ...17 G3
Ivydale SKEL WN8 ...17 G3
Ivydale Dr LEIGH WN7 ...65 H1
Ivy Farm Gdns
    GOL/RIS/CU WA3 ...72 C5
Ivy Cv LHULT M38 ...41 E4
Ivy House Rd GOL/RIS/CU WA3...63 G5
Ivy Rd BOLS/LL BL3 ...70 C1
    WGNNW/ST WN6 ...
Ivy St BOLS/LL BL3 ...38 A1
Ivy St WGNNW/ST WN6 ...2 B5

Jack's La WHTN BL5 ...36 D1
Jackson St WALK M28 ...41 H4
    WGNE/HIN WN2 ...35 F1
Jacob St WGNE/HIN WN2 ...36 A2
James Cl WGNS/IIMK WN5 ...2 C7
James Pl WCNNW/ST WN6 ...5 F5
James Pl WGNE/HIN WN2 ...36 B1
James Sq WGNNW/ST WN6 ...5 E5
James St ATH M46 ...53 F2
    WGNE/HIN WN2 ...48 D4
    WGNS/IIMK WN3 ...34 C2
    WGNS/IIMK WN3 ...35 H3
Jasmine Rd
    WGNW/BIL/O WN5 * ...33 E1
Jean Av LEIGH WN7 ...64 D4
Jeffrey St LEIGH WN7 ...64 D1
Jellicoe La RNFD/HAY WA11...68 D1
Jenkinson St WGNE/HIN WN2...25 F5
Jennet Hey AIMK WN4 ...47 G5
Jennet's La GOL/RIS/CU WA3...65 H5
Jessica Wy LEIGH WN7 ...51 H5
Johnson Av NEWLW WA12 ...69 E4
Johnson La WGNE/HIN WN2 ...50 B2
Johnson St ATH M46 ...52 B2
    TYLD M29 ...53 H2
    WGNW/BIL/O WN5 ...32 C2
John St AIMK WN4 ...61 G1
    BOLS/LL BL3 ...70 B1
    LEIGH WN7 ...64 B1
    TYLD M29 ...53 H2
    WGN WN1 ...3 F5
    WGNE/HIN WN2 ...37 E5
    WGNS/IIMK WN3 ...33 H3
Jonathan Fold LEIGH WN7 ...66 A1
Jonquil Dr LHULT M38 ...55 E1
Jubilee Av WGNW/BIL/O WN5...31 G4
Jubilee Crs RNFD/HAY WA11...68 C2
Jubilee Dr SKEL WN8 ...16 D5
Jubilee Houses WALK M28...41 H5
Junction Rd RNFD/HAY WA11...43 F2
Junction Rd West HOR/BR BL6...15 H5
Junction Ter WGNS/IIMK WN3...34 D2
June Av LEIGH WN7 ...64 B1
Juniper Dr WGNE/HIN WN2 ...36 C5
Jupiter Gv WGNS/IIMK WN5 ...47 F1
Jury St LEIGH WN7 ...51 H4
Justene Cl GOL/RIS/CU WA3...62 B4
Jutland Gv WHTN BL5 ...25 H4

Kane Ct GOL/RIS/CU WA3 ...63 H5
Karen Rd WGN WN1 ...3 H5
Kay Cl WGN WN1 ...3 F5
Kay St ATH M46 ...53 E1
Kaye St LEIGH WN7 ...64 C1
    WGNNW/ST WN6 ...2 A3
Keats St LEIGH WN7 ...51 G4
Keats Wy WGNW/BIL/O WN2...49 G2
Keble Gv LEIGH WN7 ...65 F3
Keble Rd WGNE/HIN WN2 ...36 B3
Kellaton Ct WGNS/IIMK WN5 *...34 D2
Kelibank Rd WGNS/IIMK WN5...33 F5
Kellet Cl WGNW/BIL/O WN5 ...21 E4
Kells Gv WGNNW/ST WN6 ...21 G5
Kellsall Cl WALK WN4 * ...60 A2
Kelvin Cl WGNS/IIMK WN5...47 G1
Kelway Ter WGN WN1 ...3 F2
Kempton La NEWLW WA12 ...69 G4
Kendal Cl RNFD/HAY WA11 ...43 E1
Kendal Dr RNFD/HAY WA11 ...43 E2
Kendal Gv WALK M28 ...55 G4
    LEIGH WN7 ...64 C1
Kendal Rd WALK M28 ...54 D4
    WGNE/HIN WN2 ...23 F5
    WGNE/HIN WN2 ...36 B3
Kendal St WGNNW/ST WN6 ...2 A3
Kendrew Rd BOLS/LL BL3...27 H1
Kendrick Pl WGN WN1 ...3 G4
Kenford Dr WGNS/IIMK WN3...47 F1
Kenhall Rd LEIGH WN7 ...65 H2
Kenilworth Dr LEIGH WN7 ...53 F4
    WGNE/HIN WN2 ...36 C4
Kenilworth Rd
    GOL/RIS/CU WA3 ...71 F2
Kenmore Gv AIMK WN4 ...60 A3
Kennedy Rd TYLD M29 ...54 C4
Kennet Cl WHTN BL5 ...25 H4
Kenneth Av LEIGH WN7 ...51 G5
Kenneth Gv LEIGH WN7 ...51 G5
Kenney Wy LEIGH WN7 ...53 F4
Kensington Rd
    WGNW/BIL/O WN5 ...33 E5
Kent Av WGNE/HIN WN2 ...49 F1
Kent St WALK M28 ...55 F1

Kentmere Av RNFD/HAY WA11...58 B5
Kentmere Dr TYLD M29 ...54 A4
Kentmere Gv FWTH BL4 ...41 E1
Kent Rd ATH M46 ...38 D4
    TYLD M29 ...53 C1
Kent St LEIGH WN7 ...66 A2
    WGN WN1 ...3 F6
Kenway RNFD/HAY WA11 ...43 F5
Kenwood Av LEIGH WN7 ...65 F1
Kenwood Cl LEIGH WN7 ...65 H2
Kenyon Gv LHULT M38 ...40 D4
Kenyon La GOL/RIS/CU WA3 ...71 G3
Kenyon Rd WGN WN1 ...2 C1
    WGNNW/ST WN6 ...5 E5
Kenyons La North
    RNFD/HAY WA11 ...68 C1
Kenyon's La South
    RNFD/HAY WA11 ...68 C1
Kenyon St LEIGH WN7 ...51 G3
Kenyon Ter LEIGH WN7 ...51 G3
Kenyon Wy LHULT M38 ...40 D5
Kerans Dr WHTN BL5 ...25 G5
Kerfoot's La SKEL WN8 ...16 E5
Kerfoot St LEIGH WN7 ...65 H2
Kermishaw Nook TYLD M29...53 H5
Kersal Av LHULT M38 ...41 G4
Kershaw St TYLD M29 ...53 H2
Kershaw Wy NEWLW WA12 ...69 F4
Kestrel Pk SKEL WN8 ...17 H1
Kestrel Av LHULT M38 ...41 F4
Kestrel Dr AIMK WN4 ...48 B5
Kestrel Ms SKEL WN8 ...17 H1
Keswick Pl WGNE/HIN WN2 ...35 F1
Keswick Wy RNFD/HAY WA11...43 E1
Kid Glove Rd GOL/RIS/CU WA3...62 C5
Kielder Cl AIMK WN4 ...47 G4
Kilbuck La RNFD/HAY WA11...68 D1
Kilburn Av AIMK WN4 ...61 F3
Kilburn Clase LEIGH WN7 ...51 G2
Kilburn Dr WGNNW/ST WN6...17 F5
Kilburn Gv WGNS/IIMK WN5...33 E5
Kilburn Rd BOLS/LL BL3 ...31 F3
Kildale Cl BOLS/LL BL3 ...27 H1
Kildare St FWTH BL4 ...41 H1
    WGNE/HIN WN2 ...35 H1
    WGNW/BIL/O WN5 ...33 G2
Killington Cl WGNS/IIMK WN3...48 A1
Killingworth Ms
    Kiln La SKEL WN8 ...14 C1
Kiln La SKEL WN8 ...17 H1
The Kilphin HOR/BR BL6 ...15 G2
Kilsby Cl HOR/BR BL6 ...15 H4
Kilshaw St WGNW/BIL/O WN5...32 D3
Kimberley Pl AIMK WN4 ...61 F3
Kimberly St WGNNW/ST WN6...21 H4
Kincraig Cl BOLS/LL BL3 ...27 F1
Kinder Gv AIMK WN4 ...47 G5
Kingfisher Ct AIMK WN4 ...48 A5
Kingfisher Dr FWTH BL4 ...41 E1
Kingfisher Pk SKEL WN8 ...17 H1
King George Cl AIMK WN4 ...61 F1
King George Rd
    RNFD/HAY WA11 ...68 D2
King's Av GOL/RIS/CU WA3 ...71 G2
Kingsbury Ct SKEL WN8 ...17 H1
King's Crs TYLD M29 ...53 F3
Kingscroft Cts WGN WN1 ...22 B1
Kingsdown Rd
    WGNE/HIN WN2 ...49 G4
Kingsfield Wy TYLD M29 ...54 A4
King's Gdns LEIGH WN7 ...65 H1
Kingshill Ct WGNNW/ST WN6...10 C3
Kingsley Av WGNS/IIMK WN3...34 A4
Kingsley Rd WALK M28 ...41 H4
Kingsley St LEIGH WN7 ...51 F4
Kingsmead Ct
    GOL/RIS/CU WA3 ...77 H4
Kingsmede WGN WN1 ...22 A1
King's Moss La
    RNFD/HAY WA11 ...44 B4
Kingsoak Cl WGN WN1 ...3 H5
King's Rd AIMK WN4 ...60 D1
    WGNS/IIMK WN3 ...70 B2
Kingston Cl WGNS/IIMK WN3...34 A5
King St LEIGH WN7 ...65 E2
    WGN WN1 ...2 D4
    WGNE/HIN WN2 ...35 F1
    WGNE/HIN WN2 ...36 C3
    WHTN BL5 ...26 A5
King St West WGN WN1 ...2 C5
Kingsway WGN WN1 ...3 J7
Kingswood Crs
    WGNE/HIN WN2 ...35 E2
Kinlet Rd WGNW/BIL/O WN5...32 D4
Kinnerly Gv WALK M28 ...55 F3
Kinniside Ct WGNS/IIMK WN5...47 H1
Kinross Av AIMK WN4 ...59 H2
Kinsley Dr WALK M28 ...55 F3
Kintbury St WGNE/HIN WN2...49 E4
Kipling Av WGNE/HIN WN2...36 C4
Kipling Cv LEIGH WN7 ...51 G4
Kirby Av ATH M46 ...38 D5
Kirby Rd AIMK WN4 ...61 F1
Kiribati Wy LEIGH WN7 ...51 H5
Kirkbeck Gdns SKEL WN8 ...30 C1
Kirkebrook Rd BOLS/LL BL3...27 G1
Kirkfell Dr TYLD M29 ...54 A4
Kirkhall La LEIGH WN7 ...51 H5
Kirkham Av GOL/RIS/CU WA3*...71 F3
Kirkham Rd LEIGH WN7 ...64 C4
Kirkham St LHULT M38 ...41 G3
Kirkless St WGNE/HIN WN2...23 F2
Kirkless Vis WGNE/HIN WN2...23 F2
Kirkpatrick St WGNE/HIN WN2...36 A1
Kirkstead Wy GOL/RIS/CU WA3...70 B1
Kirkstile Crs WGNS/IIMK WN3...47 F1

Kirkstone WGNW/BIL/O WN5 ...32 D1
Kirkwood Cl WGNE/HIN WN2...23 E3
Kite Cv LEIGH WN7 ...41 E1
Kitt Green Rd
    WGNW/BIL/O WN5 ...20 D5
Kittiwake Cl TYLD M29 ...53 H4
Kiveton Cl WALK M28 ...55 H1
Kiveton Dr AIMK WN4 ...61 H1
Knaresborough Rd
    WGNE/HIN WN2 ...36 B4
Knightscliffe Crs
    WGNNW/ST WN6 ...8 C4
Knightshill Crs
    WGNNW/ST WN6 ...21 G4
Knightswood BOLS/LL BL3 ...27 G2
Knowles Av WGNS/IIMK WN3...33 G4
Knowles Pl WGN WN1 ...2 C1
Knowles St WGNS/IIMK WN3 *...34 C5
Knowsley Av ATH M46 ...38 D4
    GOL/RIS/CU WA3 ...62 C5
Knowsley Dr LEIGH WN7 ...64 C4
Knowsley Gv HOR/BR BL6 ...14 C1
Knowsley Rd WGNE/HIN WN2...21 H2
Knowsley St LEIGH WN7 ...64 C4
Knowsley Vw RNFD/HAY WA11...42 D3
Knutshaw Crs BOLS/LL BL3...27 F5

Laburnum Av ATH M46 ...39 F5
    LEIGH WN7 ...51 H3
    WGNS/IIMK WN5 ...33 G2
Laburnum Dr SKEL WN8 ...16 C4
Laburnum Gv HOR/BR BL6 ...14 D1
    TYLD M29 ...54 C2
Laburnum Rd
    GOL/RIS/CU WA3 ...71 G1
Laburnum St AIMK WN4 ...61 E4
    ATH M46 ...39 F5
Ladies La WGNE/HIN WN2 ...23 F5
Ladybarn Av GOL/RIS/CU WA3...70 A2
Ladybridge Av WALK M28 ...55 H5
Ladyhill Vw WALK M28 ...55 G4
Lady La WGNS/IIMK WN5 ...33 H4
Ladymere Dr WALK M28 ...55 F4
Ladysmith Av AIMK WN4 ...61 F3
Ladywell Av LHULT M38 ...41 F5
Ladywell Cv LHULT M38 ...41 F5
Lafford La SKEL WN8 ...17 H1
Laithwaite Rd
    WGNW/BIL/O WN5 ...33 E1
Lakeland Av AIMK WN4 ...61 H2
Lake Side WGNW/BIL/O WN5...31 H2
Lake Side LEIGH WN7 ...52 C5
Lakeside Av WGNW/BIL/O WN5...31 H5
Lakeside Cl RNFD/HAY WA11...58 A5
Lakeside Gdns
    RNFD/HAY WA11 ...43 E5
Lakes Ter LEIGH WN7 ...51 H5
Lakes Ter LEIGH WN7 ...52 B5
Lamberhead Rd
    WGNW/BIL/O WN5 ...32 A5
Lambeth St ATH M46 ...38 C5
Lambley Cl LEIGH WN7 ...51 G3
Lambourne Gv WALK M28*...55 H1
Lamb St WGN WN1 ...3 G2
Lanark Av WGNW/BIL/O WN5...32 C5
Lancaster Av ATH M46 ...38 C5
    GOL/RIS/CU WA3 ...62 B4
    TYLD M29 ...39 F5
Lancaster Cl NEWLW WA12...68 C4
Lancaster Crs SKEL WN8 ...16 D4
Lancaster Rd TYLD M29 ...36 C3
    WGNW/BIL/O WN5 ...20 D5
Lancaster St WGNS/IIMK WN3...34 C2
Lance Wood Pl
    WGNW/BIL/O WN5 ...33 E2
Landau Dr LHULT M38 ...41 E5
Landedmans WHTN BL5 ...38 A1
Land Gate La AIMK WN4 ...47 H4
Landor Cl GOL/RIS/CU WA3 ...71 F1
Landrace Dr WALK M28 ...55 G5
Landside LEIGH WN7 ...65 E4
Land Head Av
    GOL/RIS/CU WA3 ...71 F1
Langdale Av GOL/RIS/CU WA3...62 D5
    WGN WN1 ...22 A1
    WGNE/HIN WN2 ...23 G5
Langdale Gv WGNE/HIN WN2...49 G3
Langdale Rd WGNE/HIN WN2...36 B3
    WGNW/BIL/O WN5 ...20 C5
Langdale St FWTH BL4 ...41 H1
    LEIGH WN7 ...64 D1
Langfield Cl GOL/RIS/CU WA3...72 C5
Langfield GOL/RIS/CU WA3 ...72 C5
Langford Dr LEIGH WN7 ...64 D4
Langham Rd WGNNW/ST WN6...10 B5
Langholm Cl WGNS/IIMK WN3...47 E1
Langholme Pl AIMK WN4 ...59 H2
Langley Cl GOL/RIS/CU WA3...62 D5
    WGNNW/ST WN6 ...10 B3
Langley St WGNE/HIN WN2...49 E3
Langset Av WGNE/HIN WN2...36 C5
Langton Cl NEWLW WA12 ...10 B1
Langton Pl WGNNW/ST WN6...10 B3
Langton St LEIGH WN7 ...65 E2
Langtree Cl WALK M28 ...55 G3
Langtree La WGNNW/ST WN6...10 B3
Langworthy Av LHULT M38...41 G5
Lansbury St WGNW/BIL/O WN5...32 D3
Lansdowne Dr WALK M28...55 H3
Lansdowne Rd ATH M46 ...39 G3
Lapwing Cl GOL/RIS/CU WA3...71 F1
Larch Av WGNW/BIL/O WN5...32 D2

Larch Cl GOL/RIS/CU WA3 ...71 G3
    SKEL WN8 ...16 D4
Larch Crs WGN WN1 ...58 C1
Larch Gv ATH M46 ...38 D4
Larch Rd LEIGH WN7 ...64 C1
    RNFD/HAY WA11 ...68 B2
Larchwood Dr WGN WN1 ...22 A1
Larkfield Av LHULT M38 ...41 E3
    WGN WN1 ...22 A1
Larkfield Cl LEIGH WN7 ...17 C1
Larkhill Av WGNNW/ST WN6...10 C2
Larkspur Cl LEIGH WN7 ...65 E3
Latham Av NEWLW WA12 ...69 F5
Latham La WGNW/BIL/O WN5...20 B5
Latham Rd HOR/BR BL6 ...7 H4
Lathom Dr RNFD/HAY WA11...43 E4
Latimer Cl WGNW/BIL/O WN5 *...32 A1
Launceston Rd
    WGNE/HIN WN2 ...37 F5
Laurel Crs WGNE/HIN WN2...36 D5
Laurel St ATH M46 ...38 D4
    LEIGH WN7 ...
Laurel Cv AIMK WN4 ...61 E2
    GOL/RIS/CU WA3 ...71 E1
    LEIGH WN7 ...51 H3
Lavender Rd WGNNW/BIL...21 G2
Lawns Av SKEL WN8 ...31 F3
Lawnswood Dr TYLD M29 ...54 C2
Lawnwood Av WGNE/HIN WN2...49 E2
Lawson Av LEIGH WN7 ...51 H2
Laxey Av ATH M46 ...53 F1
Laxey Crs LEIGH WN7 ...51 H4
Layland Av GOL/RIS/CU WA3...72 D5
Layton Cl WGNW/BIL/O WN5...33 E3
Lazenby Crs AIMK WN4 ...60 C5
Lazonby Av WGNE/HIN WN2...24 C3
Leacroft AIMK WN4 ...47 F5
Leadale Cl WGNNW/ST WN6...10 A1
Leader St WGN WN1 ...
    WGNW/BIL/O WN5 ...32 D2
Leafield Fold ...
Leafield Dr WALK M28 ...55 F5
Lea Gate Cl WGNS/IIMK WN3...33 F5
Leal Holme Av WGNE/HIN WN2...23 F3
Lea St WGNS/IIMK WN5 ...33 H1
Leavale Cl LHULT M38 ...41 E4
Lea Vw WGN WN1 ...3 J5
Leaway WGNE/HIN WN2 ...3 J6
Leckenby Cl WALK M28 ...55 F5
Ledburn Cl WGNS/IIMK WN5...17 G2
Ledbury St LEIGH WN7 ...52 A5
Ledmore Gv AIMK WN4 ...60 A3
Lee Bank WHTN BL5 ...25 H4
Leeds St WGNS/IIMK WN3 ...2 A6
Lee Fold TYLD M29 ...54 B3
Lee La WGNE/HIN WN2 ...49 G3
Lee St ATH M46 ...53 E1
Leeswood SKEL WN8 ...17 G2
Legh St AIMK WN4 ...70 B1
Leicester Av WGNE/HIN WN2...36 C2
Leicester Rd TYLD M29 ...53 H1
Leigh Ar WGN WN1 * ...2 C4
Leigh Rd WALK M28 ...52 B3
    WGNE/HIN WN2 ...51 E2
    WHTN BL5 ...26 A5
Leigh St LEIGH WN7 ...64 B1
    WGN WN1 ...3 F6
    WGNE/HIN WN2 ...51 E2
    WHTN BL5 ...25 H4
Leighton Av ATH M46 ...38 C5
Leighton Dr LEIGH WN7 ...64 A5
Leighton St ATH M46 ...38 C5
Leighton St TYLD M29 ...53 H2
Leopold St WGNW/BIL/O WN5...32 C3
Lessingham Av WGN WN1 ...22 A2
Lester Rd LHULT M38 ...40 D3
Levens Pl WGNE/HIN WN2 ...23 F5
    WGNW/BIL/O WN5 ...32 D1
Lever St TYLD M29 ...53 H2
    WHTN BL5 ...25 H2
Lewis Cl CHLY/EC PR7 ...6 D1
    WGNS/IIMK WN3 ...33 H3
Leyburn Cl WGN WN1 ...3 J3
Ley Crs TYLD M29 ...54 A5
Leyland Av GOL/RIS/CU WA3...62 D5
Leyland Green Rd AIMK WN4...59 H1
Leyland Mill La WGN WN1 ...22 A1
Leyland Rd RNFD/HAY WA11...43 E5
Leyland St WGNE/HIN WN2...35 H4
    WGNW/BIL/O WN5 ...32 D2
Ley Rd TYLD M29 ...53 H4
Library St WGN WN1 ...2 D5
    WHTN BL5 ...26 A5
Lichfield Av GOL/RIS/CU WA3...71 E1
    TYLD M29 ...54 A5
Lichfield Gv AIMK WN4 ...61 F4
Lichfield St WGNW/BIL/O WN5...32 D3
Lidgate Cl WGNW/BIL/O WN5...20 B5
Lidgett St WALK M28 ...41 H5
Lightbourne Av LEIGH WN7...64 D3
Light Oaks Rd
    GOL/RIS/CU WA3 ...73 H3
Lightshaw La GOL/RIS/CU WA3...55 G5
Lilac Av AIMK WN4 ...60 A1
    LEIGH WN7 ...51 H4
    WGNNW/ST WN6 ...21 H2
Lilac Gdns WGNS/IIMK WN3...33 E4
Lilac Gv SKEL WN8 ...16 D4
Lilford St ATH M46 ...52 C5
Lilford Cl WGNE/HIN WN2 * ...
    LEIGH WN7 ...64 D2
Lilian Dr WGNNW/ST WN6 ...21 H2
Lily La WGNE/HIN WN2 ...49 F3
Lily Lane E AIMK WN4 ...61 H1
Lily St AIMK WN4 ...61 H1
Lime Av LEIGH WN7 ...51 H3
Lime Cv WGNE/HIN WN2 ...49 G4
Limefield WGN WN1 ...2 E4
Limefield Dr SKEL WN8 ...30 B1

Lime Gv *GOL/RIS/CU* WA3 ....**71** E3
RNFD/HAY WA11 ....**43** E5
SKEL WN8 ....**16** D4
WGNE/HIN WN2 ....**36** C5
Limes Av *WGNNW/ST* WN6 ....**11** E4
Lime Trees *GOL/RIS/CU* WA3 ....**72** C5
GOL/RIS/CU WA3 ....**72** C5
WGNNW/ST WN6 ....**10** D5
Lime St *ATH* M46 ....**38** A5
TYLD M29 ....**53** F2
WN5 ....**2** E4
Lime V *WGNS/IIMK* WN5 ....**35** E4
Lime Vale Rd
WGNNW/BIL/O WN5 ....**58** B3
Linbeck Gv *GOL/RIS/CU* WA3 ....**63** F5
Lincoln Av *GOL/RIS/CU* WA3 ....**63** E5
Lincoln Cl *GOL/RIS/CU* WA3 ....**72** B1
TYLD M29 ....**53** G2
Lincoln Dr *AIMK* WN4 ....**61** F4
WGNE/HIN WN2 ....**13** E5
Lincoln Pl *WGNW/BIL/O* WN5 ....**20** D5
Lincroft Rd *WGNE/HIN* WN2 ....**36** D5
Lindale Cl *WALK* M28 ....**54** D4
Lindale Rd *WALK* M28 ....**54** D4
Linden Av *AIMK* WN4 ....**60** C1
ATH M46 ....**52** C1
Linden Gv *LEIGH* WN7 ....**51** H4
WGNE/HIN WN2 ....**51** H4
RNFD/HAY WA11 ....**43** F1
Linden Ms *WALK* M28 ....**55** E5
Linden Rd *WALK* M28 ....**55** E5
Lindens *SKEL* WN8 ....**17** C1
Linden St *WGNW/BIL/O* WN5 ....**32** D3
Lindholme *SKEL* WN8 ....**17** H2
Lindisfarne Av
GOL/RIS/CU WA3 ....**72** B1
Lindley Av *WGNW/BIL/O* WN5 ....**33** E3
Linley St *LEIGH* WN7 * **65** F1
Lindow St *LEIGH* WN7 ....**64** C1
Lindsay St *HOR/BR* BL6 ....**14** C1
Lindsay Ter *WGNE/HIN* WN2 ....**12** C5
Lingards Dr *TYLD* M29 ....**66** D2
Lingards La *TYLD* M29 ....**66** D2
Lingard St *LEIGH* WN7 ....**65** G2
Ling Dr *ATH* M46 ....**53** E1
Lingfield Cl *FWTH* BL4 ....**41** H1
Lingfield Crs *WGNNW/ST* WN6 ....**21** F2
Lingmell Av *RNFD/HAY* WA11 ....**58** A5
Lingmoor Cl *WGNS/IIMK* WN3 ....**47** H2
Lingmoor Dr *TYLD* M29 ....**54** A3
Linkfield Dr *WALK* M28 ....**55** E5
Links Dr *HOR/BR* BL6 ....**15** G3
Links Rd *HOR/BR* BL6 ....**15** G3
Linkway Av *AIMK* WN4 ....**61** H1
The Linkway *HOR/BR* BL6 ....**14** B2
Linley Cl *WGNNW/ST* WN6 ....**22** D1
Linley Rd *WGNW/BIL/O* WN5 ....**33** E5
Linnet Dr *LEIGH* WN7 ....**65** C1
Linney Sq *WN1* **3** G4
Linstock Wy *ATH* M46 ....**38** B5
Linton Av *GOL/RIS/CU* WA3 ....**62** A4
Linwood Cl *WGNE/HIN* WN2 ....**36** C5
Lion La *HOR/BR* BL6 ....**7** H5
Liptrot St *WGNW/BIL/O* WN5 ....**33** C1
Liscard St *ATH* M46 ....**38** C5
Little Factory St *TYLD* M29 ....**53** G2
Littlegate *WHTN* BL5 ....**37** H5
Little La *WGNS/IIMK* WN3 ....**33** F4
Little London *WGN* WN1 ....**2** D5
Little Pasture *LEIGH* WN7 ....**51** G4
Little Scotland *HOR/BR* BL6 ....**7** F3
Littleton Gv *WGNNW/ST* WN6 ....**5** F5
Liverpool Rd *AIMK* WN4 ....**60** D4
RNFD/HAY WA11 ....**55** G5
SKEL WN8 ....**16** C5
WGNE/HIN WN2 ....**35** G5
Liza St *LEIGH* WN7 ....**51** H3
Lloyd Ct *LEIGH* WN7 * **51** H4
Local Board St *WGNE/HIN* WN2 ....**3** K7
Loch St *WGNW/BIL/O* WN5 ....**20** D1
Lockerbie Pl *WGNS/IIMK* WN3 ....**47** F1
Locker La *AIMK* WN4 ....**62** A2
Lockett Rd *AIMK* WN4 ....**48** A5
Lock La *HOR/BR* BL6 ....**26** D1
Locks Vw *WN1* **3** J5
Lodge Av *ATH* M46 ....**53** F2
Lodge Gv *ATH* M46 ....**53** F2
Lodge La *ATH* M46
LEIGH WN7 ....**66** B2
NEWLW WA12 ....**61** E5
RNFD/HAY WA11 ....**42** B2
Lodge Rd *ATH* M46 ....**53** F2
WGNW/BIL/O WN5 ....**31** H4
Loeminster Pl *WGNE/HIN* WN2 ....**3** J7
Logwood Av
WGNW/BIL/O WN5 ....**33** E1
Logwood Pl
WGNW/BIL/O WN5 ....**21** F5
Loire Dr *WGNW/BIL/O* WN5 ....**21** G5
Lomax St *WGNE/HIN* WN2 ....**49** F1
Lombard St *ATH* M46 ....**38** C5
London Cl *WGNW/BIL/O* WN5 ....**21** F5
London Flds
WGNW/BIL/O WN5 ....**58** D1
Longbrook *WGNNW/ST* WN6 ....**9** G4
Long Cswy *ATH* M46 ....**52** C4
Longcroft *TYLD* M29 ....**66** B2
Longendale Rd
WGNNW/ST WN6 ....**10** A2
Longfellow Cl *WGNS/IIMK* WN3 ....**33** H3
Longhey *SKEL* WN8 ....**17** H1
Longhurst Rd *WGNE/HIN* WN2 ....**36** C4
Long La *SKEL* WN8 ....**30** B5
WGNE/HIN WN2 ....**36** D4
WHTN BL5 ....**25** F3
Longmead Av *WN4* **61** F2
Longridge Av
WGNNW/ST WN6 ....**10** C2
Longshaw Av
WGNW/BIL/O WN5 ....**45** H2
Longshaw Cl
WGNW/BIL/O WN5 ....**45** H2

Longshaw Common
WGNW/BIL/O WN5 ....**45** H3
Longshaw Dr *WALK* M28 ....**41** H4
Longshaw Old Rd
WGNW/BIL/O WN5 ....**45** H2
Longshoot Cl *LEIGH* WN7 * **3** F3
Longton Av *GOL/RIS/CU* WA3 ....**70** D1
Longton St *WGNE/HIN* WN2 ....**35** H4
Longwall Av *WALK* M28 ....**55** H5
Longwood Ct *RNFD/HAY* WA11 ....**56** C5
Longworth Av *HOR/BR* BL6 ....**14** C1
Lonsdale Av *LEIGH* WN7 ....**64** C4
Lonsdale Wk
RNFD/HAY WA11 ....**43** F2
Lord Av *ATH* M46 * **53** F2
Lord Gv *ATH* M46 ....**53** F2
Lords Fold *RNFD/HAY* WA11 ....**42** D4
Lord St *WGNW/BIL/O* WN5 * **61** G2
ATH M46 ....**53** F2
GOL/RIS/CU WA3 ....**77** H4
LEIGH WN7 ....**65** E1
TYLD M29 ....**53** H1
WGN WN1 ....**2** D2
WGNE/HIN WN2 ....**35** F1
WGNE/HIN WN2 ....**36** A3
WHTN BL5 ....**25** H4
Lord St South *LEIGH* WN7 ....**65** F1
Lordy Cl *WGNNW/ST* WN6 ....**11** E3
Lorne St *AIMK* WN4 ....**60** C1
Lorton Cl *WALK* M28 ....**55** G5
Lostock Cl *WGNW/BIL/O* WN5 ....**58** D1
Lostock Junction La
HOR/BR BL6 ....**15** H4
Lostock La *HOR/BR* BL6 ....**15** F5
Lostock Park Dr *HOR/BR* BL6 ....**15** F5
Lostock Rd *WHTN* BL5 ....**25** H4
Loughrigg Av *RNFD/HAY* WA11 ....**58** A5
Loughrigg Cl *TYLD* M29 ....**54** A4
Louise Gdns *WHTN* BL5 ....**37** H2
Lovers' La *ATH* M46 ....**52** A4
Low Bank Rd *AIMK* WN4 ....**60** B2
Lowcroft *SKEL* WN8 ....**17** H2
Lowe Av *ATH* M46 ....**38** D3
Lower Drake Fold *WHTN* BL5 ....**37** G3
Lower Green La *TYLD* M29 ....**67** F4
Lower House Dr *HOR/BR* BL6 ....**15** H4
Lower Landedmans *WHTN* BL5 ....**38** A1
Lower Leigh Rd *WHTN* BL5 ....**38** A4
Lower Longshoot *WGN* WN1 ....**3** F4
Lower Lyndon Av
WGNNW/ST WN6 ....**9** F4
Lower Makinson Fold
HOR/BR BL6 ....**14** C1
Lower New Rw *WALK* M28 ....**55** F2
Lower St Stephen St
WGNNW/ST WN6 ....**21** H5
Lower Southfield *WHTN* BL5 ....**37** H1
Lower St *FWTH* BL4 ....**41** G1
Lower St *GOL/RIS/CU* WA3 ....**70** B1
Loweswater Av *TYLD* M29 ....**53** H4
Loweswater Rd *FWTH* BL4 ....**40** D1
Lowfield Gdns
GOL/RIS/CU WA3 ....**73** H2
Low Gn *ATH* M46 ....**39** C3
Lowood St *LEIGH* WN7 ....**64** C1
Lowside Av *HOR/BR* BL6 ....**15** H4
Lowther Av *GOL/RIS/CU* WA3 ....**71** G5
Lowther Dr *LEIGH* WN7 ....**53** F4
Lowton Gdns *GOL/RIS/CU* WA3 ....**70** C4
Lowton Rd *GOL/RIS/CU* WA3 ....**62** C5
Loxton Crs *WGNS/IIMK* WN3 ....**34** A5
Luciol Cl *TYLD* M29 ....**54** B2
Ludlow Cl *SKEL* WN8 ....**17** H1
Ludlow Av *WGNE/HIN* WN2 ....**36** D4
Ludlow Dr *LEIGH* WN7 ....**53** F4
Ludlow St *WGNNW/ST* WN6 ....**4** D4
Ludovic Ter *WGN* WN1 ....**22** B1
Luke St *AIMK* WN4 ....**61** C1
Lulworth *SKEL* WN8 ....**17** H1
Lulworth Av *WGNE/HIN* WN2 ....**36** D4
Lulworth Rd *BOLS/LL* BL3 ....**27** H2
Lune Gv *LEIGH* WN7 ....**64** B1
Lunehurst *GOL/RIS/CU* WA3 ....**71** F1
Lune Rd *WGNE/HIN* WN2 ....**36** A4
Luntswood Gv *NEWLW* WA12 ....**68** D5
Lupin Dr *RNFD/HAY* WA11 ....**68** C5
Lurdin La *WGN* WN1 ....**11** E3
Luton Gv *ATH* M46 ....**38** C5
Lychgate *WGNE/HIN* WN2 * **49** G1
Lydford Gn *WGNNW/ST* WN6 ....**10** C2
Lyefield Av *WGN* WN1 ....**3** J3
Lymefield Dr *WALK* M28 ....**55** F3
Lyme St *RNFD/HAY* WA11 ....**68** C1
WALK M28 ....**41** F5
Lymn St *WGNE/HIN* WN2 ....**36** B1
Lynbridge Cl
WGNE/HIN WN2 ....**35** F1
Lyndale *SKEL* WN8 ....**31** H3
Lyndhurst *SKEL* WN8 ....**17** H1
Lyndon Av *WGNNW/ST* WN6 ....**9** C3
Lynmouth Cl *WGNNW/ST* WN6 ....**21** F1
Lynstock Wy *HOR/BR* BL6 ....**14** D4
Lynton Av *WGNNW/ST* WN6 ....**8** B3
Lynton Rd *TYLD* M29 ....**54** C3
Lynton St *LEIGH* WN7 ....**51** H3
Lynwood Av *GOL/RIS/CU* WA3 ....**71** E3
Lynwood Cl *SKEL* WN8 ....**30** A5
Lynwood Gv *ATH* M46 ....**38** C5
Lyon Rd *WGNNW/ST* WN6 ....**21** H3
Lyon St *WN4* **47** C4
WGNS/IIMK WN3 ....**33** H3
Lytham Rd *AIMK* WN4 ....**60** C1

M

Mabel St *WGNW/BIL/O* WN5 ....**33** F2
WHTN BL5 ....**38** A2
Maberry Cl *WGNNW/ST* WN6 ....**45** H2
Macauley Pl *WGNS/IIMK* WN3 ....**33** G4
Macclesfield Cl

WGNE/HIN WN2 ....**35** H3
WGNE/HIN WN2 ....**41** F1
Macdonald Av *FWTH* BL4 ....**41** F1
Macdonald St
WGNW/BIL/O WN5 ....**32** C2
Mackenzie Av
WGNW/BIL/O WN5 ....**33** H5
Madams Wood Rd *WALK* M28 ....**41** E5
Madeley Dr *WGNS/IIMK* WN3 ....**46** D1
Maden St *TYLD* M29 ....**53** C5
Maesbrook Dr *TYLD* M29 ....**53** H5
Mafeking Pl *AIMK* WN4 ....**61** F3
Magdalen Dr *AIMK* WN4 ....**60** C2
Maggots Nook Rd
RNFD/HAY WA11 ....**43** F2
Maiden Cl *SKEL* WN8 ....**16** B3
Maidstone Cl *WGNE/HIN* WN2 ....**51** F1
Main La *GOL/RIS/CU* WA3 ....**77** F1
Mains Av *WGNE/HIN* WN2 ....**49** E4
Main St *WGNW/BIL/O* WN5 ....**58** D1
Makants Cl *ATH* M46 ....**39** G2
TYLD M29 ....**54** D3
Makerfield Dr *NEWLW* WA12 ....**68** D5
Makerfield Wy
WGNE/HIN WN2 ....**35** G1
Makinson Ar *WGN* WN1 * **2** C4
Makinson Av *WGNE/HIN* WN2 ....**36** A1
Maldon Cl *WGNE/HIN* WN2 ....**3** J1
Maldon Rd *WGNW/BIL/O* WN5 ....**10** C2
Malham Av *WGNS/IIMK* WN3 ....**47** H1
Malham Cl *LEIGH* WN7 ....**64** B1
Malika Pl *AIMK* WN4 * **60** C1
Mallory Dr *LEIGH* WN7 ....**65** C1
Mallowdale *WALK* M28 ....**55** G3
Malpas Av *WGN* WN1 ....**3** F2
Malton Av *BOLS/LL* BL3 ....**27** H1
GOL/RIS/CU WA3 ....**71** F2
Malton Cl *LEIGH* WN7 ....**51** F5
Malton Rd *WALK* M28 ....**55** H5
Malverley Dr *LEIGH* WN7 ....**65** H1
Malvern Av *ATH* M46 ....**39** G3
WGNE/HIN WN2 ....**36** D4
Malvern Cl *AIMK* WN4 ....**61** E2
WGNS/IIMK WN3 ....**32** D5
Malvern Crs *WGNS/IIMK* WN3 ....**54** A5
Malvern St *WGNNW/ST* WN6 ....**4** D4
Malvern Ter *LEIGH* WN7 ....**65** E3
Manchester Rd *HOR/BR* BL6 ....**13** F2
LEIGH WN7 ....**65** H2
TYLD M29 ....**54** B3
WGNE/HIN WN2 ....**35** F1
WHTN BL5 ....**26** A3
Manchester Rd East
WALK M28 ....**41** G5
Manchester Rd West
TYLD M58 ....**40** D3
Mandeville Cl
WGNE/HIN WN2 ....**47** E1
Manfield *SKEL* WN8 ....**17** F2
Manley Av *GOL/RIS/CU* WA3 ....**62** A4
Manley Cl *LEIGH* WN7 ....**51** G3
Manley Crs *WHTN* BL5 ....**26** C4
Manley St *WGNS/IIMK* WN3 ....**34** D2
Manning Av *WGNNW/ST* WN6 ....**21** H3
NEWLW WA12 ....**68** D5
Manor Av *GOL/RIS/CU* WA3 ....**70** D1
Manor Cl *AIMK* WN4 ....**59** H3
Manor Ct *GOL/RIS/CU* WA3 ....**70** D1
Manor Gv *LEIGH* WN7 ....**64** D2
SKEL WN8 ....**17** E4
WGNE/HIN WN2 ....**12** C5
WGNS/IIMK WN3 ....**20** C5
Manor House Cl
RNFD/HAY WA11 ....**57** H4
Manor House Dr *SKEL* WN8 ....**30** B5
Manorial Dr *LHULT* M38 ....**40** D3
Manor Pl *WGNW/BIL/O* WN5 ....**35** E2
Manor Rd *RNFD/HAY* WA11 ....**68** D2
TYLD M29 ....**54** B5
Manor St *FWTH* BL4 ....**41** H1
GOL/RIS/CU WA3 ....**62** C5
WGN WN1 ....**33** G2
WGNE/HIN WN2 ....**36** A5
Mansart Cl *AIMK* WN4 ....**61** E1
Mansel Av *WGNNW/ST* WN6 ....**4** A1
Manse Gdns *NEWLW* WA12 ....**69** G5
Mansell Wy *HOR/BR* BL6 ....**14** C2
Mansfield St *GOL/RIS/CU* WA3 ....**61** H5
Maple Av *ATH* M46 ....**38** C4
TYLD M29 ....**71** G2
WALK M28 ....**41** H4
WGNE/HIN WN2 ....**36** D4
Maple Cl *WGNW/BIL/O* WN5 ....**58** C1
Maple Crs *LEIGH* WN7 ....**51** H4
Maple Dr *WGNE/HIN* WN2 ....**49** C4
Maplefield Dr *WALK* M28 ....**55** H5
Maple Gv *WGNNW/ST* WN6 ....**21** H2
Maple St *AIMK* WN4 ....**47** H5
Maplewood *SKEL* WN8 ....**17** F1
Marbury Gv *WGNE/HIN* WN2 ....**10** B2
Marchbank *WGNE/HIN* WN2 ....**23** F5
Marchbank Rd *SKEL* WN8 ....**16** D4
Mardale Ct *ATH* M46 ....**38** D5
Margaret Av *WGNE/HIN* WN2 ....**20** D1
Margaret St *WGNE/HIN* WN2 ....**36** A2
Margery St *LEIGH* WN7 ....**21** H4
Margrove Cha *HOR/BR* BL6 ....**14** B2
Marian Rd *RNFD/HAY* WA11 ....**68** B2
Marigold St *WGNE/HIN* WN2 ....**35** E1
Marina Dr *WGNW/BIL/O* WN5 ....**33** G3
Marion Pl *WGNE/HIN* WN2 ....**36** B1
Maritime Cl *NEWLW* WA12 ....**69** F4
Market Ap *AIMK* WN4 ....**61** E3
Market Pl *CHLY/EC* PR7 * **7** E1
LEIGH WN7 ....**65** E1
WGN WN1 ....**2** D5
WGNNW/ST WN6 ....**10** B1
WHTN BL5 ....**26** A4
CHLY/EC PR7 * **7** F1
NEWLW WA12 ....**82** D5

TYLD M29 ....**53** G2
WGN WN1 ....**2** C4
WGNNW/ST WN6 ....**36** A1
WHTN BL5 ....**25** H5
Marklands Rd *WGNE/HIN* WN2 ....**66** D2
Markland St *WGN* WN1 ....**2** D5
Mark St *WALK* M28 ....**41** H4
Marland *SKEL* WN8 ....**17** F1
Marlborough Av
WGNS/IIMK WN3 ....**35** E4
Marlborough Rd *HOR/BR* BL6 ....**15** F2
Marlbrook Dr *WHTN* BL5 ....**37** H5
Marlbrook Ms *WHTN* BL5 * **38** A5
Marl Gv *WGNW/BIL/O* WN5 ....**33** C4
Marlow Ct *CHLY/EC* PR7 ....**7** E1
Marlowe Cl *WGNS/IIMK* WN3 ....**33** H5
Marnland Gv *BOLS/LL* BL3 ....**27** F1
Marple Gv *WGNNW/ST* WN6 ....**4** B5
Marrick Cl *WGNS/IIMK* WN3 ....**47** H1
Marsden St *WALK* M28 ....**55** E5
WGN WN1 ....**3** G4
WGNS/IIMK WN3 ....**34** D4
WGNW/BIL/O WN5 ....**33** E5
WHTN BL5 ....**25** H5
Marshall St *LEIGH* WN7 ....**64** C2
Marsham Rd *WHTN* BL5 ....**38** A2
Marshbank *WHTN* BL5 ....**26** B4
Marshbrook Cl
WGNE/HIN WN2 ....**36** D2
Marsh Brook Fold *WHTN* BL5 ....**36** D1
Marsh Gn *WGNW/BIL/O* WN5 ....**20** C2
Marsh La *WN1* **2** C3
Marsh Rd *LHULT* M38 ....**41** G4
Marsh Rw *WGNE/HIN* WN2 ....**36** B5
Marsh St *WHTN* BL5 ....**25** H4
Marston Cl *WGNE/HIN* WN2 ....**69** E5
Marsland Green La *TYLD* M29 ....**66** B2
Marston Cl *HOR/BR* BL6 ....**15** F2
NEWLW WA12 ....**69** E4
Martindale Crs
WGNE/HIN WN2 ....**33** F2
Martindale Rd
RNFD/HAY WA11 ....**58** A4
Martinsclough *HOR/BR* BL6 ....**14** D4
Martins Ct *WGNE/HIN* WN2 ....**36** D2
Martins La *WGNE/HIN* WN2 ....**30** A1
Martin St *ATH* M46 ....**59** E5
Martland Av *GOL/RIS/CU* WA3 ....**71** E2
WGNNW/ST WN6 ....**9** E5
Martland Crs *GOL/RIS/CU* WA3 ....**71** E2
Martland Mill La
WGNW/BIL/O WN5 ....**20** C2
Martlew Dr *ATH* M46 ....**59** G4
Marton Gv *WGNW/BIL/O* WN5 ....**32** C4
Marton Dr *ATH* M46 ....**39** F4
Marton St *WGN* WN1 * **2** C3
Marus Av *WGNS/IIMK* WN3 ....**33** G5
Marwick Cl *WGNNW/ST* WN6 ....**5** E5
Maryfield Cl *WGNS/IIMK* WN3 ....**70** B2
Mary Hulton Ct *WHTN* BL5 ....**26** B5
Marylebone Pl *AIMK* WN4 ....**61** F4
Mary St *TYLD* M29 ....**53** H2
Masefield Av *LEIGH* WN7 ....**65** G2
WGNS/IIMK WN3 ....**33** G4
Masefield Dr *FWTH* BL4 ....**41** H2
Mason Cl *AIMK* WN4 ....**61** C2
Mason St *WGNE/HIN* WN2 ....**49** G3
WGNS/IIMK WN3 ....**2** A6
Massam Ct *RNFD/HAY* WA11 ....**43** F5
Mather Av *GOL/RIS/CU* WA3 ....**71** F3
Mather Fold Rd *WALK* M28 ....**55** G2
Mather La *LEIGH* WN7 ....**65** G3
Mather St *ATH* M46 ....**39** E3
Matheson Dr
WGNW/BIL/O WN5 ....**21** E5
Matlock Cl *ATH* M46 ....**53** E1
Maunby Gdns *LHULT* M38 ....**41** H5
May Av *LEIGH* WN7 ....**51** G5
Mayfair Dr *ATH* M46 ....**39** G4
WGNS/IIMK WN3 ....**24** A3
Mayfield Av *FWTH* BL4 ....**41** H1
Mayfield Gv *GOL/RIS/CU* WA3 ....**72** B1
Mayfield Rd *SKEL* WN8 ....**30** D1
Mayfield St *AIMK* WN4 * **60** D3
WGNE/HIN WN2 ....**36** A1
May St *GOL/RIS/CU* WA3 ....**62** C4
LEIGH WN7 ....**66** B1
Maythorn Av *GOL/RIS/CU* WA3 ....**77** H5
May Tree Dr *WN1* **22** A3
Maytree Wk *SKEL* WN8 ....**17** C1
McCormack Dr *WGN* WN1 ....**2** D1
Meadowbank Av *ATH* M46 ....**39** G4
Meadowbank Gdns
GOL/RIS/CU WA3 ....**73** H2
Meadowbrook Cl *HOR/BR* BL6 ....**26** D2
Meadow Cl *LEIGH* WN7 ....**64** D4
SKEL WN8 ....**16** C3
Meadow Clough *SKEL* WN8 ....**17** C1
Meadowcroft *WGNE/HIN* WN2 ....**47** G5
SKEL WN8 ....**17** C1
WHTN BL5 ....**38** A1
Meadowfield *HOR/BR* BL6 ....**15** G3
SKEL WN8 ....**30** D1
Meadowfield Dr *WALK* M28 ....**55** F3
Meadow Pit La
WGNE/HIN WN2 ....**12** C2
Meadows Cl *WGNE/HIN* WN2 ....**36** D3
Meadows Gn *GOL/RIS/CU* WA3 ....**71** F4
Meadowside Av *AIMK* WN4 ....**61** E4
Meadowside Rd
WGNW/BIL/O WN5 ....**36** D4
Meadows St *WGNNW/ST* WN6 ....**21** H4
Meadow St *CHLYE* PR6 ....**7** F1
Meadowvale Dr
WGNW/BIL/O WN5 ....**32** D2
Meadow Wk *FWTH* BL4 ....**41** F1

Meadow Wy *HOR/BR* BL6 ....**13** F1
Meads Gv *TYLD* M29 ....**54** B5
Meadway *GOL/RIS/CU* WA3 ....**77** E1
SKEL WN8 ....**17** F1
TYLD M29 ....**54** C2
WGNE/HIN WN2 ....**3** J7
Mealhouse Ct *ATH* M46 ....**38** D5
Mealhouse La *ATH* M46 ....**38** D5
Meanley Rd *TYLD* M29 ....**53** G4
Meanley St *TYLD* M29 ....**53** G2
Medlar Wy *AIMK* WN4 ....**60** C1
Medlock Rd *WGNE/HIN* WN2 ....**49** F1
Medway Cl *AIMK* WN4 * **47** G5
LEIGH WN7 ....**72** B1
Medway Dr *WGNW/BIL/O* WN5 ....**33** E2
Medway Rd *WGNW/BIL/O* WN5 ....**55** G3
Megfield *WHTN* BL5 ....**37** H2
Melbreck *SKEL* WN8 ....**17** F1
Melbury Dr *HOR/BR* BL6 ....**15** E2
Melford Dr *AIMK* WN4 ....**60** D2
WGNW/BIL/O WN5 ....**32** C2
Melling Cl *LEIGH* WN7 ....**65** E5
Mellings Av *WGNW/BIL/O* WN5 * **45** H2
Melling Rd *WGNW/BIL/O* WN5 ....**33** F3
Melling Wy *WGNS/IIMK* WN3 ....**47** G2
Mellor Brook Dr
WGNE/HIN WN2 * **49** F1
Mellor Gv *WGNW/BIL/O* WN5 ....**5** F5
Mellor Dr *WALK* M28 ....**55** H2
Melmerby Cl *AIMK* WN4 ....**60** C3
Melrose Av *LEIGH* WN7 ....**51** G2
Melrose Crs *AIMK* WN4 ....**59** H3
Melrose Dr *WGNS/IIMK* WN3 ....**34** A5
Melton Cl *TYLD* M29 ....**54** A3
WALK M28 ....**54** A3
Melverley St *WGNS/IIMK* WN3 ....**33** H1
Mendip Av *WGNS/IIMK* WN3 ....**32** D5
Mercer St *NEWLW* WA12 ....**69** G5
Merchants Crs
GOL/RIS/CU WA3 * **63** F5
Mere Av *LEIGH* WN7 ....**64** C1
Mere Cl *SKEL* WN8 ....**17** E3
Merefield Cl *WGNE/HIN* WN2 ....**36** B4
Mere Fold *WALK* M28 ....**41** G5
Mere Gv *RNFD/HAY* WA11 ....**58** A5
Mereland Cl *WGNE/HIN* WN2 ....**47** E1
Mere Rd *AIMK* WN4 ....**70** A5
NEWLW WA12 ....**70** A5
Mere St *LEIGH* WN7 ....**64** C1
WGNW/BIL/O WN5 ....**33** G2
Merewood *SKEL* WN8 ....**17** E1
Merlewood Dr *TYLD* M29 ....**54** A3
Mersey Cl *WGNE/HIN* WN2 ....**37** F5
Mersey Rd *WGNE/HIN* WN2 ....**49** E1
WGNW/BIL/O WN5 ....**32** A1
Mersey St *LEIGH* WN7 ....**64** B2
Merton Gv *TYLD* M29 ....**54** B5
Merton Rd *WGNS/IIMK* WN3 ....**32** C4
Mervyn Pl *WGNS/IIMK* WN3 ....**33** H4
Mesnes Av *WGNS/IIMK* WN3 ....**33** H3
Mesnes Park Ter *WGN* WN1 ....**2** B5
Mesnes Rd *WGN* WN1 ....**22** B5
Mesnes St *WGN* WN1 ....**2** C4
Mesnes Ter *WGN* WN1 * **2** C4
Metal Box Wy *WHTN* BL5 ....**26** A3
Metcalfe Ct *LHULT* M38 * **41** E4
The Mews *WGNS/IIMK* WN3 ....**36** A3
Meynell Dr *LEIGH* WN7 ....**65** E4
Meyrick St *WGNW/BIL/O* WN5 ....**33** G2
Mickleton *ATH* M46 ....**39** F4
Middlebrook Dr *HOR/BR* BL6 ....**15** H4
Middlecot Cl
WGNS/IIMK WN3 ....**31** H3
Middleton *SKEL* WN8 ....**17** F1
Midland Cl *LEIGH* WN7 ....**51** F5
Miles La *WGNNW/ST* WN6 ....**8** D5
Milford Rd *WGNE/HIN* WN2 ....**3** K1
Milford St *WGNS/IIMK* WN3 ....**34** D2
Milk St *TYLD* M29 ....**53** H2
WGNS/IIMK WN3 ....**2** C6
Mill Bank *WGNNW/ST* WN6 ....**8** C3
Millbeck Farm
WGNNW/ST WN6 ....**33** E3
Millbeck La *RNFD/HAY* WA11 ....**58** A5
Millbrook Av *ATH* M46 ....**39** F5
Millbrook Cl *GOL/RIS/CU* WA3 ....**73** H4
SKEL WN8 ....**16** D3
Millcroft Av *WGNW/BIL/O* WN5 ....**33** E2
Milldale Cl *ATH* M46 ....**39** G5
HOR/BR BL6 ....**15** G3
Milldale Rd *LEIGH* WN7 ....**64** A5
Miller's La *LEIGH* WN7 ....**53** E2
Millfield Dr *WALK* M28 ....**41** G5
Millfield La *RNFD/HAY* WA11 ....**60** B5
Millgate *WGN* WN1 ....**2** D4
Millgreen Cl *SKEL* WN8 ....**30** D1
Mill Hill *LHULT* M38 ....**40** D2
Mill House Vw *SKEL* WN8 ....**31** F1
Millingford Av
GOL/RIS/CU WA3 ....**62** A4
Millingford Gv *AIMK* WN4 ....**61** E3
Mill La *LEIGH* WN7 ....**65** G2
RNFD/HAY WA11 ....**56** D2
SKEL WN8 ....**17** E5
SKEL WN8 ....**30** C2
WGNNW/ST WN6 ....**8** B3
WHTN BL5 ....**37** H4
Mill Meadow *WGN* WN1 ....**2** E6
Mill Rd *WGNW/BIL/O* WN5 ....**31** G3
ATH M46 ....**53** F2
GOL/RIS/CU WA3 ....**70** B1
LEIGH WN7 ....**51** H4
WALK M28 ....**55** F4
WGNE/HIN WN2 ....**36** A3
WHTN BL5 ....**2** B6
Millstone Cl *WGNE/HIN* WN2 ....**23** B2
Milne Av *AIMK* WN4 ....**60** D1
Milnes Av *LEIGH* WN7 ....**65** E4
Milton Crs *FWTH* BL4 ....**41** G2
Milton Gv *WGN* WN1 ....**22** B2
WGNW/BIL/O WN5 ....**32** B2

WGNW/BIL/O WN5 .....45 G2
Milton Rd GOL/RIS/CU WA3 .....71 E2
Milton St LEIGH WN7 .....64 D1
Minehead Av LEIGH WN7 .....51 G1
Mine Wy RNFD/HAY WA11 * 68 C2
Minster Gv TYLD M29 .....54 A4
Minstrel Cl WGNE/HIN WN2 .....49 G4
Mirfield Cl GOL/RIS/CU WA3 .....71 E2
Miriam Gv LEIGH WN7 .....51 G1
Miry La WHTN BL5 .....2 B4
Mitchell Rd WGNW/BIL/O WN5 .....58 D1
Mitchell St AIMK WN4 .....61 F4
GOL/RIS/CU WA3 .....70 B2
LEIGH WN7 .....64 A1
WGNE/HIN WN2 .....3 F5
WGNW/BIL/O WN5 .....33 F2
Mitton Cl GOL/RIS/CU WA3 .....72 C4
Moat House St
WGNE/HIN WN2 .....35 F1
Molyneux Rd WHTN BL5 .....26 C4
Molyneux St WGN WN1 .....3 F4
Mona St WGN WN1 .....2 B4
Monica Ter AIMK WN4 .....61 E4
Monmouth Crs AIMK WN4 .....61 F4
Monsford Rd WGNE/HIN WN2 .....23 F3
Montfort Cl WHTN BL5 .....37 G2
Montrey Crs AIMK WN4 .....61 F4
Montrose Av
WGNW/BIL/O WN5 .....32 D1
Monument Man WGN WN1 * 2 D1
Monument Rd WGN WN1 .....2 D1
Monyash Vw WGNE/HIN WN2 .....36 C5
Moody St WGNNW/ST WN6 .....10 B1
Moor Av WGNNW/ST WN6 .....8 D2
Moor Dr SKEL WN8 .....30 A1
Moore Dr RNFD/HAY WA11 .....68 C3
Moore La WGNNW/ST WN6 .....5 E5
Moore St WGN WN1 .....3 H5
Moore St East WGN WN1 .....3 G2
Moorfield WALK M28 .....55 E4
Moorfield Crs GOL/RIS/CU WA3 .....71 H2
Moorfield St WGNE/HIN WN2 .....35 G5
Moorgate Dr TYLD M29 .....54 B5
Moorhey Rd LHULT M38 .....41 F2
Moorings Cl WGN WN1 .....3 J5
Moorland Dr LHULT M38 .....41 F2
Moorland Rd AIMK WN4 .....61 H1
WGNE/HIN WN2 .....35 H5
Moorlands Av LEIGH WN7 .....65 G3
Moorlands Vw BOLS/LL BL3 .....27 H5
Moor La LEIGH WN7 .....51 H5
Moor Rd WGNW/BIL/O WN5 .....31 H2
Moorside Av FWTH BL4 .....41 G1
Moorside Wk
WGNW/BIL/O WN5 .....20 C5
Morden Av AIMK WN4 .....61 E3
Moresby Cl LEIGH WN7 .....64 C1
Moreton Cl GOL/RIS/CU WA3 .....62 A5
Moreton Dr LEIGH WN7 .....71 E1
Morley's La TYLD M29 .....66 D3
Morley St ATH M46 .....38 D5
Mornington Rd ATH M46 .....39 G2
WGNE/HIN WN2 .....36 D3
Morris Fold Dr HOR/BR BL6 .....13 H4
Morris Rd WGN WN1 .....30 D1
Morris St TYLD M29 .....53 G2
WGN WN1 .....2 E4
WGNE/HIN WN2 .....36 A3
WGNS/IIMK WN3 .....34 D4
Mortlake Cl LHULT M38 .....41 E5
Mort La TYLD M29 .....53 G5
Morton Av WGNS/IIMK WN3 .....34 A3
Morton Ct WGNS/IIMK WN3 .....34 A3
Mort St TYLD M29 .....53 G2
WGNE/HIN WN2 .....36 D3
WGNNW/ST WN6 .....21 H4
Morville Dr WGNS/IIMK WN3 .....34 A4
Mosedale Av RNFD/HAY WA11 .....58 A5
Mosedale Cl TYLD M29 .....54 B5
Mosley Common Rd TYLD M29 .....54 D5
Moss Av LEIGH WN7 .....65 G1
WGNS/IIMK WN3 .....31 G5
Moss Bank Rd
RNFD/HAY WA11 .....57 H5
Mossborough Rd
WGNW/BIL/O WN5 * 56 A1
Mossbrook Dr LHULT M38 .....40 D2
Moss Brow RNFD/HAY WA11 .....42 D4
Mossdale Rd AIMK WN4 .....47 H5
Moss Fold TYLD M29 .....54 B4
Moss Gv WGNNW/ST WN6 .....10 B2
Mosslands Gv BOLS/LL BL3 .....27 G5
Moss La GOL/RIS/CU WA3 .....74 A4
GOL/RIS/CU WA3 .....74 A4
RNFD/HAY WA11 .....57 H1
SKEL WN8 .....29 E2
TYLD M29 .....66 D5
WGNE/HIN WN2 .....35 F5
Moss Lane Vw SKEL WN8 .....29 G1
Moss Meadow WHTN BL5 .....25 H5
Moss Nook La
RNFD/HAY WA11 .....42 D5
Moss Rd WGNW/BIL/O WN5 .....31 G5
Moss St WGNNW/ST WN6 .....21 H4
WGNS/IIMK WN3 .....35 G5
WGNW/BIL/O WN5 * 32 C3
Moss Ter AIMK WN4 .....61 G3
Mossy Lea Fold
WGNNW/ST WN6 .....4 A4
Mottram Dr WGNS/IIMK WN3 .....34 A3
Mountain Dr WALK M28 .....55 G4
Mountain St WALK M28 .....41 H4
Mount Crs WGNW/BIL/O WN5 .....32 A2
Mountmorres Cl WHTN BL5 .....39 G1
Mount Pleasant St
HOR/BR BL6 .....14 C1
Mount Skip La LHULT M38 .....41 E4
Mount St HOR/BR BL6 .....14 C1
The Mount SKEL WN8 * 17 G5
Mount Vw WGNS/IIMK WN3 .....34 C3
Mountwood SKEL WN8 .....17 F1
Moxon Wy AIMK WN4 .....61 G2
Muirfield Cl BOLS/LL BL3 .....27 G2

Muirfield Dr TYLD M29 .....54 B4
Mulberry Av GOL/RIS/CU WA3 .....71 G2
Mulberry Cl WGNE/HIN WN2 .....33 E2
Mullein Cl GOL/RIS/CU WA3 .....71 E1
Mullins Av NEWLW WA12 .....69 F4
Muncaster Dr RNFD/HAY WA11 .....43 F4
Munro Av WGNS/IIMK WN3 .....33 H3
Murphy Cl WGNS/IIMK WN3 .....33 H3
Murray St ATH M46 .....52 C1
Mycroft Cl LEIGH WN7 .....51 H5
Myrtle Av AIMK WN4 .....61 G5
LEIGH WN7 .....51 H4
Myrtle Gv WGNW/BIL/O WN5 * 58 C2
Myrtle St WGN WN1 .....2 B4

N

Naburn Dr WGNNW/BIL/O WN5 .....31 H3
Nairn Cl WGNNW/ST WN6 .....10 A1
Nangreaves St LEIGH WN7 .....64 B1
Narborough Cl
WGNE/HIN WN2 .....36 B4
Nathan Dr RNFD/HAY WA11 .....68 A4
Naunton Av LEIGH WN7 .....64 B1
Navenby Rd WGNS/IIMK WN3 .....47 H1
Navigation Cl LEIGH WN7 .....64 D2
Naylor St GOL/RIS/CU WA3 .....70 C1
Naylorfarm Av
WGNNW/ST WN6 .....9 E5
Naylor St ATH M46 .....38 D5
Neild Gdns LEIGH WN7 .....64 D2
Nel Pan La LEIGH WN7 .....51 F5
Nelson Av WGNE/HIN WN2 .....23 F5
Nelson St ATH M46 .....38 C5
TYLD M29 .....54 A3
WGNE/HIN WN2 .....36 A2
Nene Gv WGNE/HIN WN2 .....36 B4
Netherby Rd WGNNW/ST WN6 .....21 H2
Netherfields LEIGH WN7 .....51 G4
Neverstitch Cl WGNE/HIN WN2 .....17 E3
Neverstitch Rd SKEL WN8 .....16 C3
Neville St WGNE/HIN WN2 .....35 F5
Newark Rd WGNE/HIN WN2 .....35 H4
Newark St WGNNW/ST WN6 .....21 G4
New Bank St TYLD M29 * 53 H5
New Barn Av AIMK WN4 .....61 F3
New Barn La LEIGH WN7 .....64 D4
Newbeck Cl HOR/BR BL6 .....14 C1
Newbridge Cl AIMK WN4 .....60 A5
Newbrook Rd ATH M46 .....39 G2
Newbury Cl WGNS/IIMK WN3 .....33 G5
Newby Sq WGNNW/BIL/O WN5 * 32 C3
New City Rd WALK M28 .....55 F5
Newcombe Dr LHULT M38 .....41 E2
New Drake Gn WHTN BL5 .....37 H3
Newearth Rd WALK M28 .....55 H2
New Ellesmere Ap WALK M28 .....41 H4
Newenden Rd WGN WN1 .....22 A1
New Fold WGNS/IIMK WN3 .....31 H4
Newgate Dr LHULT M38 .....41 G2
Newgate Rd SKEL WN8 .....30 C1
New Hall Ms HOR/BR BL6 .....15 H1
Newhart St WALK M28 .....55 H1
Newhaven Av LEIGH WN7 .....52 A3
Newholme Gdns LHULT M38 .....41 H5
Newhouse Dr WGNS/IIMK WN3 .....47 E2
Newland Av
WGNW/BIL/O WN5 .....33 G3
Newland Ms GOL/RIS/CU WA3 .....72 D4
Newland Rd TYLD M29 .....53 H5
Newlands Dr GOL/RIS/CU WA3 .....70 C1
HOR/BR BL6 .....13 F3
Newlands Rd LEIGH WN7 .....64 D3
New La LEIGH WN7 .....77 H5
New Lester Cl TYLD M29 .....54 A2
New Lester Wy LHULT M38 .....40 D4
New Ldg WGN WN1 .....22 B3
Newlyn Dr AIMK WN4 .....61 E4
SKEL WN8 .....30 A1
Newman Av WGNNW/ST WN6 .....21 H3
New La RNFD/HAY WA11 .....43 E1
Newstead Dr BOLS/LL BL3 .....27 H5
Newstead Rd WGNS/IIMK WN3 .....33 H5
New St WGNE/HIN WN2 .....49 F2
WGNW/BIL/O WN5 .....32 C3
New Tempest Rd HOR/BR BL6 .....26 D1
Newton Cl WGN WN1 * 2 E1
Newton La NEWLW WA12 .....76 A2
Newton Park Dr NEWLW WA12 .....76 A2
Newton Rd GOL/RIS/CU WA3 .....71 F3
WARRN/WOL WA2 .....76 A4
Newton St LEIGH WN7 .....65 E1
New York BOLS/LL BL3 .....27 H5
Nicol Mere Dr AIMK WN4 .....47 H5
Nicol Rd AIMK WN4 .....60 D1
Nightingale Rd HOR/BR BL6 .....7 H4
Nipe La SKEL WN8 .....30 A1
Nixons La SKEL WN8 .....30 A1
Noble St LEIGH WN7 * 65 F1
Nook La GOL/RIS/CU WA3 .....70 C1
TYLD M29 .....67 G4
The Nook WGNNW/ST WN6 .....8 D3
Norbreck Cl WGNE/HIN WN2 .....21 H3
Norbury Av WGNE/HIN WN2 .....35 H3
Norbury St LEIGH WN7 .....64 C1
Norfolk Cl WGNE/HIN WN2 .....36 D2
Norfolk Rd ATH M46 .....39 G5
WGNE/HIN WN2 .....45 H2
Norfolk St WGNNW/BIL/O WN5 .....21 H3
WGNW/BIL/O WN5 .....33 G2

Norley Hall Av
WGNW/BIL/O WN5 .....32 D2
Norley Rd LEIGH WN7 .....64 A2
WGNW/BIL/O WN5 .....32 D2
Norman Av RNFD/HAY WA11 .....68 D2
Normanby Rd WALK M28 .....55 H2
Normanby St
WGNW/BIL/O WN5 .....32 C2
Normanton Cl
WGNE/HIN WN2 .....21 F1
Norris St FWTH BL4 .....41 H1
Northcroft WGNE/HIN WN2 .....5 K3
North Edge LEIGH WN7 .....52 C5
Northfield LEIGH WN7 .....17 G1
North Florida Rd
RNFD/HAY WA11 .....68 A1
North Gv WALK M28 .....41 H5
North La TYLD M29 .....67 F3
Northolt Av LEIGH WN7 .....52 A3
North Rd ATH M46 .....38 C3
North St AIMK WN4 .....61 G1
ATH M46 .....39 F5
LEIGH WN7 .....65 G2
NEWLW WA12 .....69 G4
RNFD/HAY WA11 .....68 B3
Northumberland St WGN WN1 .....3 G3
Northway SKEL WN8 .....17 G4
WGN WN1 .....2 C5
Northways WGNNW/ST WN6 .....8 D4
Northwell St LEIGH WN7 .....51 H5
Northwich Cl WGNS/IIMK WN3 .....32 D5
Northwood Av NEWLW WA12 .....70 A5
Norton Cl WALK M28 .....54 D4
Norweb Wy LEIGH WN7 .....65 G3
Norwich Av AIMK WN4 .....61 G4
GOL/RIS/CU WA3 .....71 G2
Norwick Cl BOLS/LL BL3 .....27 F1
Norwood Av AIMK WN4 .....47 G5
GOL/RIS/CU WA3 .....71 F2
WGNNW/ST WN6 .....53 H5
Norwood Gv RNFD/HAY WA11 .....21 H2
Nostell Rd AIMK WN4 .....60 D1
Nottingham Pl WGN WN1 .....3 H2
Nuttall St ATH M46 .....39 F5
Nutt St WGN WN1 .....3 G2

O

Oak Av GOL/RIS/CU WA3 .....70 C1
RNFD/HAY WA11 .....68 B2
WGNE/HIN WN2 .....36 D5
WGNE/HIN WN2 .....49 H4
WGNW/BIL/O WN5 .....10 C2
Oakbank WGNE/HIN WN2 .....35 G5
Oakbarton HOR/BR BL6 .....26 C1
Oak Crs SKEL WN8 .....16 C4
Oakdale Dr TYLD M29 .....54 B5
Oakenden Cl AIMK WN4 .....47 H5
Oakengates WGNNW/ST WN6 .....10 C1
Oakfield Av ATH M46 .....38 D4
WGNW/BIL/O WN5 .....62 A5
Oakfield Crs WGNE/HIN WN2 .....37 H5
Oakfield Dr LHULT M38 .....40 D3
Oakfield Gv FWTH BL4 .....41 H2
Oakhead La WGNE/HIN WN2 .....65 H3
Oak Hill Cl WGN WN1 .....3 H1
Oaklands Rd GOL/RIS/CU WA3 .....71 G2
Oaklea WGNNW/ST WN6 .....4 B5
Oakleigh SKEL WN8 .....44 A1
Oakley Av WGNS/IIMK WN3 .....45 G5
Oakley Dr WGNW/BIL/O WN5 .....33 F2
The Oaklings WGNE/HIN WN2 .....36 D5
Oak St ATH M46 .....52 B2
GOL/RIS/CU WA3 .....71 H5
LEIGH WN7 .....65 E3
TYLD M29 .....53 H2
WGN WN1 .....3 G5
Oak Tree Cl AIMK WN4 .....52 B2
Oak Tree Ct SKEL WN8 .....18 A2
Oakwood SKEL WN8 .....18 A2
Oakwood Av AIMK WN4 .....60 D4
Oakwood Cl WGNE/HIN WN2 .....21 H4
Oakwood Dr LEIGH WN7 .....64 D5
Oban Dr AIMK WN4 .....60 A4
Oban Wy WGNE/HIN WN2 * 13 E5
Okell Gv LEIGH WN7 .....9 H1
Old Beechfield Gdns
WGNNW/ST WN6 .....9 H1
Old Boston RNFD/HAY WA11 .....68 D4
Oldbridge Dr WGNE/HIN WN2 .....36 A2
Old Colliery Yd AIMK WN4 .....60 C3
Old Engine La SKEL WN8 .....18 B3
Oldfield Cl WHTN BL5 .....26 A5
Old Fold WGNW/BIL/O WN5 .....32 C2
Old Fold Rd WGNE/HIN WN2 .....13 E5
Old Greenwood La
HOR/BR BL6 .....14 C1
Old Hall Clough HOR/BR BL6 .....15 H1
Old Hall Dr AIMK WN4 .....60 D4
Old Hall Gdns RNFD/HAY WA11 .....43 F5
Old Hall La HOR/BR BL6 .....15 H1
WHTN BL5 .....37 H3
Old Hall Mill La LEIGH WN7 .....52 B3
Old Hall St WGNS/IIMK WN3 .....34 C2
Old La LHULT M38 .....41 F2
RNFD/HAY WA11 .....9 G4
WGNNW/ST WN6 .....9 G4
WGN WN1 .....2 C5
Old Manor Pk ATH M46 .....52 B1
Old Moss La GOL/RIS/CU WA3 .....4 C5
Old Pepper La WGNNW/ST WN6 .....4 C5
Old Rd AIMK WN4 .....60 D1
Old School House La
WARRN/WOL WA2 .....76 B5
Old School La CHLY/EC PR7 .....6 D2
Old School Pl AIMK WN4 .....60 D3
Oldstead Gv BOLS/LL BL3 .....27 G1
Old Town Cl SKEL WN8 .....16 C5
Old Town Wy SKEL WN8 .....16 C5

Old Vicarage WHTN BL5 .....37 H3
Old Wells Cl LHULT M38 .....41 F2
Olive Gv SKEL WN8 .....16 D4
WGNE/HIN WN2 .....21 G2
Oliver St ATH M46 .....39 E5
Ollerton Cl WGNE/HIN WN2 .....23 F3
Opal Gv LEIGH WN7 .....64 D2
Orchard Av WALK M28 .....55 H2
Orchard Cl LEIGH WN7 .....52 A4
WGNE/HIN WN2 .....9 F5
Orchard La LEIGH WN7 .....52 A4
The Orchards
WGNW/BIL/O WN5 .....31 H5
Orchard St AIMK WN4 .....61 F3
WGN WN1 .....2 E4
The Orchard WHTN BL5 .....25 H4
Orchid Cl AIMK WN4 .....31 E2
Ordsall Av LHULT M38 .....40 D4
Orford Cl LEIGH WN7 .....65 G4
Organ St LEIGH WN7 .....64 D1
WGNE/HIN WN2 .....37 E5
Oriel Rd AIMK WN4 .....60 C2
Oriole Cl WALK M28 .....55 G3
Oriole Dr WALK M28 .....55 G3
Ormsby Cl WGNNW/ST WN6 .....10 B1
Ormside Cl WGNE/HIN WN2 .....35 H4
Ormskirk Rd RNFD/HAY WA11 .....42 C1
SKEL WN8 .....16 E4
SKEL WN8 .....17 G5
WGNW/BIL/O WN5 .....33 E3
Ormston Gv LEIGH WN7 .....64 D2
Orpington St
WGNW/BIL/O WN5 .....32 D2
Orrell Ar WGN WN1 .....2 C4
Ordsall Av LHULT M38 * 2 C4
Orrell Hall Cl
WGNW/BIL/O WN5 .....32 C1
Orrell Gdns WGNW/BIL/O WN5 .....32 A2
Orrell Rd WGNW/BIL/O WN5 .....33 H1
Orrell St WGNW/BIL/O WN5 .....33 H1
Orton Wy AIMK WN4 .....60 C5
Osborne St ATH M46 .....39 E5
Osborne Gv LEIGH WN7 .....53 E5
Osborne Rd AIMK WN4 .....60 D2
GOL/RIS/CU WA3 .....71 F2
Oscott Av LHULT M38 .....41 F3
Osprey Av WHTN BL5 .....25 H4
The Ospreys WGNS/IIMK WN3 .....32 D5
Otterwood Sq
WGNE/HIN WN2 .....21 F1
Oulton Cl LEIGH WN7 .....65 F2
The Oval WGNNW/ST WN6 .....21 H4
Overbeck Cl WGNNW/ST WN6 .....21 H1
Overdene Cl HOR/BR BL6 .....15 G4
Overdene Rd WGNS/IIMK WN3 .....33 E5
Overton St LEIGH WN7 .....64 D2
Owenington Gv LHULT M38 .....41 F3
Owen St LEIGH WN7 * 64 C1
Owlwood Cl LHULT M38 .....40 D5
Owlwood Dr LHULT M38 .....40 D5
Oxburgh Rd WGNS/IIMK WN3 .....33 E5
Oxford Ct WGN WN1 .....3 J3
Oxford St ATH M46 .....38 D5
HOR/BR BL6 .....15 E2
SKEL WN8 .....16 D4
WGNW/BIL/O WN5 .....32 A1
Oxford St CHLY/EC PR7 .....7 E1
LEIGH WN7 .....52 A4
Ox Hey Cl HOR/BR BL6 .....14 D2
Ox Hey La HOR/BR BL6 .....14 D3
Oxhouse Rd
WGNW/BIL/O WN5 .....31 H4
Oxlea Gv WHTN BL5 .....37 H3

P

Paddock Cl ATH M46 .....39 F3
Paddock Ri WGNNW/ST WN6 .....21 F2
Paddock Rd SKEL WN8 .....29 H3
The Paddock AIMK WN4 .....47 G5
Padiham Cl LEIGH WN7 .....65 F1
Pagefield St WGNNW/ST WN6 .....21 H4
Pagefield Cl WGNNW/ST WN6 .....21 H4
Palace Ar AIMK WN4 .....61 E3
Palatine Cl WGNS/IIMK WN3 .....33 F4
Palatine Sq LEIGH WN7 .....64 C1
Palewood Cl WGN WN1 .....3 G2
Palin St WGNE/HIN WN2 .....36 A2
Palm Av AIMK WN4 .....60 A1
Palm St WGNE/HIN WN2 .....36 B4
Palmer Gv LEIGH WN7 .....51 H2
Palmerston St WGNE/HIN WN2 .....33 E2
Panton St HOR/BR BL6 .....14 C1
Parbrook La WGNE/HIN WN2 .....9 G3
The Parchments
NEWLW WA12 .....69 G5
Paris Av WGNS/IIMK WN3 .....32 D5
Park Av GOL/RIS/CU WA3 .....62 A4
WGNE/HIN WN2 .....9 G3
Park Bank ATH M46 .....39 G2
Park Crs WGN WN1 .....2 A3
Park Crs West WGN WN1 .....2 A3
Parkdale TYLD M29 .....67 E1
Park Edge WHTN BL5 .....38 B1
Parkend Dr CHLY/EC PR7 .....64 C4
Parkfield WGNE/HIN WN2 .....54 A5
Parkfield Av FWTH BL4 .....41 H1
TYLD M29 .....54 A5
Parkfield Cl LEIGH WN7 .....52 B4
TYLD M29 .....54 A5
Parkfield Dr TYLD M29 .....54 C2
Parkfields WGNE/HIN WN2 .....38 A2
Parkham Cl WHTN BL5 .....38 A2
Park Hey Dr WGNNW/ST WN6 .....8 D3
Parklands RNFD/HAY WA11 .....43 E4
SKEL WN8 .....18 A3
Parklands Dr WGNE/HIN WN2 .....12 D4
Park La LEIGH WN7 .....65 H2
WGNE/HIN WN2 .....49 G4

Park Meadow WHTN BL5 .....26 B5
Park Rd CHLY/EC PR7 .....6 D1
NEWLW WA12 .....70 A2
WALK M28 .....55 H2
WGNE/HIN WN2 .....36 B5
WGNNW/ST WN6 .....10 B2
WGNNW/ST WN6 .....21 H4
WGNW/BIL/O WN5 .....32 B2
WGNW/BIL/O WN5 .....45 H2
WHTN BL5 .....26 A5
Parkside Av AIMK WN4 .....36 B2
Parkside Crs
WGNW/BIL/O WN5 .....32 A2
Parkside Rd NEWLW WA12 .....76 C3
Parks Nook FWTH BL4 .....41 H1
The Parks RNFD/HAY WA11 .....61 E5
Park St ATH M46 .....39 F4
TYLD M29 .....53 H2
WGNS/IIMK WN3 .....34 A2
Park Vw AIMK WN4 .....61 E4
WGNE/HIN WN2 .....49 G2
WGNW/BIL/O WN5 * 32 C3
Parkway LHULT M38 .....40 D5
WHTN BL5 .....37 G3
Parkway Gv LHULT M38 .....40 D4
Parkwood Cl WGNS/IIMK WN3 .....34 D2
Parkwood Dr WHTN BL5 .....55 H1
Parliament St SKEL WN8 .....19 F5
WGNS/IIMK WN3 .....34 C2
Parnell Cl TYLD M29 .....67 E1
Parr Fold Av WALK M28 .....55 H2
Parr St TYLD M29 .....53 G3
Parsonage Brow SKEL WN8 .....30 D1
Parsonage Cl SKEL WN8 .....30 D1
Parsonage Rd WALK M28 .....55 H1
WALK M28 .....55 H1
Parsonage Wy LEIGH WN7 .....51 H5
Parson's Brow
RNFD/HAY WA11 .....42 D3
Parson's Wk WGN WN1 .....2 B3
Partington St
WGNW/BIL/O WN5 .....21 F5
Part St WHTN BL5 .....25 H3
Pasture Cl AIMK WN4 .....61 H1
Pasture Dr GOL/RIS/CU WA3 .....77 H5
Pasture La RNFD/HAY WA11 .....56 B2
Pateley Sq WGNNW/ST WN6 .....22 A3
Patricroft Rd WGNE/HIN WN2 .....35 E2
Patterdale Pl WGNE/HIN WN2 .....35 F1
Patterdale Rd AIMK WN4 .....61 H1
LEIGH WN7 .....65 H2
Patterson St BOLS/LL BL3 .....27 H1
NEWLW WA12 .....69 E5
Pauline St WGNE/HIN WN2 .....37 E1
Paxton Pl SKEL WN8 .....29 H4
Peace St ATH M46 .....39 F5
TYLD M29 .....53 H2
Peach Gv RNFD/HAY WA11 * 68 B2
Peacock Fold LEIGH WN7 .....51 G5
Peak Av ATH M46 .....38 C5
Pearl St WGNNW/ST WN6 .....22 A3
Pear Tree Ct WGNE/HIN WN2 .....12 D4
Pear Tree Gv TYLD M29 .....54 D2
Peebles Cl AIMK WN4 .....59 H2
Peel Dr LHULT M38 .....39 F5
Peel Hall Av TYLD M29 .....41 E4
Peel La LHULT M38 .....41 E5
TYLD M29 .....67 E2
Peel Park Crs LHULT M38 .....41 E4
Peel Rd SKEL WN8 .....30 B3
Peel St LEIGH WN7 .....64 D1
WHTN BL5 .....25 H4
Peelwood Av LHULT M38 .....41 F3
Peelwood Gv ATH M46 .....53 F1
Pemberton Rd
WGNS/IIMK WN3 .....46 C2
Pemberton St LHULT M38 .....41 G4
Pembroke Rd
WGNE/HIN WN2 .....37 F5
WGNS/IIMK WN3 .....21 E4
Penbury Rd WGN WN1 .....11 E5
Pendeen Cl TYLD M29 .....53 H3
Pendennis Crs WGNE/HIN WN2 .....36 D5
Pendlebury Fold BOLS/LL BL3 .....27 E3
Pendlebury La WGN WN1 .....11 F4
Pendle Cl SKEL WN8 .....30 A5
Pendle Ct WGNW/BIL/O WN5 .....32 A2
Pendle Pl SKEL WN8 .....30 A4
Pendle Rd GOL/RIS/CU WA3 .....62 D5
Penketh Av TYLD M29 .....53 H3
Penketh Pl SKEL WN8 .....29 H3
Penketh St WGNNW/ST WN6 .....2 A1
Penleach Av LEIGH WN7 .....65 G1
Pennell Dr WGNS/IIMK WN3 .....46 C1
Pennine Av WGNS/IIMK WN3 .....32 D5
Pennine La GOL/RIS/CU WA3 .....51 F3
Pennine Pl SKEL WN8 .....29 G2
Pennington Av LEIGH WN7 .....64 D4
Pennington Cl LHULT M38 .....40 D4
WGNE/HIN WN2 .....24 B4
Pennington Gdns LEIGH WN7 .....64 D3
Pennington Green La
WGNE/HIN WN2 .....24 A3
Pennington La
WGNE/HIN WN2 .....11 H1
RNFD/HAY WA11 .....42 D1
Pennington Rd LEIGH WN7 .....65 E3
Pennington St
WGNE/HIN WN2 .....36 A2
Pennygate Cl WGNE/HIN WN2 .....36 A2
Pennyhurst St
WGNS/IIMK WN3 .....33 H1
Penny La RNFD/HAY WA11 .....68 D3
Penrhyn Gv ATH M46 .....38 D3
Penrice Fold WALK M28 .....55 G4
Penrith Crs AIMK WN4 .....61 G2
Penrose Pl SKEL WN8 .....30 A5

Penshaw Av WGNS/IIMK WN3 ....34 A5
Penson St WCN WN1 ....3 C1
Pepper La WGNNW/ST WN6 ....4 C4
Pepper Mill La WGN WN1 ....2 E7
Pepperwood Dr
  WGNS/IIMK WN3 ....47 F1
Pepys Pl WGNS/IIMK WN3 ....33 H4
Perch St WGN WN1 ....3 G3
Percival Wy WGNE/HIN WN2 ....55 H4
Peregrine Dr LEIGH WN7 ....65 C1
Perryn Pl WGNNW/ST WN6 ......10 C1
Perth Av WGNE/HIN WN2 ....23 F5
Petersfield Gdns
  GOL/RIS/CU WA3 ....72 D5
Peter St AIMK WN4 ....61 F3
  GOL/RIS/CU WA3 ....70 B1
  LEIGH WN7 ....65 C2
  TYLD M29 ....53 C2
  WGNE/HIN WN2 ....30 C5
  WHTN BL5 ....36 C1
Petrel Cl TYLD M29 ....53 H5
Petticoat La WGNE/HIN WN2 ....35 G1
Petworth Av WGNS/IIMK WN3 ...47 E1
Pewfist Gn WHTN BL5 ....37 H2
The Pewfist Spinney
  WHTN BL5 ....37 G1
The Pewfist WHTN BL5 ....37 H1
Pheasant Cl WALK M28 ....55 C5
Philip Cl WCNW/BIL/O WN5 .....53 H5
Phillips St LEIGH WN7 ....51 H5
Phipps St WALK M28 ....81 H4
Picadilly WGN WN1 ....55 D1
Pickley Gdns LEIGH WN7 ....51 H2
Picksley St LEIGH WN7 ....65 C2
Pickthorn Cl WGNE/HIN WN2 ...35 C5
Pickup St WGNE/HIN WN2 ....3 K7
Piele Rd RNFD/HAY WA11 ....68 E2
Pierpont St NEWLW WA12 ....70 B2
Piggott St FWTH BL4 ....45 F1
Pigot St WGNNW/BIL/O WN5 ....32 C2
Pike Av ATH M46 ....52 B1
Pikelaw Pl SKEL WN8 ....29 H3
Pilgrims Wy WGNNW/ST WN6 ..10 D3
Pilkington St
  RNFD/HAY WA11 ....43 E5
  WGNE/HIN WN2 ....36 A2
Pilling Pl SKEL WN8 ....29 H3
Pilling St LEIGH WN7 ....51 H5
Pisley Cl WGNNW/BIL/O WN5 ...20 B4
Pimblett Rd RNFD/HAY WA11 ...68 B2
Pimblett St GOL/RIS/CU WA3 *..70 B2
Pimbo La SKEL WN8 ....30 C5
Pimbo Rd RNFD/HAY WA11 ......48 A1
  SKEL WN8 ....29 H3
Pine Cl SKEL WN8 ....17 E4
Pine Dr RNFD/HAY WA11 ....42 D4
Pine Gv GOL/RIS/CU WA3 ....70 D1
  WHTN BL5 ....37 H1
The Pines LEIGH WN7 ....53 F2
Pine St TYLD M29 ....53 H2
Pinevale WGNNW/ST WN6 ......10 D3
Pine Vw WGNS/IIMK WN3 ....35 E3
Pinewood AIMK WN4 ....60 D4
  SKEL WN8 ....18 A2
Pinewood Cl WGNE/HIN WN2 ...49 E4
Pinewood Crs WGNE/HIN WN2 ..35 E2
  WGNW/BIL/O WN5 ....31 H2
Pinfold Cl WHTN BL5 ....37 C2
Pinfold Pl SKEL WN8 ....30 A4
Pinfold Rd WALK M28 ....55 H2
Pinfold St WGNE/HIN WN2 ......35 F1
Pingot Rd WGNNW/BIL/O WN5 ..3 C4
The Pingot LEIGH WN7 ....64 C1
The Pipers GOL/RIS/CU WA3 ....71 C1
Pit Hey Pl SKEL WN8 ....29 H3
Pitt St WGNS/IIMK WN3 ....2 B6
Plane Av WGNW/BIL/O WN5 ....33 F1
Plane Tree Gv
  RNFD/HAY WA11 * 68 D2
Plank La LEIGH WN7 ....63 H2
Plantation Av WALK M28 ....41 H4
Plantation Gates
  WGN WN1 ....22 D3
Platt Cft LEIGH WN7 ....55 F3
Platt Fold Rd LEIGH WN7 ....52 B5
Platt Fold St LEIGH WN7 ....65 F1
Platt Hill Av BOLS/LL BL3 ....27 H1
Platt La WGN WN1 ....3 C4
  WGNE/HIN WN2 ....36 A3
  WHTN BL5 ....36 C1
Platt St LEIGH WN7 ....52 A5
  WGNE/HIN WN2 ....49 F1
Pleasance Wy NEWLW WA12 ...69 F5
Plodder La WHTN BL5 ....27 H5
Ploughfields WHTN BL5 ....25 H2
Plover Wy GOL/RIS/CU WA3 ....71 F1
Plymouth Gv
  WGNNW/ST WN6 ....10 D3
Pocket Nook La
  WGNS/IIMK WN3 ....71 H1
Pocket Nook Rd HOR/BR BL6 ...26 C2
Poet's Nook LEIGH WN7 ....53 H5
Poke St WGNW/BIL/O WN5 .....32 C2
Polegate Dr WGNE/HIN WN2 ...51 F1
Pole St WGNNW/ST WN6 ....10 B1
Pond St GOL/RIS/CU WA3 ....71 H1
Pondwater Cl WALK M28 ....41 E5
Poolstock Cl WGNS/IIMK WN3 ..34 A3
Poolstock La
  WGNS/IIMK WN3 ....33 H4
Pool Wk WGNE/HIN WN2 ....36 A4
  WGNS/IIMK WN3 ....34 A2
Poplar Av AIMK WN4 ....60 A1
  HOR/BR BL6 ....14 C2
  WGNW/BIL/O WN5 ....13 E2
Poplar Dr SKEL WN8 ....17 E4
Poplar Gv LEIGH WN7 ....51 E1
  WHTN BL5 ....25 H5
The Poplars CHLY/EC PR7 ....7 E1
  LEIGH WN7 ....53 E1
Poplar St GOL/RIS/CU WA3 ....62 C5
  LEIGH WN7 ....65 E3

  TYLD M29 ....53 H2
Porlock Cl WGNE/HIN WN2 ......47 F4
Porter Av NEWLW WA12 ....69 F4
Porterfield Dr TYLD M29 ....53 H5
Porters Wood Cl
  WGNW/BIL/O WN5 * 32 C1
Porthleven Crs TYLD M29 ....54 B5
Portland Cl WGNE/HIN WN2 ....49 F2
Portland Rd WALK M28 ....41 H5
Portland St NEWLW WA12 ......68 C5
  WGNW/BIL/O WN5 ....63 C3
Potter Pl SKEL WN8 ....30 A3
Pottery Rd WGNS/IIMK WN3 ....33 H1
Pottery Ter WGNS/IIMK WN3 ....2 A7
Poulton Dr AIMK WN4 * 60 C2
Powell La WGNW/BIL/O WN5 ...58 C5
Powell St WGN WN1 ....49 E2
  WGNE/HIN WN2 ....49 G2
Pownall St LEIGH WN7 ....65 F1
Powys St ATH M46 ....53 F2
Prefect Wy WGNW/BIL/O WN5 ..20 D5
Presbyterian Fold
  WGNE/HIN WN2 ....36 A2
Prescot Av ATH M46 ....39 F4
  TYLD M29 ....54 B2
Prescott La GOL/RIS/CU WA3 ...62 A4
  WGNW/BIL/O WN5 ....20 C5
Prescott Rd SKEL WN8 ....30 B4
Prescott St GOL/RIS/CU WA3 ...62 B5
  LEIGH WN7 ....65 F1
  WALK M28 ....41 C5
  WGNE/HIN WN2 ....36 A3
  WGNE/HIN WN2 ....21 H5
Prestbury Av WGNS/IIMK WN3 .33 F5
Prestt Gv WGNS/IIMK WN3 .....33 G5
Prestwich Av WGNS/IIMK WN3 .46 B4
Prestwich St ATH M46 ....38 C4
Pretoria Rd AIMK WN4 ....60 D2
Priestners Wy LEIGH WN7 ....51 H5
Primrose Av WALK M28 ....55 G1
Primrose Bank WALK M28 ......55 G1
Primrose Dr RNFD/HAY WA11 ...68 B2
  WGNW/BIL/O WN5 * 33 F1
Primrose La WGNNW/ST WN6 ...5 F1
Primrose St LEIGH WN7 ....64 C1
Primrose St North TYLD M29 ....53 H2
Primrose Vw AIMK WN4 ....61 E4
Primula Dr WGNE/HIN WN2 ....71 E1
Prince's Av TYLD M29 ....53 H5
Princes Gdns LEIGH WN7 ....65 H1
Prince's Pk WGNNW/ST WN6 ...20 A1
Princess Av AIMK WN4 ....61 F5
  ATH M46 ....68 D2
  RNFD/HAY WA11 ....68 D2
Princess Rd AIMK WN4 ....61 E3
  HOR/BR BL6 ....15 C3
  WGNNW/ST WN6 ....20 D1
Princess St LEIGH WN7 * 65 F1
  WGNE/HIN WN2 ....35 H5
  WGNS/IIMK WN3 ....2 A4
Prince St AIMK WN4 ....60 D1
  LEIGH WN7 ....53 F2
Printshop La ATH M46 ....54 B4
Priorswood Pl SKEL WN8 ....30 C4
Priory Av LEIGH WN7 ....51 G2
Priory Cl WGNW/BIL/O WN5 ....32 C3
Priory Nook SKEL WN8 ....17 G5
Priory Rd SKEL WN8 ....60 C1
  WGN WN1 ....31 F1
The Priory WARRN/WOL WA2 ...76 B5
Proctor Cl WGNS/IIMK WN3 ....55 H1
Prodesse Ct WGNE/HIN WN2 ...36 A2
Progress St WGNE/HIN WN2 ....48 C3
Prospect Pl FWTH BL4 ....41 H1
  SKEL WN8 ....30 C3
Prospect Rd
  WGNNW/ST WN6 ....10 B3
Prospect St TYLD M29 ....53 G2
Provost Av WGNE/HIN WN2 ....36 A3
Pryce Av WGNE/HIN WN2 ....52 B1
Pryor Av WALK M28 ....36 A4
Pump St WGNE/HIN WN2 ......35 H1
Punch La BOLS/LL BL3 ....27 E5
The Pungle WHTN BL5 ....37 G3
Purbeck Dr HOR/BR BL6 ....15 E2
Purbeck Wy TYLD M29 ....52 D5
Pye Cl RNFD/HAY WA11 ....69 E1
Pyke St WGN WN1 ....3 F2

R

Radbourne Gv BOLS/LL BL3 ....27 G1
Radcliffe Gv LEIGH WN7 ....52 A4
Radnor Cl LEIGH WN7 ....36 D5
Radnor Dr LEIGH WN7 ....52 B4
Radway TYLD M29 ....53 H2
Rail Cl RNFD/HAY WA11 ....43 E1
  LEIGH WN7 ....64 D1
  SKEL WN8 ....16 C5
Railway St ATH M46 ....38 C4
  WGNE/HIN WN2 ....36 B1
  WGNNW/ST WN6 ....21 H4
Rainbow Dr ATH M46 ....39 E4
Rainford By-Pass
  RNFD/HAY WA11 ....42 C4
  RNFD/HAY WA11 ....28 B4
  WGNW/BIL/O WN5 ....58 A1
Raithby Dr WGNS/IIMK WN3 ...33 H5
Rampit Cl RNFD/HAY WA11 .....68 C2
Ramsay Av FWTH BL4 ....41 G1
Ramsden Cl WGNS/IIMK WN3 ..35 H4
Ramsey Cl AIMK WN4 ....61 E4
Ramsey St LEIGH WN7 * 53 F1
Ramsey St WGNE/HIN WN2 .....65 F2
Ram St LHULT M38 ....41 E4
Randall Av WGNNW/ST WN6 ...5 H5
Randle Av LEIGH WN7 ....42 D3
Randle Brook Ct
  RNFD/HAY WA11 ....42 D3
Rands Clough Dr WALK M28 ....55 C5
Rancar Steet WGNE/HIN WN2 ..37 F5
Ranmore Av AIMK WN4 ....60 A2
Ranworth Dr GOL/RIS/CU WA3 .71 F2
Rassey Cl WGNNW/ST WN6 ....10 D3
Ratcliffe Rd WGNE/HIN WN2 ....55 A5
Ratcliffe St LEIGH WN7 ....52 A5
  TYLD M29 ....54 A2
  WGNNW/ST WN6 ....21 H4
Rathen Av WGNE/HIN WN2 .....23 F4
Ravenhead Dr SKEL WN8 ....30 D1
Ravenhead Wy SKEL WN8 ......30 D1
Rands La BOLS/LL BL3 * 27 H1
Ravenscraig Rd LHULT M38 .....41 G2
Ravenswood Av
  WGNS/IIMK WN3 ....35 E3
Ravenswood Dr
  WGNE/HIN WN2 ....36 B2
Rawsthorne St TYLD M29 ....54 C3
Rawthey Pl WGNE/HIN WN2 ...49 E1
Raydale Cl GOL/RIS/CU WA3 ...63 F5
Rayden Crs WHTN BL5 ....37 H2
Rayner Av WGNE/HIN WN2 .....36 B5
Recreation Av AIMK WN4 ....61 G2
Recreation Dr
  WGNW/BIL/O WN5 ....58 D1
Rectory Av GOL/RIS/CU WA3 ...70 D1
Rectory Gdns WHTN BL5 ....37 H4
Rectory La WGNNW/ST WN6 ...10 C1
Rectory Rd AIMK WN4 ....60 A1
Red Bank Av NEWLW WA12 ....76 A5
Red Barn Rd
  WGNW/BIL/O WN5 ....45 E5
Redbrook Rd WGNS/IIMK WN3 .34 C2
Redburn Cl WGNS/IIMK WN3 ...34 A2
Red Cat La RNFD/HAY WA11 ....57 C1
Red Delph La RNFD/HAY WA11 .50 C3
Redford Cl LEIGH WN7 ....65 F1
Redgate Rd AIMK WN4 ....48 A5
Redgrave Ri WGNS/IIMK WN3 ..33 E5
Red Hill Wy WGNE/HIN WN2 ...36 A2
Redland Ct WGNE/HIN WN2 ....48 D4
Redmain Cl GOL/RIS/CU WA3 ...71 F1
Redmayne Ci NEWLW WA12 ....69 E5
Rednal Wk WGNS/IIMK WN3 ...34 A2
Redpol Av LEIGH WN7 ....52 C5
Redpoll Cl WALK M28 ....55 G4
Red Rock La WGNE/HIN WN2 ...11 G2
Redshank Cl NEWLW WA12 .....69 F5
Redshank Gv LEIGH WN7 ....52 C5
Redstart Cl WGNE/HIN WN2 ....71 F1
Redstock Cl WHTN BL5 ....26 B4
Red St ATH M46 ....39 F5
Redwater Cl WALK M28 ....55 F5
Red Waters LEIGH WN7 ....51 H5
Redwood WGNE/HIN WN2 ......9 G4
Redwood Av
  WGNNW/ST WN6 ....21 G2
  WGNW/BIL/O WN5 ....32 B2
Reed Crs WGNS/IIMK WN3 .....55 H3
Reedley Dr WALK M28 ....55 H5
Reeds Brow RNFD/HAY WA11 ..43 C3
Reedy La WGNE/HIN WN2 ......56 A3
Reedsmere Cl
  WGNW/BIL/O WN5 ....33 G2
Reepham Cl WGNS/IIMK WN3 ..33 E5
Reeves St LEIGH WN7 ....52 A1
Reeve St GOL/RIS/CU WA3 .....72 A1
Regaby Gv WGNE/HIN WN2 ....36 D3
Regency Cl WGN WN1 ....2 B4
Regent Av AIMK WN4 ....60 C1
  LHULT M38 ....41 H4
Regent Dr HOR/BR BL6 ....15 C3
Regents Hl HOR/BR BL6 ....15 H4
Regent St ATH M46 ....53 F1
  WGNE/HIN WN2 ....36 A1
Regina Crs LEIGH WN7 ....55 F5
Reginald St BOLS/LL BL3 * 27 H1
Renfrew Cl WGNS/IIMK WN3 ...33 H5
Renfrew Dr BOLS/LL BL3 ....27 G2
Renfrew Rd WGNE/HIN WN2 ...13 E5
Renwick Sq AIMK WN4 ....61 E4
Repington Av WGNE/HIN WN2 .35 H4
Reservoir St WGNE/HIN WN2 ...23 F5
  WGNE/HIN WN2 ....36 A1
Restormel Av WGNE/HIN WN2 .13 G4
Reynolds Cl WHTN BL5 ....39 G2
Reynolds Dr WHTN BL5 ....39 G1

Rhyl Fold LEIGH WN7 * 66 B1
Ribbesford Rd
  WGNS/IIMK WN3 ....32 D4
Ribble Crs WGNW/BIL/O WN5 ..58 B5
Ribble Dr WALK M28 ....55 E5
  WGNNW/ST WN6 ....32 D1
Ribble Gv LEIGH WN7 ....64 B1
Ribble Rd WGNE/HIN WN2 .....47 F1
  WGNNW/ST WN6 ....4 C5
Richard Gwyn Cl WHTN BL5 ....37 G2
Richards St WGNS/IIMK WN3 ...34 C2
Richmond Cl GOL/RIS/CU WA3 .72 C5
  WGN WN1 ....3 F4
Richmond Dr LEIGH WN7 ....53 F4
Richmond Gv LEIGH WN7 ....53 E5
Richmond Hl
  WGNW/BIL/O WN5 ....32 D2
Richmond Rd AIMK WN4 ....60 C1
  WALK M28 ....36 D5
Richmond St WGN WN1 ....2 B4
  WGNS/IIMK WN3 ....33 H3
Ridge Av WGN WN1 ....11 E3
Ridgeway GOL/RIS/CU WA3 ....71 F2
Ridgewell Av GOL/RIS/CU WA3 .58 A1
Ridgmont Dr WALK M28 ....55 E5
Ridgway HOR/BR BL6 ....7 H5
Riding Cl TYLD M29 ....54 C4
Riding La AIMK WN4 ....61 H1
Ridyard St LHULT M38 ....41 H4
  WGNW/BIL/O WN5 ....58 D1
  WGNW/BIL/O WN5 ....33 F1
Rigby Av HOR/BR BL6 * 7 H5
Rigby Gv LHULT M38 ....40 D4
Rigbys Houses CHLY/EC PR7 *..6 D1
Rigby La AIMK WN4 ....60 C5
Rigby St AIMK WN4 ....60 D5
  GOL/RIS/CU WA3 ....70 B1
  WGNE/HIN WN2 ....36 B2
Riley La WGNE/HIN WN2 ....12 C3
Riley Sq WGN WN1 ....3 F4
Riley St ATH M46 ....52 B2
Rimington Av
  GOL/RIS/CU WA3 ....62 D5
Rindle Rd TYLD M29 ....55 H1
Ringley Av GOL/RIS/CU WA3 ...62 A5
Ringway Av LEIGH WN7 ....52 A5
Ripley Dr LEIGH WN7 ....52 A5
  WGNS/IIMK WN3 ....32 D4
Ripon Av GOL/RIS/CU WA3 .....71 E1
Ripon Cl NEWLW WA12 ....69 E5
Ripon Dr AIMK WN4 ....61 H2
The Rise WGNNW/ST WN6 .....20 D2
Riverdale Cl WGNNW/ST WN6 ..21 E2
Riverside Av WGNE/HIN WN2 ..52 B5
Riversmeade LEIGH WN7 ....52 A5
Rivers St WGNW/BIL/O WN5 ...31 H2
River Wy WGN WN1 ....2 D5
Rivington Av GOL/RIS/CU WA3 .22 A3
  WGN WN1 ....35 G5
  WGNE/HIN WN2 ....22 A3
Rivington Dr SKEL WN8 ....31 F1
Rivington Pl CHLY/EC PR7 ......50 C2
Rivington Rd ATH M46 ....52 B1
Rivington Wy WGNNW/ST WN6 .10 C2
Rixton Dr TYLD M29 ....54 A3
Roach Gn WGN WN1 ....3 H5
Roadside Ct GOL/RIS/CU WA3 ..70 D1
Robertshaw St LEIGH WN7 .....51 H4
Robert St ATH M46 * 53 F5
  WGNE/HIN WN2 ....35 F5
Robin Dr WGNNW/ST WN6 .....4 C5
Robin Hill La WGNNW/ST WN6 .10 D2
Robin Park Rd
  WGNW/BIL/O WN5 ....21 F5
Robin's La RNFD/HAY WA11 ....44 C3
Rob La NEWLW WA12 ....69 H5
Robson Wy GOL/RIS/CU WA3 ..71 G1
Roby MI SKEL WN8 ....19 E2
Roby Well Wy
  WGNW/BIL/O WN5 ....58 C1
Rochester Av WALK M28 ....55 H2
Rochester Cl GOL/RIS/CU WA3 .70 B1
Roch PI WGNE/HIN WN2 ....49 E1
Rockbourne Cl
  WGNS/IIMK WN3 ....36 A4
Rockingham Dr
  WGNE/HIN WN2 ....35 H4
Rock St GOL/RIS/CU WA3 ......62 C5
Rocky Bank Ter
  WGNS/IIMK WN3 * 34 D3
Rodgers Cl WHTN BL5 ....37 H2
Rodgers Wy WHTN BL5 ....37 H2
Rodney St ATH M46 * 52 D1
  WGN WN1 ....2 D6
Roebuck St WGNE/HIN WN2 ...37 F5
Roecliffe St WGNS/IIMK WN3 ..34 A2
Rogerton Cl LEIGH WN7 ....65 G2
Rokeby Av GOL/RIS/CU WA3 ...63 E5
Rokeden NEWLW WA12 ....69 G5
Roman Rd AIMK WN4 ....60 D1
Romford Av LEIGH WN7 ....52 A5
Romford Pl WGNE/HIN WN2 ...36 A3
Romford St WGNE/HIN WN2 ...36 A3
Romiley Dr SKEL WN8 ....17 E5
Romiley Sq WGNS/IIMK WN3 ..10 B2
Romney Wy WGN WN1 ....22 A2
Romsey Gv WGNS/IIMK WN3 ..47 E1
Roocroft Sq HOR/BR BL6 ....7 H5
Rookery Av LEIGH WN7 ....56 B1
Rookery La RNFD/HAY WA11 ...56 B1
The Rookery NEWLW WA12 ....69 G5
Roscoe Ct WHTN BL5 ....38 A1
Roscoe St WGN WN1 ....3 C6
Rose Acre WALK M28 ....55 H5
Rose Av RNFD/HAY WA11 ......68 D3
  WGNE/HIN WN2 ....49 G4
  WGNE/HIN WN2 ....21 G2
Rosebank HOR/BR BL6 ....15 H5
Rose Bank LEIGH WN7 ....53 F1
Roseberry Rd AIMK WN4 ....60 D1

Rosebery St WHTN BL5 ....26 A5
Rosebridge Ct WGN WN1 * 3 J6
Rosebridge Wy WGN WN1 ......3 J6
Rosebury Av LEIGH WN7 ....65 F1
Rosebury Cv GOL/RIS/CU WA3 .52 C5
Rose Crs SKEL WN8 ....16 D4
Rosedale Av ATH M46 ....38 D5
  GOL/RIS/CU WA3 ....70 D2
Rosedale Dr LEIGH WN7 ....65 H1
Rose Dr RNFD/HAY WA11 ....37 C2
Rose Hill Av WGNW/BIL/O WN5 .32 D2
Rose Hill Vw AIMK WN4 ....47 E4
Rosemary Crs WGN WN1 ....22 C3
Rosemary Dr NEWLW WA12 ....76 A1
Rosemary La WHTN BL5 ....40 A2
Rose Pl RNFD/HAY WA11 ....56 B1
Rose St WGN WN1 ....3 J6
  WGNE/HIN WN2 ....37 F2
Rosewood Cl WGNE/HIN WN2 ..37 F2
Rosewood Cl WALK M28 ....49 G4
Rosina Cl AIMK WN4 ....47 C5
Rosley Rd WGNS/IIMK WN3 ....34 A5
Rossall Crs LEIGH WN7 ....65 F3
Ross Cl WGNE/HIN WN2 ....58 D1
  GOL/RIS/CU WA3 ....10 D3
Rossdale Gv WGNNW/ST WN6 .10 D3
Rossett Cl WGNS/IIMK WN3 ....47 E1
Rostherne Av GOL/RIS/CU WA3 .71 E1
Rosthwaite Cl WGNS/IIMK WN3 .47 H1
Rosthwaite Gv
  RNFD/HAY WA11 ....58 A5
Rothay St LEIGH WN7 ....65 C2
Rothwell Crs LHULT M38 ....40 D2
Rothwell La LHULT M38 ....40 D3
Rothwell Rd GOL/RIS/CU WA3 .62 D5
Roughlea Av
  GOL/RIS/CU WA3 ....72 C5
Round House Av WGN WN1 ....3 H2
Roundmoor Rd
  WGNNW/ST WN6 ....10 D3
Round Thorn
  GOL/RIS/CU WA3 ....77 H5
Rowanthorn La WHTN BL5 .....37 H1
Rowan Av GOL/RIS/CU WA3 ...71 G2
  HOR/BR BL6 ....14 D1
  WGNE/HIN WN2 ....21 G2
Rowanhill WGN WN1 ....3 F2
Rowan La SKEL WN8 ....17 G1
Rowbottom Sq WGN WN1 ......2 C4
Rowe St TYLD M29 * 54 A3
Rowland St ATH M46 ....39 E5
Rowton Ri WGN WN1 ....11 E2
Roxby Cl WALK M28 ....41 G5
Royal Ar WGN WN1 ....2 D4
Royal Dr LEIGH WN7 ....53 E5
Royden Av WGNS/IIMK WN3 ...47 G1
Royden Crs WGNW/BIL/O WN5 .58 D1
Royden Rd WGNW/BIL/O WN5 .58 D1
Royston Cl GOL/RIS/CU WA3 ...71 F1
Ruabon Crs WGNE/HIN WN2 ...34 C2
Ruby Gv LEIGH WN7 ....64 D2
Rowal Dr WGNNW/ST WN6 .....5 F5
Ruecroft Cl WGNNW/ST WN6 ..10 D3
Rufford Cl TYLD M29 ....66 C2
Rufford Rd RNFD/HAY WA11 ...43 E3
Rugby Dr WGNW/BIL/O WN5 ...20 A5
Rugby Rd LEIGH WN7 ....68 E3
Rumworth Rd HOR/BR BL6 .....15 H4
Runshaw Av WGNNW/ST WN6 ..8 D2
Rupert St WGN WN1 ....3 F6
Rushdene WGNS/IIMK WN3 ....33 H4
Rushmoor Av AIMK WN4 ....61 H2
Rushton Av LEIGH WN7 ....51 C5
  WGNE/HIN WN2 ....69 E5
  WGNS/IIMK WN3 ....33 C5
Russeldene Rd
  WGNS/IIMK WN3 ....33 F5
Russell Ct LHULT M38 ....41 H5
Russell St ATH M46 ....38 D5
  LHULT M38 ....41 H5
  WGNE/HIN WN2 ....23 F5
Rutherford Dr WHTN BL5 ....39 G1
Rutland Av GOL/RIS/CU WA3 ...39 G5
  GOL/RIS/CU WA3 ....52 C5
Rutland Dr AIMK WN4 ....61 F2
Rutland Gv FWTH BL4 * 41 H1
Rutland Rd TYLD M29 ....53 G1
  WALK M28 ....55 H2
Rutland St LEIGH WN7 ....66 B2
Rydal Av WGNE/HIN WN2 ......36 B3
  WGNW/BIL/O WN5 ....32 A1
Rydal Cl AIMK WN4 ....61 F2
  HOR/BR BL6 ....53 H4
  TYLD M29 ....41 E1
Rydal Gv FWTH BL4 ....41 E1
Rydal Pl WGNE/HIN WN2 ....23 G5
Rydal Rd LEIGH WN7 ....64 D1
Ryder Gv LEIGH WN7 ....65 H4
Ryde St BOLS/LL BL3 * 27 H1
  WGNW/BIL/O WN5 ....33 F2
Ryecroft Av GOL/RIS/CU WA3 ..63 F5
Ryecroft Dr WHTN BL5 ....26 B5
Ryeford Cl WGNE/HIN WN2 ....58 D1
Rye Hl WHTN BL5 ....26 A5
Ryelands WHTN BL5 ....26 A5
Ryelands Cl WHTN BL5 * 26 A5
Rylands St WGNNW/ST WN6 ...21 H3
Ryton Cl WGNS/IIMK WN3 .....34 A2

S

Sabden Brook Dr
  WGNE/HIN WN2 * 49 E1
Saddleback Cl WALK M28 ....55 C5
Saddleback Crs
  WGNW/BIL/O WN5 ....32 C1
Saddleback Rd

WGNW/BIL/O WN5 ....32 C1
Saffron Cl GOL/RIS/CU WA3 ....71 F1
St Aidan's Cl
WGNW/BIL/O WN5 ....45 H5
St Albans Cl RNFD/HAY WA11 .....68 C2
St Ambrose Rd TYLD M29 ....66 D1
St Andrew's Crs
WGNE/HIN WN2......................36 A3
St Andrews Dr LEIGH WN7 ....65 H1
WGNNW/ST WN6......................21 G3
St Andrews Rd HOR/BR BL6 ....15 F3
St Anne's Av ATH M46..................53 F2
St Anne's Ct WGNNW/ST WN6 ....9 E5
St Anne's Dr WGNNW/ST WN6........9 F5
St Aubyn's Rd WGN WN1 * 22 B2
St Austell Av TYLD M29...............54 B3
St Christopher Ct
WGNNW/ST WN6 * 20 D1
St Clare Ter HOR/BR BL6 * 15 E2
St Clement's Rd WGN WN1 ....22 B2
St Clement's St
WGNS/IIMK WN3 ....35 E4
St David's Crs WGNE/HIN WN2 ....12 C5
St Elizabeth's Rd
WGNE/HIN WN2......................12 C5
St George's Av WHTN BL5 ....37 H2
St Georges Ct TYLD M29..............53 G3
St George's Pl ATH M46 * 38 C4
St George's St TYLD M29 ....53 G3
St Gregorys Cl FWTH BL4 ....41 H1
St Helens Rd LEIGH WN7 ....64 B5
RNFD/HAY WA11........................56 C4
WHTN BL5...................................27 G4
St James Crs WGNE/HIN WN2 ......50 C3
St James Gv WGNS/IIMK WN3 ......34 A2
St James' Rd WGNW/BIL/O WN5....31 G4
St James St FWTH BL4 ....41 G1
WHTN BL5...................................38 A3
St John's Av WHTN BL5...............25 G2
St Johns Ct HOR/BR BL6..............26 C1
St John's Rd HOR/BR BL6.............26 C2
WALK M28..................................54 D4
WGNE/HIN WN2.........................12 C5
St John's St WGNE/HIN WN2 ....49 G3
St John St ATH M46 ....39 E5
WALK M28..................................41 H4
WGNW/BIL/O WN5 ....32 C2
St Johns Wd HOR/BR BL6.............26 C1
St Katherines Dr HOR/BR BL6 ....7 H4
St Leonard's Av HOR/BR BL6........15 E1
St Luke's Av GOL/RIS/CU WA3 .....71 E1
St Luke's Dr WGNW/BIL/O WN5....31 G4
St Malo Rd WGN WN1 ....22 B1
St Mark's Av
WGNW/BIL/O WN5 ....33 G1
St Mary's Av
WGNW/BIL/O WN5 ....58 B2
St Mary's Cl ATH M46 ....39 F5
WGNE/HIN WN2 * 12 C5
St Mary's Rd WALK M28 ....41 H4
WGNE/HIN WN2.........................12 C4
St Mary's Wy LEIGH WN7 * 65 E1
St Matthew's Cl
WGNS/IIMK WN3 ....32 D4
St Michael's Av ATH M46 ....52 B2
St Michael's Ct WGN WN1 ....2 D1
St Nicholas Rd
GOL/RIS/CU WA3.........................63 H5
St Oswalds Rd AIMK WN4.............60 D4
St Patrick St WGN WN1 ....3 F5
St Patricks Wy WGN WN1 ....3 F5
St Paul's Av WGNS/IIMK WN3 ......33 G4
St Stephen's Av WGN WN1 ....3 H1
St Stephens Cl TYLD M29 ....66 D1
St Stephen's Rd
WGNNW/ST WN6............................9 H1
St Thomas's Ct SKEL WN8 * 31 F1
St Thomas St WGNS/IIMK WN3 ......2 C7
St Wilfrid's Rd
WGNNW/ST WN6..........................10 C2
Salcombe Cl WGN WN1....................3 H1
Sale La TYLD M29..........................54 C2
Salesbury Wy WGNS/IIMK WN3.....33 H5
Salford Rd WHTN BL5 ....27 H5
Salisbury Av WGNE/HIN WN2 ....36 B2
Salisbury Rd AIMK WN4 * 60 D1
HOR/BR BL6................................14 D1
RNFD/HAY WA11..........................60 B5
Salisbury St GOL/RIS/CU WA3 ......70 B1
Salisbury Wy TYLD M29 ....54 A3
Salkeld Av AIMK WN4 ....60 C3
Sallowfields
WGNW/BIL/O WN5 ....31 G3
Salmon St WGN WN1 * 3 G2
Saltergate BOLS/LL BL3 ....27 G1
Salters Ct ATH M46 ....39 E5
Salterton Dr BOLS/LL BL3.............27 G3
Saltram Rd WGNS/IIMK WN3 ....32 D4
Salvin Cl AIMK WN4......................61 G3
Salwick Cl WGNS/IIMK WN3 ....33 F4
Samuel St ATH M46......................53 G2
Sandalwood WHTN BL5 ....37 G2
Sandalwood Dr
WGNNW/ST WN6..........................21 G2
Sandbrook Gdns
WGNW/BIL/O WN5 ....31 G3
Sandbrook Rd
WGNW/BIL/O WN5 ....31 F3
Sanderling Cl WHTN BL5...............37 G2
Sanderling Dr LEIGH WN7 ....65 F1
Sanderson's Cft LEIGH WN7...........65 H2
Sanderson St LEIGH WN7...............64 D1
Sandfield Cl GOL/RIS/CU WA3 ....71 F1
Sandfield Crs GOL/RIS/CU WA3 .....73 H2
Sandfield Dr HOR/BR BL6..............15 H4
Sandgate Cl LEIGH WN7 ....52 A5
Sandiacre WGNNW/ST WN6...........10 B2
Sandiway Cl WHTN BL5..................25 G5
Sandling Dr GOL/RIS/CU WA3 ....62 B4
Sandon Gv RNFD/HAY WA11 ....43 F5
Sandown Cl GOL/RIS/CU WA3 * 73 E5
Sandown Rd WGNNW/ST WN6 ....21 F2
Sandpiper Cl FWTH BL4 ....41 E1
NEWLW WA12...............................69 F5
Sandpiper Rd WGNS/IIMK WN3....32 C4
Sandringham Cl CHLY/EC PR7........6 D1
WGNW/BIL/O WN5 ....33 F3
Sandringham Dr LEIGH WN7 ....53 F4
Sandringham Rd WALK M28 ....55 F5
WGNE/HIN WN2............................36 B4
Sandstone Rd
WGNS/IIMK WN3 ....47 E1
Sandwash Cl RNFD/HAY WA11 ......56 C2
Sandway WGNNW/ST WN6 ....21 G3
Sandwith Cl WGNS/IIMK WN3 ....48 A1
Sandyacre Cl WHTN BL5 ....39 H2
Sandy Brow La
GOL/RIS/CU WA3..........................77 F2
Sandycroft Av WGN WN1................2 C2
Sandy La GOL/RIS/CU WA3............63 H4
GOL/RIS/CU WA3 ....77 H3
NEWLW WA12...............................70 A1
RNFD/HAY WA11...........................57 G5
SKEL WN8.....................................16 C4
TYLD M29.....................................66 D2
TYLD M29.....................................67 E5
WGNE/HIN WN2............................36 D2
WGNW/BIL/O WN5 ....31 G4
Sandy Pk WGNE/HIN WN2 ....36 D2
Sandy Wy WGNE/HIN WN2.............36 C2
Sankey St GOL/RIS/CU WA3..........70 B1
Santon Dr GOL/RIS/CU WA3..........71 F1
Sarah St WGNE/HIN WN2 ....51 E1
Sarsfield Av GOL/RIS/CU WA3 ......71 E1
Satinwood Cl AIMK WN4 ....60 C3
Sawley Av GOL/RIS/CU WA3 ....63 E5
WGNNW/ST WN6...........................21 G2
Sawyer Dr AIMK WN4 ....61 G3
Saxthorpe Cl
WGNS/IIMK WN3 ....33 E5
Scafell Dr WGNW/BIL/O WN5........32 C2
Scafell Gv WGNE/HIN WN2............49 G1
Scargill Rd BOLS/LL BL3 ....27 H1
Scarisbrick Rd
RNFD/HAY WA11...........................43 E4
Scarisbrick St WGN WN1 ....2 D2
Scarth Pk SKEL WN8 ....29 H1
Schofield Gdns LEIGH WN7 ....64 D3
Schofield La ATH M46 ....38 A5
Schofield St LEIGH WN7 ....64 D3
Scholefield La WGN WN1 ....3 F4
Scholes WGN WN1 ....3 F4
Scholes Av WGN WN1......................3 G2
School Brow
WGNW/BIL/O WN5 ....58 D1
School Dr WGNW/BIL/O WN5.........58 D1
School Houses SKEL WN8 * 17 G5
School La AIMK WN4 ....59 H3
SKEL WN8.....................................16 D3
SKEL WN8.....................................19 E2
SKEL WN8.....................................31 F1
WGN WN1.......................................2 E4
WGNE/HIN WN2............................11 H2
WGNE/HIN WN2............................12 A4
WGNNW/ST WN6...........................10 A1
School St AIMK WN4 ....61 G1
ATH M46 ....52 C1
GOL/RIS/CU WA3..........................70 B1
LEIGH WN7 ....51 H3
TYLD M29.....................................53 G3
TYLD M29.....................................53 G5
WGN WN1.......................................2 E4
WGNE/HIN WN2..............................3 K6
WGNE/HIN WN2............................49 G2
WHTN BL5.....................................25 H5
School Ter GOL/RIS/CU WA3 * 70 B1
School Wy WGNW/BIL/O WN5........32 D2
Scot La WGNE/HIN WN2 ....13 E4
Scotland Pl WHTN BL5 ...
Scott Av WGNE/HIN WN2 ....36 B2
Scott Rd GOL/RIS/CU WA3 ....63 E5
Scott St LEIGH WN7.......................64 C1
TYLD M29.....................................67 F2
WGNNW/ST WN6.............................2 A3
WHTN BL5.....................................25 H3
Seaforth Av ATH M46 ....38 D4
Seaman Wy WGNE/HIN WN2 ....35 G1
Seascale Crs WGN WN1...................22 B2
Seathwaite Cl TYLD M29 ....53 H4
Seathwaite Rd FWTH BL4................41 E1
Seatoller Pl WGNW/BIL/O WN5 ......32 C1
Seaton Pl SKEL WN8 ....16 D2
Second Av ATH M46 ....39 E4
TYLD M29.....................................53 G2
WGNNW/ST WN6...........................21 H3
Seddon Cl ATH M46 ....38 D5
Seddon House Dr
WGNNW/ST WN6...........................21 F2
Seddon Pl SKEL WN8......................16 D2
Seddon St LHULT M38....................41 E3
WHTN BL5.....................................25 H2
Sedgefield Dr
WGNNW/ST WN6...........................21 F2
Sedgely WGNNW/ST WN6................10 D3
Sedgley Dr WHTN BL5....................37 H3
Sedgwick Cl ATH M46 ....39 F5
WHTN BL5.....................................38 A2
Sedwyn St WGN WN1 ....3 G2
Seedley Av LHULT M38 ....41 G4
Sefton Av ATH M46 ....38 D3
WGNW/BIL/O WN5 ....31 G3
Sefton Cl WGNW/BIL/O WN5 ....31 G3
Sefton Fold Dr
WGNW/BIL/O WN5 ....58 C1
Sefton Fold Gdns
WGNW/BIL/O WN5 ....58 C1
Sefton La HOR/BR BL6 ....14 C1
Sefton Rd AIMK WN4 ....47 G5
WGNS/IIMK WN3 ....33 G4
WGNW/BIL/O WN5 ....31 G3
Sefton St LEIGH WN7 ....65 E1
Sefton Vw WGNW/BIL/O WN5.........31 G3
Selbourne Cl WHTN BL5 ....26 B4
Selbourne St LEIGH WN7 ....64 C1
Selby Dr WGNS/IIMK WN3 ....32 D4
Selby Pl SKEL WN8.........................16 C2
Selkirk Av AIMK WN4......................60 A2
Selkirk Gv WGNW/BIL/O WN5 ....20 C5
Selside WGNS/IIMK WN3.................48 A1
Selwyn Cl NEWLW WA12.................69 E4
Selwyn St LEIGH WN7 ....52 A5
Senecar Cl WGNE/HIN WN2 ....23 G3
Sennicar La WGN WN1 ....11 F5
Sephton St WGNS/IIMK WN3 ....35 E2
Seven Oaks LEIGH WN7 ....52 B5
Seven Stars Rd
WGNS/IIMK WN3 ....33 H1
Severn Cl WGNW/BIL/O WN5..........58 C2
Severn Dr WGNE/HIN WN2..............37 F5
WGNW/BIL/O WN5 ....32 D2
Severn Rd AIMK WN4 ....61 H1
Severn St LEIGH WN7 ....65 G2
Sewell Wy LHULT M38.....................41 E5
Shadwell Gv LEIGH WN7.................51 F3
Shaftesbury Av HOR/BR BL6..........15 E2
Shaftesbury Rd
WGNW/BIL/O WN5 ....20 B5
Shaftesbury St
WGNNW/ST WN6...........................21 G2
Shaftway Cl RNFD/HAY WA11 ....68 C2
Shakerley La TYLD M29 ....39 G4
Shakerley Rd TYLD M29 ....53 G2
Shakespeare Gv
WGNS/IIMK WN3 ....33 H4
Shalbourne Rd WALK M28 ....41 H5
Shap Ga WGNW/BIL/O WN5 ....32 C1
Shared St WGN WN1 ....3 F6
Sharon Sq WGNE/HIN WN2 ....49 E3
Sharp St WGNS/IIMK WN3 ....34 D2
Shawbrook Av WALK M28 ....55 G3
Shawbury Cl HOR/BR BL6 ....13 E1
Shaw St AIMK WN4 ....61 E1
RNFD/HAY WA11...........................68 B3
WGN WN1.......................................2 D2
Shearwater Av TYLD M29 ....53 H3
Shearwater Dr WALK M28 ....41 H5
WHTN BL5.....................................37 G2
Shefford Crs WGNS/IIMK WN3.......46 D1
The Sheilings GOL/RIS/CU WA3.....71 G1
Shelburne Dr WGNE/HIN WN2........35 H4
Sheldon Av WGNNW/ST WN6.............5 F5
Sheldwich Cl LEIGH WN7 ....65 E3
Shelley Dr WGNE/HIN WN2 ....49 G2
WGNW/BIL/O WN5 ....32 B2
Shelley Rd LHULT M38 * 41 F3
Shelley St LEIGH WN7 ....51 F4
Shellingford Cl
WGNNW/ST WN6.............................8 C3
Shepherds Cl HOR/BR BL6 ....7 H4
Shepton Av WGNE/HIN WN2 ....49 F2
Sheraton Cl WGNW/BIL/O WN5.......20 C4
Sherborne Av WGNE/HIN WN2 ......36 D3
Sherborne Rd
WGNW/BIL/O WN5 ....20 B5
Sherbourne Pl
WGNS/IIMK WN3 ....34 D3
Sheridan Av GOL/RIS/CU WA3........71 E2
Sheriffs Dr TYLD M29 ....54 C2
Sherlock Av RNFD/HAY WA11 ....68 B2
Sherrat St SKEL WN8.....................16 C4
Sherwood Av AIMK WN4 * 61 F2
TYLD M29.....................................53 H5
Sherwood Crs WGNE/HIN WN2 ......49 F1
WGNW/BIL/O WN5 ....33 E1
Sherwood Dr SKEL WN8.................18 A2
WGNW/BIL/O WN5 ....33 E1
Sherwood Gv LEIGH WN7...............65 G4
WGNW/BIL/O WN5 ....33 E1
Shevington La WGNNW/ST WN6 .....9 G1
Shevington Moor
WGNNW/ST WN6.............................4 B5
Shildon Cl WGNE/HIN WN2..............3 K1
Shillingten Cl LHULT M38 ....41 E5
Shipham Cl LEIGH WN7 ....51 G3
Ship Yd WGN WN1 ....2 D5
Shires Cl WGNE/HIN WN2 ....36 B4
Shirewell Rd
WGNW/BIL/O WN5 ....31 H3
Shortland Pl WGNE/HIN WN2 ....50 D3
Short St GOL/RIS/CU WA3 * 62 C5
RNFD/HAY WA11...........................68 B3
WGNW/BIL/O WN5 ....32 C2
Shrewsbury Cl
WGNE/HIN WN2............................36 C2
Shurdington Rd ATH M46 ....39 G3
Shuttle Hillock Rd
WGNE/HIN WN2............................50 C4
Shuttle St TYLD M29 ....53 G2
WGNE/HIN WN2............................36 B2
Sibley Av AIMK WN4 ....61 G2
Sidbrook St WGNE/HIN WN2 ....35 H3
Siddeley St LEIGH WN7 ....64 C1
Siddow Common LEIGH WN7 ....65 F3
Siding La RNFD/HAY WA11.............42 C2
Sidmouth Gv WGNS/IIMK WN3 ....33 F5
Sidney St LEIGH WN7 ....65 F1
Silcock St GOL/RIS/CU WA3 ....70 B1
Silk St LEIGH WN7 ....65 E1
WHTN BL5 * 25 H4
Sillitoe Dr WGNNW/ST WN6 ....21 H4
Silsbury Gv WGNNW/ST WN6..........10 D2
Silsden Av GOL/RIS/CU WA3..........72 A1
Silver Birch Gv AIMK WN4 ....60 D1
Silverdale WGN WN1 ....2 C1
Silverdale Av WGNE/HIN WN2 ....23 F5
Silverdale Ct WGN WN1 ....3 F5
Silverdale Rd NEWLW WA12............69 E5
WGNE/HIN WN2............................36 C3
WGNW/BIL/O WN5 ....20 C5
Silver St WGNE/HIN WN2 ....49 G1
Silver Ter WGN WN1 ....2 E5
Silvington Wy WGNE/HIN WN2 ....23 F3
Simfield Cl WGNNW/ST WN6 ....10 A1
Simpkin St WGNE/HIN WN2 ....49 G2
Simpson Gv WALK M28 ....55 F5
Simpson Rd WALK M28...................55 F5
Sinclair Pl WGNW/BIL/O WN5 ....21 F5
Singleton Gv WHTN BL5 ....26 C5
Siskin Cl LEIGH WN7......................65 G1
Sittingbourne Rd WGN WN1 ....22 B1
Sixpools Gv WALK M28 ....55 H3
Size House Pl LEIGH WN7 * 65 F2
Skelton St AIMK WN4 ....47 G5
Skiddaw Pl WGNW/BIL/O WN5 ....32 D2
Skipton Av WGNE/HIN WN2............36 D4
Skull House La
WGNNW/ST WN6.............................8 C2
Skull House Ms
WGNNW/ST WN6.............................8 B2
Slackey Fold WGNE/HIN WN2 ....51 E2
Slack La WHTN BL5 ....26 A3
Slag La GOL/RIS/CU WA3 ....63 G4
Slaidburn Cl WGNS/IIMK WN3 ....33 H5
Slaidburn Crs GOL/RIS/CU WA3....62 A4
Slate La SKEL WN8.........................16 B3
Slater's Nook WHTN BL5.................25 H4
Slater St North LEIGH WN7 ....64 C1
Sledbrook St
WGNW/BIL/O WN5 * 32 D3
Smallbridge Cl WALK M28 ....55 H3
Smallbrook La LEIGH WN7 ....37 H5
Smalley St WGNNW/ST WN6 ....10 B1
Smallshaw Cl AIMK WN4.................60 D4
Smethurst La
WGNW/BIL/O WN5 ....32 D3
Smethurst Park Hall
WGNW/BIL/O WN5 ....45 F1
Smethurst Rd
WGNW/BIL/O WN5 ....45 F1
Smethurst St
WGNW/BIL/O WN5 ....32 D3
Smith Av WGNW/BIL/O WN5 ....20 C5
Smith Brow HOR/BR BL6 ....7 H5
Smith Fold La WALK M28 ....41 F5
Smith's La WGNE/HIN WN2 ....50 D3
Smith St ATH M46 * 38 D5
LEIGH WN7 ....65 F1
SKEL WN8.....................................16 C4
WGNE/HIN WN2............................12 D5
Smithwood Av
WGNE/HIN WN2............................36 C2
Smithy Brow GOL/RIS/CU WA3 ......77 G5
Smithy Gn WGNE/HIN WN2 ....3 K6
Smithy Hl BOLS/LL BL3 ....27 H1
Smithy La GOL/RIS/CU WA3 ....77 H5
Smithy St LEIGH WN7 ....65 E2
Smock La AIMK WN4 ....59 H2
Snowden Av WGNS/IIMK WN3........33 H4
Snowshill Dr WGNS/IIMK WN3.......32 D4
Snydale Cl WHTN BL5 ....26 B3
Snydale Wy BOLS/LL BL3 ....27 E3
Soane Cl AIMK WN4........................61 G3
Soham Cl WGNE/HIN WN2 ....36 B4
Soho St WGNW/BIL/O WN5 ....33 G1
Sole St WGN WN1............................3 H2
Solway Cl AIMK WN4 ....60 D2
Somerset Av TYLD M29 ....39 G5
Somerset Rd ATH M46 ....38 C4
WGNW/BIL/O WN5 ....32 D2
Somerville Rd WGN WN1 ....22 B1
Sonning Dr BOLS/LL BL3................27 H3
Sougher's La AIMK WN4 ....47 G5
South Av LEIGH WN7......................65 H3
Southcourt LEIGH WN7 ....52 C5
Southdown Dr WALK M28 ....55 E5
Southern's Fold
WGNE/HIN WN2............................23 F2
Southern's La
RNFD/HAY WA11...........................43 F5
Southern St
WGNW/BIL/O WN5 ....33 E3
Southery Av WGNS/IIMK WN3.......33 E5
Southfield WGNE/HIN WN2 ....49 G1
Southfield Dr WHTN BL5 ....37 H1
South Gdns TYLD M29 * 66 D1
South Gv WALK M28 ....55 H1
South Hey LEIGH WN7 ....64 B1
Southlands Av
WGNNW/ST WN6...........................10 B2
South La TYLD M29 ....66 D1
Southover WHTN BL5 ....37 H2
South St ATH M46 ....53 F2
South Vw ATH M46 ....38 D5
Southward Rd
RNFD/HAY WA11...........................68 D2
Southway SKEL WN8 ....17 H4
Southwell Cl GOL/RIS/CU WA3 ......70 D1
Southworth La
WARRN/WOL WA2 ....77 E5
Southworth Rd NEWLW WA12 ....70 A5
Sovereign Cl GOL/RIS/CU WA3 ......71 F2
Sovereign Fold Rd LEIGH WN7 ....51 H2
Sovereign Rd WGN WN1...................2 E7
Spa Crs LHULT M38 ....41 F2
Spa Gv LHULT M38.........................41 F2
Spa La BRSC L40...........................16 A1
LHULT M38...................................41 F2
Spa Rd ATH M46............................38 D3
Sparta Av WALK M28......................55 H1
Spawell Cl GOL/RIS/CU WA3..........63 F5
Speakmana Dr
WGNNW/ST WN6.............................8 B4
Speakman Av LEIGH WN7 ....65 G1
NEWLW WA12...............................69 E4
Speedwell Cl GOL/RIS/CU WA3 ......71 F1
Spelding Dr WGNNW/ST WN6 ....21 E2
Spencer Rd WGN WN1 ....22 A2
Spencer Rd West
WGNNW/ST WN6...........................21 H2
Spencers La SKEL WN8 ....17 G5
WGNW/BIL/O WN5 ....31 G1
Spenlow LEIGH WN7 ....65 H3
Spey Cl WGNNW/ST WN6 ....10 A1
Spilsby Sq WGNS/IIMK WN3 ....47 H1
Spindle Hillock AIMK WN4 ....60 A2
Spindlepoint Dr WALK M28 ....55 H3
Spindle Wk WHTN BL5 ....26 A3
Spindlewood Rd
WGNS/IIMK WN3 ....34 D2
Spiningdale LHULT M38 ....40 C2
Spinnerette Cl LEIGH WN7 ....65 F1
The Spinney RNFD/HAY WA11 ....43 E4
WGNW/BIL/O WN5 ....33 F3
Spinning Jenny Wy
LEIGH WN7 ....65 E2
Spion Kop AIMK WN4 ....60 D3
Spiredale Brow
WGNNW/ST WN6...........................10 C1
Spires Gdns WARRN/WOL WA2 ......76 B5
Sportsman St LEIGH WN7..............64 C1
Springbourne
WGNNW/ST WN6...........................21 G3
Springburn Cl WALK M28 ....55 F5
Spring Fld RNFD/HAY WA11...........42 D1
Springfield Av GOL/RIS/CU WA3....70 A1
Springfield Rd ATH M46 ....39 F4
HOR/BR BL6.................................14 C2
WGNE/HIN WN2............................35 G2
WGNNW/ST WN6...........................21 G3
Springfield St WGN WN1 ....2 D1
Spring Gdns WGN WN1 ....2 B5
Spring Gv WGN WN1 ....3 F6
Springmount GOL/RIS/CU WA3 ......71 F2
Springpool WGNS/IIMK WN3 ....46 C1
Spring Rd WGNW/BIL/O WN5 ....20 A5
Spring St WGN WN1 ....3 F6
WGNS/IIMK WN3 ....34 D4
Spruce Cl GOL/RIS/CU WA3 ....71 G2
Spruce Rd WGNNW/ST WN6............21 F2
Squires La TYLD M29 ....53 F3
Stadium Wy
WGNW/BIL/O WN5 ....21 F4
Stafford Rd WALK M28 ....55 H2
Stafford St LEIGH WN7 ....66 A2
SKEL WN8.....................................16 C3
WGNE/HIN WN2............................35 H3
Stainburn Cl WGNNW/ST WN6..........8 C4
Stainer Cl NEWLW WA12.................69 E4
Stainforth Cl GOL/RIS/CU WA3 .....72 C5
Stairgate WGN WN1 ....2 D5
Stamford St ATH M46 ....39 F4
Stancliffe Gv WGNE/HIN WN2 ....12 D4
Standfield Dr WALK M28 ....55 F4
Standish Av WGNW/BIL/O WN5.......58 D1
Standish Dr RNFD/HAY WA11 ....43 F4
Standish Gallery WGN WN1 * 2 D4
Standishgate WGN WN1....................2 D4
Standish St TYLD M29 ....53 H3
Standish Wood La
WGNNW/ST WN6...........................10 B3
Stanedge Gv WGNS/IIMK WN3 ......48 A1
Stanhope St LEIGH WN7.................51 G5
Stanley Av RNFD/HAY WA11 ....42 D4
Stanley Cl WHTN BL5.....................38 B1
Stanley Dr LEIGH WN7 ....51 G3
Stanley Gv HOR/BR BL6 ....14 C1
Stanley La WGNE/HIN WN2 ....12 D3
Stanley Pl WGN WN1 ....3 G4
Stanley Rd SKEL WN8 ....30 D1
WGNE/HIN WN2............................12 D4
WGNE/HIN WN2............................35 F5
Stanley St ATH M46........................52 D1
WGNW/BIL/O WN5 ....33 G2
Stanley Wy SKEL WN8....................16 D2
Stanmoor Dr WGNE/HIN WN2........12 D5
Stannanought Rd SKEL WN8..........18 A2
Stansfield Cl LEIGH WN7................65 H4
Stanstead Cl WGNE/HIN WN2 ....23 E3
Stanton Cl WGNS/IIMK WN3...........34 A5
Stapleford Cl WHTN BL5.................39 H2
Staplehurst Cl WGNE/HIN WN2......51 F1
Stapleton St WGNE/HIN WN2 ....49 F1
Starling Dr FWTH BL4 ....41 E1
Startham Av
WGNW/BIL/O WN5 ....58 C3
Statham Rd SKEL WN8 ....16 C2
Station Av WGNE/HIN WN2 ....50 A2
WGNW/BIL/O WN5 ....31 G3
Station Ms AIMK WN4.....................60 A3
Station Rd AIMK WN4 ....59 H3
CHLY/EC PR7 ....7 E1
HOR/BR BL6.................................13 F1
WGN WN1.......................................2 D5
Staveley Rd SKEL WN8 ....16 D2
Stavesacre LEIGH WN7 ....65 E3
Stein Av GOL/RIS/CU WA3 ....71 F1
Stephenson St
WGNE/HIN WN2............................49 G3
Stephen St WGNE/HIN WN2............49 F1
Sterndale Av WGNNW/ST WN6 ....5 F5
Sterndale Rd WALK M28.................55 E5
Stetchworth Dr WALK M28 ....55 G4
Stevenson Cl WGNS/IIMK WN3 ....33 H3
Stevenson St WALK M28.................41 G5
Stewart Av FWTH BL4.....................41 G1
Stewart Rd WGNS/IIMK WN3..........33 H5
Stewerton Cl GOL/RIS/CU WA3 ......62 A4
Stirling Av WGNE/HIN WN2 ....23 F5
Stirling Cl LEIGH WN7 ....66 A1
Stirling Dr AIMK WN4 ....60 A2
Stirling Rd WGNE/HIN WN2 ....36 C4
Stirling St WGN WN1 ....22 A3
Stocksfield Dr LHULT M38 ....41 E3
Stockwell Cl WGNS/IIMK WN3 ....33 E5
Stoneacre HOR/BR BL6 ....15 E2
Stonebridge Cl HOR/BR BL6 ....15 H4
Stonechat Cl GOL/RIS/CU WA3 ......71 F1
WALK M28....................................55 G3
Stonecrop WGNNW/ST WN6 ....8 C1
Stone Cross La North
GOL/RIS/CU WA3..........................70 D2
Stone Cross La South
GOL/RIS/CU WA3..........................70 D3
Stonefield TYLD M29......................54 B2
Stonehaven BOLS/LL BL3...............27 G2
Stone Hvn WGNS/IIMK WN3...........47 E1
Stone Pit Cl GOL/RIS/CU WA3 ....63 F5
Stone Pit La GOL/RIS/CU WA3 ......77 G2
Stoney Brow SKEL WN8 ....19 E3
Stoney La CHLY/EC PR7 ....6 D3
Stonyhurst Av
WGNS/IIMK WN3 ....34 C2
Stonyhurst Crs
GOL/RIS/CU WA3..........................72 C4
Stopford St WGNE/HIN WN2 ....3 K6
Stopforth St WGNNW/ST WN6 ....21 H4
Stourbridge Av LHULT M38 ....41 F2
Stour Rd TYLD M29........................54 B4
Stout St LEIGH WN7 ....64 B2
Stowe Gdns LEIGH WN7 ....65 E1
Stradbroke Cl
GOL/RIS/CU WA3..........................71 H2
The Straits TYLD M29 ....54 B5
Strand Av AIMK WN4......................61 E2
The Strand AIMK WN4....................61 E2

Strange Rd AIMK WN4 60 A3
Strange St LEIGH WN7 64 A2
Stranraer Rd WGNW/BIL/O WN5 20 D4
Stratford St WGNNW/ST WN6 21 H4
Strathmore Av AIMK WN4 60 D1
Stratton Dr WGNE/HIN WN2 49 E2
Streetgate LHULT M38 41 F3
Stretton Av GOL/RIS/CU WA3 * 71 E2
WGNW/BIL/O WN5 58 D1
Stretton Cl WGNNW/ST WN6 10 B2
Strines Cl WGNE/HIN WN2 36 A2
Stringer St LEIGH WN7 65 E1
Stroud Cl WGNE/HIN WN2 23 E3
Stuart Av WGNE/HIN WN2 37 E5
Stuart Crs WGNW/BIL/O WN5 58 C1
Studley Ct TYLD M29 53 F3
Sturton Av WGNS/IIMK WN3 33 F5
Sudbrook Cl GOL/RIS/CU WA3 * 71 F1
Sudbury Cl WGNS/IIMK WN3 48 A1
Sudbury Dr HOR/BR BL6 15 H4
Suffolk Cl WGN WN1 11 E2
Suffolk Gv LEIGH WN7 64 B1
Sullivan Wy WGN WN1 3 F3
Summerfield Dr TYLD M29 54 A3
Summer St SKEL WN8 17 E1
Sumner St ATH M46 38 D5
WGNE/HIN WN2 13 E5
Sunderland Pl
WGNW/BIL/O WN5 21 E4
Sundridge Cl BOLS/LL BL3 27 H2
Sunleigh Rd WGNE/HIN WN2 36 B2
Sunningdale Gv LEIGH WN7 53 E4
Sunnybank Cl NEWLW WA12 69 F5
Sunnybank Rd TYLD M29 54 A5
Sunny Dr WGNW/BIL/O WN5 32 A2
Sunnyfields WGNS/IIMK WN3 46 D1
Sunny Garth WHTN BL5 25 H5
Sunnyside Rd AIMK WN4 47 G5
Surrey Av LEIGH WN7 66 B2
Sussex Cl WGN WN1 11 E1
WGNE/HIN WN2 36 D3
Sussex St LEIGH WN7 66 B2
Sutherland Rd
WGNS/IIMK WN3 33 H5
Sutherland St WGNE/HIN WN2 35 H3
WGNW/BIL/O WN5 33 G2
Sutton Av GOL/RIS/CU WA3 72 D5
Sutton Rd BOLS/LL BL3 27 G1
Swallowfield LEIGH WN7 65 F1
Swanfield Wk
GOL/RIS/CU WA3 62 A4
Swan La WGNE/HIN WN2 37 E4
Swan Meadow Rd
WGNS/IIMK WN3 2 A7
Swann St WGNS/IIMK WN3 2 A6
Swan Rd NEWLW WA12 68 B5
Swift St WGNW/BIL/O WN5 33 H1
Swinburn Gv
WGNW/BIL/O WN5 45 G2
Swinley La WGN WN1 22 B3
Swinley Rd WGN WN1 2 C1
Swinley St WGN WN1 2 D1
Swinside WGN WN1 3 K3
Sycamore Av GOL/RIS/CU WA3 62 B5
TYLD M29 54 C2
WGNE/HIN WN2 36 C5
WGNNW/ST WN6 21 G1
Sycamore Dr SKEL WN8 16 D3
WGNS/IIMK WN3 46 C1
Sycamore Rd ATH M46 39 F5
Syderstone Cl WGNE/HIN WN2 36 B4
Sydney Av LEIGH WN7 64 C4
Sydney St WGNE/HIN WN2 35 F5
Sykes Crs WGNS/IIMK WN3 46 D2
Syresham St WGNE/HIN WN2 49 G1

T

Taberner Cl WGNNW/ST WN6 10 C1
Taberner St WGNE/HIN WN2 49 G1
Tadmor Cl LHULT M38 41 E4
Talbot St AIMK WN4 * 61 G2
GOL/RIS/CU WA3 70 B1
Talman Gv AIMK WN4 61 G3
Tamer Gv LEIGH WN7 51 F3
The Tamneys SKEL WN8 17 E4
Tamworth Dr WGNE/HIN WN2 23 E3
Tanfields SKEL WN8 17 E4
Tanhouse Av TYLD M29 54 C4
Tan House Dr WGNS/IIMK WN3 46 D2
Tan House La WGNS/IIMK WN3 46 D1
Tanhouse Rd SKEL WN8 17 H5
Tanner's La GOL/RIS/CU WA3 70 C1
Tansley Sq WGNW/BIL/O WN5 33 E3
Tarleswood SKEL WN8 17 E4
Tarleton Av ATH M46 38 C3
Tarleton Pl BOLS/LL BL3 27 H2
Tarnbrook Dr WGNE/HIN WN2 12 C5
Tarn Cl AIMK WN4 61 E1
Tarnrigg Cl WGNS/IIMK WN3 33 F5
Tarnside Rd WGNW/BIL/O WN5 31 H2
Tarnway GOL/RIS/CU WA3 71 G2
Tarrant Cl WGNS/IIMK WN3 47 E1
Tarvin Cl GOL/RIS/CU WA3 71 F2
Tatham Gv WGNS/IIMK WN3 47 E2
Tatlock Cl WGNW/BIL/O WN5 58 D1
Tatton Dr AIMK WN4 60 C2
Taunton Av LEIGH WN7 51 G1
Tavistock Rd WGNE/HIN WN2 36 D4
Tavistock St ATH M46 38 C5
Tawd Rd SKEL WN8 17 H5
Taylor Gv WGNE/HIN WN2 37 F5
Taylor Rd RNFD/HAY WA11 68 C3
WGNE/HIN WN2 37 F5
Taylor's La WGNS/IIMK WN3 35 E5
Taylor St LEIGH WN7 51 G3
SKEL WN8 16 B4
WGNS/IIMK WN3 2 A5
Tayton Cl TYLD M29 54 B2
Taywood Rd BOLS/LL BL3 27 E3
Teal Cl WGNS/IIMK WN3 32 C4
Tebworth Dr WGNE/HIN WN2 36 B4
Teesdale Dr LEIGH WN7 65 H1
Telford Crs LEIGH WN7 51 G3
Telford St ATH M46 52 B2
Tellers Cl ATH M46 39 E5
Tempest Cha HOR/BR BL6 26 C1
Tempest Ct HOR/BR BL6 * 26 D1
Tempest Rd HOR/BR BL6 15 H5
Templegate Cl WGNNW/ST WN6 5 G5
Templeton Cl WHTN BL5 25 H5
Templeton Rd WGNE/HIN WN2 49 F2
Tenbury Dr AIMK WN4 60 C2
Tenement St WGNE/HIN WN2 49 G2
Tennyson Av LEIGH WN7 51 F3
Tennyson Dr WGN WN1 22 B2
WGNW/BIL/O WN5 45 G2
Tennyson Rd FWTH BL4 41 G2
Tensing Av ATH M46 38 D3
Tenter Dr WGNNW/ST WN6 11 E3
Tetbury Cl WGNW/BIL/O WN5 21 E4
Teversham SKEL WN8 17 E3
Tewkesbury SKEL WN8 * 16 D3
Tewkesbury Rd
GOL/RIS/CU WA3 70 C1
Thackeray Pl WGNS/IIMK WN3 33 H3
Thames Av LEIGH WN7 65 E5
Thames Dr WGNW/BIL/O WN5 32 A1
Thanet SKEL WN8 17 E3
Thanet Gv LEIGH WN7 65 F1
Thealby Cl SKEL WN8 16 D3
Thelwall Cl LEIGH WN7 64 A2
Thetford Cl WGNE/HIN WN2 36 B4
Thicknesse Av
WGNNW/ST WN6 21 G2
Thickwood Moss La
RNFD/HAY WA11 56 A1
Third Av TYLD M29 67 E2
WGNNW/ST WN6 21 H3
Thirlmere Av AIMK WN4 61 F2
SKEL WN8 31 E1
TYLD M29 53 H4
WGNE/HIN WN2 35 G1
WGNE/HIN WN2 49 G3
WGNNW/ST WN6 10 D3
WGNW/BIL/O WN5 32 A1
Thirlmere Dr LHULT M38 41 F3
Thirlmere Rd GOL/RIS/CU WA3 62 D5
HOR/BR BL6 7 H4
WGNE/HIN WN2 36 B3
WGNW/BIL/O WN5 32 C1
WHTN BL5 39 G1
Thirlmere St LEIGH WN7 64 D1
Thirsk SKEL WN8 16 D3
Thistledown Cl
WGNNW/ST WN6 21 H3
Thistleton Rd BOLS/LL BL3 27 G2
Thomas St ATH M46 39 E5
GOL/RIS/CU WA3 70 B1
WGNE/HIN WN2 37 E5
WHTN BL5 * 25 H2
Thompson St AIMK WN4 61 G2
LEIGH WN7 64 A1
WGN WN1 3 G2
Thorburn Rd
WGNW/BIL/O WN5 32 D2
Thoresby Cl WGNS/IIMK WN3 33 F5
Thornbury SKEL WN8 17 E3
Thornbury Av GOL/RIS/CU WA3 71 F2
Thornbush Cl GOL/RIS/CU WA3 63 F5
Thorneycroft LEIGH WN7 65 H1
Thorneyholme Cl HOR/BR BL6 15 H4
Thornfield Cl GOL/RIS/CU WA3 70 D1
Thornfield Crs LHULT M38 41 E3
Thornfield Gv LHULT M38 41 E3
Thornhill Rd AIMK WN4 59 H2
Thorn Lea ATH M46 53 F1
Thorn St WGNE/HIN WN2 36 A4
Thornton Cl AIMK WN4 60 C2
FWTH BL4 41 G1
LEIGH WN7 65 E5
WALK M28 54 D4
Thornton Rd WALK M28 54 D4
Thornvale WGNE/HIN WN2 49 H4
Thornway WALK M28 55 F4
Thorn Well WHTN BL5 37 H1
Thornwood SKEL WN8 17 E3
Thorpe SKEL WN8 17 E3
Three Sisters Rd AIMK WN4 48 A5
Throstle Nest Av
WGNNW/ST WN6 21 H4
Thurcroft Dr SKEL WN8 16 D3
Thurlby Cl AIMK WN4 61 G2
Thurlow GOL/RIS/CU WA3 71 F2
Thursford Gv HOR/BR BL6 13 E1
Thurston SKEL WN8 16 D3
Thurston Av WGNS/IIMK WN3 34 A5
Tideswell Av
WGNW/BIL/O WN5 20 B4
Tilbury Gv WGNNW/ST WN6 8 C3
Tilcroft SKEL WN8 16 D3
Timperley La LEIGH WN7 65 G4
Tinkersfield LEIGH WN7 51 G4
Tintagel SKEL WN8 16 C3
Tintagel Rd WGNE/HIN WN2 36 D4
Tintern Av AIMK WN4 61 G3
TYLD M29 54 B4
Tinwald Pl WGN WN1 3 J3
Tipping St WGNS/IIMK WN3 34 A2
Tithebarn Rd AIMK WN4 59 H4
Tithebarn St SKEL WN8 * 31 E1
Tithe Barn St WHTN BL5 25 H4
Tiverton Av LEIGH WN7 51 G1
SKEL WN8 16 D3
Tiverton Cl TYLD M29 54 B4
Toddington La
WGNE/HIN WN2 12 C2
Tollgreen Cl WGNE/HIN WN2 36 A4
Toll St WGNE/HIN WN2 49 F2
Tongbarn SKEL WN8 16 D3
Tontine Rd SKEL WN8 31 F2
Toothill Cl AIMK WN4 61 E1
Top Acre Rd SKEL WN8 29 H1
Torquay Dr WGNW/BIL/O WN5 45 H3
Torridon Cl WGNNW/ST WN6 10 D3
Torside Cl WGNE/HIN WN2 36 A2
Torver Cl WGNS/IIMK WN3 47 H1
Toulston Rd WGNNW/ST WN6 21 G3
Tower Gv LEIGH WN7 53 E5
Tower Hill Rd SKEL WN8 30 D3
Tower Nook SKEL WN8 30 D3
Towers Av BOLS/LL BL3 27 H1
Townfield Av AIMK WN4 61 E4
Townfields AIMK WN4 60 D3
Townsfield Rd WHTN BL5 37 H1
Townson Dr LEIGH WN7 65 E5
Tracks La WGNW/BIL/O WN5 31 G5
Trafalgar Rd WGN WN1 2 C2
WGNE/HIN WN2 36 A3
Trafford Dr LHULT M38 41 G3
Trafford Rd WGNE/HIN WN2 35 H3
Tram St WGNE/HIN WN2 49 F2
Travers St HOR/BR BL6 14 C1
Trecastell Cl WGN WN1 3 J3
Treen Rd TYLD M29 54 B3
Tregaron Gv WGNE/HIN WN2 36 D5
Trencherfield Ml
WGNS/IIMK WN3 * 2 B7
Trent Dr WALK M28 55 G1
WGNE/HIN WN2 37 F5
Trent Gv LEIGH WN7 64 B2
Trent Rd AIMK WN4 61 H1
WGNW/BIL/O WN5 32 D1
WGNW/BIL/O WN5 58 B2
Trescott Ms WGNNW/ST WN6 10 B2
Trevelyan Dr
WGNW/BIL/O WN5 45 G2
Trinity Gdns AIMK WN4 60 C2
Troon Cl BOLS/LL BL3 27 G2
Troutbeck Av NEWLW WA12 68 B5
Troutbeck Dr TYLD M29 53 H4
Troutbeck Gv RNFD/HAY WA11 58 A4
Troutbeck Ri
WGNW/BIL/O WN5 32 C2
Troutbeck Rd AIMK WN4 61 F1
Truro Rd TYLD M29 54 B3
Tucker's Hill Brow
WGNE/HIN WN2 12 C1
Tudor Av FWTH BL4 41 G1
Tudor Cl RNFD/HAY WA11 42 D3
Tudor Gv WGNS/IIMK WN3 47 F1
Tulip Dr WGNNW/ST WN6 21 G2
Tulip Rd RNFD/HAY WA11 68 C3
Tunstall La WGNW/BIL/O WN5 33 E3
Turnberry BOLS/LL BL3 27 G2
SKEL WN8 16 C3
Turnberry Cl TYLD M29 54 B3
Turncroft Wy WALK M28 55 E4
Turnditch Cl WGNNW/ST WN6 21 H1
Turner Av WGNE/HIN WN2 50 B2
Turner St LEIGH WN7 65 F2
WGN WN1 2 E4
WGNE/HIN WN2 36 A2
WHTN BL5 37 H3
Turners Yd
WGNW/BIL/O WN5 * 31 H2
Turnill Dr AIMK WN4 61 E4
Turnstone Av NEWLW WA12 69 F5
Turnstone Cl LEIGH WN7 52 B5
Turret Hall Dr GOL/RIS/CU WA3 71 F1
Turriff Gv WGNE/HIN WN2 23 F4
Turton St GOL/RIS/CU WA3 70 B1
Tweed St LEIGH WN7 65 G2
Twelve Yards Rd IRL M44 75 F5
Twiss Green Dr
GOL/RIS/CU WA3 72 D5
Twiss Green La
GOL/RIS/CU WA3 72 C5
Twist Av GOL/RIS/CU WA3 70 D1
Twist La LEIGH WN7 64 D2
Tybyrne Cl WALK M28 55 E4
Tyldesley Ar WGN WN1 * 2 D4
Tyldesley Old Rd ATH M46 53 E1
Tyldesley Pas ATH M46 53 G2
Tyldesley Rd ATH M46 53 E1
Tyne Ct WALK M28 41 H5
Tynesbank WALK M28 55 H1
Tyrer Av WGNS/IIMK WN3 33 G3

U

Ullswater Av WGNW/BIL/O WN5 32 A1
Ullswater Dr FWTH BL4 40 D1
WGNE/HIN WN2 35 G1
Ullswater Rd GOL/RIS/CU WA3 62 D5
TYLD M29 53 H4
Ullswater St LEIGH WN7 64 D1
Ulverston Rd WGNS/IIMK WN3 33 G5
Umberton Rd WHTN BL5 39 G1
Union St LEIGH WN7 65 E1
TYLD M29 53 G2
WGNE/HIN WN2 23 F5
Unsworth Av
GOL/RIS/CU WA3 63 E5
TYLD M29 54 A3
Unsworth St LEIGH WN7 51 H4
Upholland Rd
WGNW/BIL/O WN5 31 G5
Upland Dr AIMK WN4 61 G2
LHULT M38 41 E2
Upper Dicconson St WGN WN1 2 D3
Upper George St TYLD M29 53 H3
Upper Lees Dr WHTN BL5 26 B4
Upper St Stephen St
WGNNW/ST WN6 2 A4
Uppingham SKEL WN8 16 C4
Upton Cl GOL/RIS/CU WA3 71 E1
Upton La TYLD M29 54 B3
Upton Rd ATH M46 39 F4
Upwood Rd GOL/RIS/CU WA3 71 E2
Urmston Av NEWLW WA12 69 E4
Urmston St LEIGH WN7 64 C1

V

Vale Cl WGNNW/ST WN6 8 D2
Vale Cft SKEL WN8 30 D2
Valentines Rd ATH M46 52 B2
The Vale WGNNW/ST WN6 8 C2
Valiant Rd WGNW/BIL/O WN5 21 E5
Valley Rd WGNW/BIL/O WN5 33 E3
The Valley ATH M46 39 F5
Vanbrugh Gv
WGNW/BIL/O WN5 20 C4
Varley Rd BOLS/LL BL3 27 H1
Vauxhall Rd WGN WN1 3 F5
Vauze Av HOR/BR BL6 13 E1
Verda St WGNE/HIN WN2 49 F3
Vernon St LEIGH WN7 65 E1
Vicarage Cl WGNE/HIN WN2 49 F1
Vicarage La WGNNW/ST WN6 9 F5
Vicarage Rd AIMK WN4 61 E4
WALK M28 41 H4
WGNE/HIN WN2 49 G2
WGNW/BIL/O WN5 31 G4
Vicarage Rd West HOR/BR BL6 7 H5
Vicarage Sq LEIGH WN7 * 65 E1
Vicars Hall La WALK M28 67 H2
Victor Cl WGNW/BIL/O WN5 21 E5
Victoria Av WGNE/HIN WN2 50 B2
WGNNW/ST WN6 21 H4
Victoria Cl WALK M28 * 55 F5
WGNE/HIN WN2 12 C4
Victoria Crs WGNNW/ST WN6 10 B2
Victoria Pk SKEL WN8 16 B4
Victoria Rd AIMK WN4 60 A2
NEWLW WA12 69 F5
WGNE/HIN WN2 49 F2
Victoria St LEIGH WN7 51 H5
RNFD/HAY WA11 43 E4
WALK M28 55 F5
WGNE/HIN WN2 49 F1
WGNW/BIL/O WN5 33 F2
WHTN BL5 26 A5
Victoria Ter WGNE/HIN WN2 50 C3
Victoria Wy LEIGH WN7 51 H4
Vigo St WGNE/HIN WN2 23 E3
Villa Av WGNNW/ST WN6 21 H1
Village Cl SKEL WN8 16 C5
Village Vw WGNW/BIL/O WN5 58 D1
Village Wy SKEL WN8 16 C5
Vincent Wy WGNW/BIL/O WN5 21 E5
Vine Gv WGNS/IIMK WN3 2 C6
Vine St WGN WN1 3 F2
WGNE/HIN WN2 36 A2
Viola Cl WGNNW/ST WN6 5 E5
Violet St AIMK WN4 61 E4
WGNS/IIMK WN3 34 D2
Virginia Wy WGNW/BIL/O WN5 20 D5
Viscount Rd
WGNW/BIL/O WN5 21 E5
Vista Av NEWLW WA12 68 D5
Vista Rd NEWLW WA12 68 D5
Vista Wy NEWLW WA12 68 D5
Vulcan Dr WGN WN1 3 F6
Vulcan Rd WGNW/BIL/O WN5 21 E5

W

Waddington Cl
GOL/RIS/CU WA3 * 71 G1
Wade Bank WHTN BL5 26 A5
Wadsworth Dr
WGNNW/ST WN6 21 G3
Wainfleet Cl WGNS/IIMK WN3 33 F5
Wainscot Cl TYLD M29 54 A4
Wakefield Crs
WGNNW/ST WN6 10 D3
Wakefield St GOL/RIS/CU WA3 70 B2
Walcot Pl WGNS/IIMK WN3 47 H1
Waldon Cl WGNE/HIN WN2 36 C4
Waldorf Cl WGNS/IIMK WN3 47 E1
Walford Rd AIMK WN4 61 F3
Walkden Av WGN WN1 22 A3
Walkden Av East WGN WN1 2 C1
Walkdene Dr WALK M28 41 G5
Walkdens Av ATH M46 52 B1
Walkers Dr LEIGH WN7 65 F1
Walker St WHTN BL5 25 H5
The Walk ATH M46 39 E5
Wallace La WGN WN1 3 G2
Wallbrook Av
WGNW/BIL/O WN5 45 G2
Wallbrook Crs LHULT M38 41 F2
Wallcroft St SKEL WN8 16 D5
Wallgarth Cl WGNS/IIMK WN3 47 E1
Wallgate WGNS/IIMK WN3 2 B6
Walls St WGNE/HIN WN2 51 F1
Wall St WGNNW/ST WN6 21 G4
Wallwork Rd TYLD M29 54 C5
Walmer Rd WGNE/HIN WN2 36 D3
Walmesley Av
WGNS/IIMK WN3 34 B2
Walmesley Dr
RNFD/HAY WA11 56 B1
WGNE/HIN WN2 35 G1
Walmesley Rd LEIGH WN7 64 D1
Walmesley St WGN WN1 2 E6
Walmsley St NEWLW WA12 69 G5
Walney Rd WGNS/IIMK WN3 47 E1
Walnut Av WGN WN1 3 F1
Walnut Gv LEIGH WN7 52 A3
Walpole Av WGNS/IIMK WN3 33 G5
Walsh Cl NEWLW WA12 69 F4
Walter Scott Av WGN WN1 22 A1
Walters Green Crs
GOL/RIS/CU WA3 62 B4
Walter St AIMK WN4 * 61 G2
LEIGH WN7 64 A1
WGNW/BIL/O WN5 33 E2
Waltham Av GOL/RIS/CU WA3 73 H2
WGNNW/ST WN6 21 G2
Walthew House La
WGNW/BIL/O WN5 20 C4
Walthew La WGNE/HIN WN2 35 F5
WGNW/BIL/O WN5 21 E3
Walton St ATH M46 * 39 F4
CHLY/EC PR7 7 F1
Wanborough Cl LEIGH WN7 52 A4
Warbeck Cl WGNE/HIN WN2 36 B5
Warburton Pl ATH M46 39 E5
Wardend Cl LHULT M38 * 41 F2
Wardens Bank WHTN BL5 37 H3
Wardley Av WALK M28 55 G1
Wardley Rd TYLD M29 54 C3
Wardley Sq TYLD M29 54 C3
Wardley St WGNW/BIL/O WN5 32 C3
Wardlow Av
WGNW/BIL/O WN5 20 B5
Wardour St ATH M46 52 D1
Ward St WGNE/HIN WN2 36 A1
Wareing St TYLD M29 53 G3
Warlow Dr LEIGH WN7 51 G2
Warminster Gv
WGNS/IIMK WN3 47 E1
Warncliffe St
WGNW/BIL/O WN5 33 E3
Warnford St WGN WN1 22 B3
Warren Cl ATH M46 39 F4
Warren Dr NEWLW WA12 70 A5
Warrington La WGN WN1 2 E5
Warrington Rd AIMK WN4 61 E4
GOL/RIS/CU WA3 76 C1
LEIGH WN7 65 G4
NEWLW WA12 70 B3
WGNE/HIN WN2 49 F1
WGNS/IIMK WN3 33 G4
WGNS/IIMK WN3 34 D3
WGNS/IIMK WN3 47 G1
Warwick Av AIMK WN4 61 G4
Warwick Dr WGNE/HIN WN2 36 C2
Warwick Rd ATH M46 38 D3
TYLD M29 53 H1
WALK M28 55 H2
WGNE/HIN WN2 * 12 D5
Warwick St CHLY/EC PR7 7 E1
LEIGH WN7 66 A3
Wasdale Rd AIMK WN4 47 H3
Washacre WHTN BL5 38 A1
Washacre Cl WHTN BL5 38 A1
Washbrook Av WALK M28 55 G2
Washburn Cl WHTN BL5 25 H3
Wash La LEIGH WN7 65 H1
Washwood Cl LHULT M38 * 41 G2
Waterbeck Cl WGN WN1 3 J3
Water Dr WGNNW/ST WN6 11 E3
Watergate Dr WHTN BL5 40 B1
Watergate La WHTN BL5 40 B1
Waterhouse Nook CHLY/EC PR7 7 F2
Waterloo St WGNNW/ST WN6 21 H4
Watermede
WGNW/BIL/O WN5 31 H5
Waterside Dr WGNS/IIMK WN3 34 A2
Water's Nook Rd WHTN BL5 26 B5
Waters Reach WGN WN1 3 J5
Water St ATH M46 39 E5
CHLY/EC PR7 7 F1
NEWLW WA12 69 F5
WGN WN1 2 D4
Waterview Pk LEIGH WN7 64 D2
Waterworks Dr NEWLW WA12 70 A5
Waterworks La
WARRN/WOL WA2 76 C5
Watkin St WGN WN1 2 D4
Watson Av AIMK WN4 61 F3
GOL/RIS/CU WA3 62 A5
Waverley SKEL WN8 16 C4
Waverley Ct WGNS/IIMK WN3 33 E5
Waverley Gv LEIGH WN7 * 53 E5
Waverley Rd GOL/RIS/CU WA3 63 E5
WALK M28 55 G2
WGNE/HIN WN2 35 H3
Wavertree Av ATH M46 38 C4
Wayfarer Dr TYLD M29 53 H3
Wayfaring WHTN BL5 26 A3
Wearhead Cl GOL/RIS/CU WA3 70 B2
Wearish La WHTN BL5 37 F2
Weaste Av LHULT M38 41 G4
Weaver Av WALK M28 55 F1
Weaver Gv LEIGH WN7 64 B2
Webster's St WGNE/HIN WN2 49 F1
Wedgewood Dr
WGNNW/ST WN6 21 E2
Weedon Av NEWLW WA12 69 E4
Welbeck Rd AIMK WN4 61 E1
WGNS/IIMK WN3 33 F5
Welch Hill St LEIGH WN7 64 D2
Weldon Av BOLS/LL BL3 27 H3
Weldon Gv WGN WN1 3 G1
Welford Av GOL/RIS/CU WA3 70 D2
Welland Rd AIMK WN4 61 H1
Wellbrooke Cl AIMK WN4 61 F3
Wellcross Rd SKEL WN8 31 E2
Wellesley Cl NEWLW WA12 69 E4
WGNW/BIL/O WN5 21 F5
Wellfield RNFD/HAY WA11 56 B2
Wellfield Rd GOL/RIS/CU WA3 72 D5
WGNE/HIN WN2 36 D4
WGNNW/ST WN6 21 G1
Wellham Rd WGNS/IIMK WN3 34 A5
Wellington Cl SKEL WN8 18 B5
Wellington Dr TYLD M29 54 D2
Wellington Gv
WGNS/IIMK WN3 34 C3
Wellington Rd ATH M46 39 G3
Wellington St WGN WN1 3 F5
WHTN BL5 25 H3
Wells Av WGNW/BIL/O WN5 58 C1
Wells Cl TYLD M29 54 A3
Wells Dr WGNE/HIN WN2 3 J1
Wells Pl WGN WN1 3 H4
Wellstock La LHULT M38 41 E2
Well St TYLD M29 53 H3
Welton Cl LEIGH WN7 65 H1
Wendlebury Cl LEIGH WN7 64 D5
Wenlock Gv WGNE/HIN WN2 36 A4
Wenlock Rd LEIGH WN7 64 D4
WGNE/HIN WN2 36 A3
Wenlock St WGNE/HIN WN2 * 36 A4
Wensleydale Rd LEIGH WN7 65 H1
Wensley Rd GOL/RIS/CU WA3 71 F2
Wentworth Av FWTH BL4 41 H1
Wentworth Rd AIMK WN4 60 C2

Wescoe Cl WGNW/BIL/O WN5 .....31 H3
Wesley Av RNFD/HAY WA11.....68 B2
Wesley Cl WHTN BL5.....25 H5
Wesley St ATH M46 *.....35 H5
  WGNW/BIL/O WN5 .....33 E4
  WHTN BL5.....25 H5
Wessex Cl WGN WN1.....11 E1
Wessex Rd WGNW/BIL/O WN5.....21 E4
West Av GOL/RIS/CU WA3.....62 C5
  LEIGH WN7.....65 H3
  WALK M28.....41 F5
West Bank St ATH M46.....53 F2
Westbourne Av LEIGH WN7.....51 H4
Westbridge Ms WGN WN1.....2 D6
West Bridgewater St
  LEIGH WN7.....65 E2
Westbury Av WGNS/IIMK WN3 ..47 E1
Westbury Cl WHTN BL5.....26 B4
Westbury St ATH M46.....53 F2
Westcott Dr WGNS/IIMK WN3 ..32 D4
Westcroft WGNE/HIN WN2.....49 G1
Westerdale Cl TYLD M29.....54 A3
Westfield Av AIMK WN4.....60 D2
Westfield Gv WGN WN1.....22 A2
Westgate SKEL WN8.....16 C5
Westgate Dr TYLD M29.....54 B5
  WGNW/BIL/O WN5.....33 G3
West Gv WGN WN1.....22 A2
Westhead Av GOL/RIS/CU WA3..71 F1
Westinghouse Cl
  WGNS/IIMK WN3.....21 H5
Westlake Gv WGNE/HIN WN2 ..37 E4
Westland Av FWTH BL4.....41 H2
Westleigh La LEIGH WN7.....51 G1
Westlock WGNS/IIMK WN3.....34 A2
Westmead WGNNW/ST WN6.....10 B2
Westmeade Rd WALK M28.....41 H3
Westminster Dr LEIGH WN7.....53 F5
  RNFD/HAY WA11.....43 F2
Westminster St
  WGNW/BIL/O WN5 *.....33 G2
Westmoorland St WGN WN1.....3 G3
Westmorland Rd TYLD M29.....55 H1
West Mt WGN WN1.....3 F1
  WGNW/BIL/O WN5.....32 C2
Westonby Ct AIMK WN4.....61 G3
Weston Pk WGNNW/ST WN6 ..21 E3
Weston St ATH M46.....39 F4
Westrees LEIGH WN7.....52 B4
West St WGNE/HIN WN2.....23 F5
  WGNE/HIN WN1.....37 E5
  WGNNW/ST WN6.....2 A3
West Vw RNFD/HAY WA11 *.....43 E5
West Wy LHULT M38.....41 F3
Westwell Gv LEIGH WN7.....51 H3
Westwell St LEIGH WN7.....51 H3
Westwood Av WALK M28.....55 F1
Westwood La WGNS/IIMK WN3..34 C3
Westwood Pk
  WGNS/IIMK WN3.....34 B2
Westwood Rd
  WGNS/IIMK WN3.....34 B2
Westwood Ter
  WGNS/IIMK WN3 *.....34 D3
Wetheral Cl WGNE/HIN WN2 ..37 F5
Wetherby Cl NEWLW WA12 .....69 F4
Wexham Gdns
  WGNS/IIMK WN3.....35 F5
Weybourne Dr
  WGNS/IIMK WN3.....35 F5
Weymouth Dr WGNE/HIN WN2..36 D4
Whalley Av GOL/RIS/CU WA3...73 H2
  RNFD/HAY WA11.....43 E5
Whalley Cl WGNS/IIMK WN3 ...33 H5
Whalley Gv LEIGH WN7.....51 G2
Whalleys Rd SKEL WN8.....17 G1
Wharfedale WHTN BL5.....26 A3
Wharmby Rd RNFD/HAY WA11 ..68 B3
Wharncliffe St
  WGNE/HIN WN2 *.....36 A3
Wharton Hall Cl TYLD M29.....54 A2
Wharton La LHULT M38.....40 D3
Wheatacre AIMK WN4.....16 D5
Wheatlea Rd WGNS/IIMK WN3 ..45 E5
Wheatley Av NEWLW WA12 .....69 F4
Wheatsheaf Wk
  WGNNW/ST WN6.....10 A1
Whelley WGN WN1.....23 E3
  WGNE/HIN WN1.....23 E3
Whimbrel Rd TYLD M29.....54 B4
Whinchat Av NEWLW WA12 .....69 F5
Whinchat Cl WGNE/HIN WN2..23 H1
Whinfield Cl WGNNW/ST WN6..21 H5
Whins Crest HOR/BR BL6.....15 H3
Whinslee Dr HOR/BR BL6.....15 H3
Whistlecroft Ct
  WGNS/IIMK WN3.....35 E2
Whistley St WGNE/HIN WN2 ...35 G5
Whitbeam Gv WGNE/HIN WN2..50 B1
Whitburn Cl AIMK WN4.....60 A2
  BOLS/LL BL3.....27 F1

Whiteacre WGNNW/ST WN6 .....4 B5
Whitebeam Wk WHTN BL5.....26 A3
Whitecroft Av
  GOL/RIS/CU WA3.....63 F5
Whitecroft Rd
  WGNS/IIMK WN3.....47 H1
Whitegate BOLS/LL BL3.....28 D3
Whitehall Av WGNNW/ST WN6 ..8 D2
Whitehall St WGNS/IIMK WN3 *..32 D1
Whitehey Rd SKEL WN8.....16 D5
White Horse Gv WHTN BL5.....26 B3
White Lady Cl WALK M28.....41 E5
Whiteledge Rd SKEL WN8.....17 G5
White Lodge Dr AIMK WN4.....61 G2
White Moss Rd SKEL WN8.....28 B1
White Moss Rd South
  SKEL WN8.....28 C1
Whiteside Av WGNE/HIN WN2..36 A1
  WGNNW/ST WN6.....21 H4
Whitestock SKEL WN8.....16 D5
White St LEIGH WN7.....65 H2
  WGNW/BIL/O WN5.....32 C2
Whitewood Cl AIMK WN4.....47 H5
Whitfield St LEIGH WN7.....65 H2
Whitledge Gn AIMK WN4.....61 F3
Whitledge Rd AIMK WN4.....60 D1
Whitley Crs WGN WN1.....22 A1
  WGN WN1.....49 C4
Whitley Rd SKEL WN8.....19 F2
Whitlow Av GOL/RIS/CU WA3..62 A5
Whitsbury Av WGNE/HIN WN2..36 A4
Whitstone Dr SKEL WN8.....30 A1
Whitsundale WHTN BL5.....26 A3
Whitt St WGNS/IIMK WN3.....47 F1
Whitwell Cl WGNNW/ST WN6......5 H5
Wichbrook Rd WALK M28.....41 E5
Wicheaves Crs WALK M28.....41 E5
The Wicherlies LHULT M38.....41 E5
Widdow's St LEIGH WN7.....65 G2
Widdrington Rd WGN WN1.....2 E1
Wiend WGN WN1.....2 D5
Wigan Gallery WGN WN1 *.....2 D4
Wigan La WGN WN1.....2 D2
  WGN WN1.....11 E5
Wigan Lower Rd
  WGNNW/ST WN6.....20 D1
Wigan Pier WGNS/IIMK WN3 *....2 A7
Wigan Rd AIMK WN4.....47 C4
  AIMK WN4.....52 A1
  BOLS/LL BL3.....27 F2
  GOL/RIS/CU WA3.....62 C1
  LEIGH WN7.....51 F4
  SKEL WN8.....17 E5
  WGNE/HIN WN2.....23 F2
  WGNNW/ST WN6.....9 H5
  WGNW/BIL/O WN5.....46 A4
  WHTN BL5.....36 D1
Wigan Sq WGN WN1 *.....2 C4
Wigan Upper Rd LEIGH WN7..49 F1
Wightman Av NEWLW WA12 ...69 F4
Wigshaw Cl LEIGH WN7.....65 E5
Wilbraham St LEIGH WN7.....64 B1
  WHTN BL5.....35 H5
Wilcock Rd RNFD/HAY WA11...68 D1
Wilcock St WGNS/IIMK WN3.....33 H1
Wilcove SKEL WN8.....17 E4
Wild Arum Cl GOL/RIS/CU WA3..71 F1
Wildbrook Cl LHULT M38.....40 D5
Wildbrook Gv LHULT M38.....40 D5
Wildbrook Rd LHULT M38.....40 D4
Wildings Old La
  GOL/RIS/CU WA3.....77 H4
Wilding St WGNS/IIMK WN3....34 D3
Wilds Pas LEIGH WN7.....65 E2
Wilfred St WGNW/BIL/O WN5..33 G1
Wilfrid's Pl WGNNW/ST WN6..10 B1
Wilkesley Av WGNNW/ST WN6..10 A2
Wilkinson St LEIGH WN7.....64 D1
Willard Av WGNW/BIL/O WN5..31 G5
Williams Av NEWLW WA12 .....69 F4
William St LEIGH WN7 .....64 B1
  WGNE/HIN WN2.....36 B3
  WGNS/IIMK WN3.....34 C2
Willow Av NEWLW WA12 .....69 G5
  TYLD M29.....53 H5
Willow Bank Est NEWLW WA12..76 A1
Willowbrook Dr
  WGNNW/ST WN6.....9 G3
Willow Crs LEIGH WN7.....51 H3
Willowcroft Av
  WGNE/HIN WN2.....24 C2
Willow Dr SKEL WN8.....16 C4
  WGNE/HIN WN2.....36 C5
Willowfield Gv AIMK WN4.....60 D4
Willow Gv AIMK WN4.....61 H1
  GOL/RIS/CU WA3.....62 B5
Willow Hey SKEL WN8.....17 E4
Willow Ldg WGNE/HIN WN2..49 G2
Willow Rd NEWLW WA12 .....69 G5
  RNFD/HAY WA11.....68 B2
  WGNNW/ST WN6.....21 G1

Willow St ATH M46.....38 D4
Willow Tree Cl WGN WN1.....22 A1
Willow Wk SKEL WN8.....17 C1
Wilmot Dr GOL/RIS/CU WA3....70 A2
Wilsford Cl GOL/RIS/CU WA3..62 C5
Wilshaw Av WGNW/BIL/O WN5..31 H5
Wilson Av WGN WN1.....22 A3
Wilson Fold Av HOR/BR BL6...15 E1
Wilson St LEIGH WN7.....23 E3
Wilton La GOL/RIS/CU WA3....71 H4
Wilton Rd WGNNW/ST WN6......9 F4
Wilton St AIMK WN4.....47 G5
  WGN WN1.....2 E7
Wiltshire Pl WGNW/BIL/O WN5..32 D2
Wimberry Hill Rd WHTN BL5..25 C2
Wimborne Cl HOR/BR BL6.....15 E1
Wimborne Rd
  WGNE/HIN WN2.....20 B5
Winchcombe Cl LEIGH WN7....64 C3
Winchester Av AIMK WN4.....60 D5
  WGN WN1.....54 B4
Winchester Cl
  WGNW/BIL/O WN5.....32 A1
Winchester Gv
  WGNS/IIMK WN3.....34 C2
Winchester Rd
  RNFD/HAY WA11.....60 B5
  WGNS/IIMK WN3.....45 G2
Windale WALK M28.....41 G5
Windermere Av ATH M46.....39 E3
Windermere Dr
  RNFD/HAY WA11.....43 E1
  WGNE/HIN WN2.....64 D1
  WGNE/HIN WN2.....40 D1
  LEIGH WN7.....35 F1
  WGNE/HIN WN2.....36 B3
  WGNE/HIN WN2.....49 C3
  WGNW/BIL/O WN5.....20 A5
Windermere St WGN WN1.....3 C5
Windlehurst Dr WALK M28.....55 C4
Windleshaw St
  WGNS/IIMK WN3.....34 D2
Windmill Cl WALK M28.....41 H5
  WGN WN1.....3 H4
Windmill Hts SKEL WN8.....18 D5
Windmill La TYLD M29.....66 C2
Windmill Rd WALK M28.....41 H3
Windrows SKEL WN8.....17 E4
Windrush Dr WHTN BL5.....26 A4
Windsor Av CHLY/EC PR7.....6 D1
  LHULT M38.....41 G3
  TYLD M29.....53 G5
Windsor Crs WGNE/HIN WN2..13 E5
Windsor Dr RNFD/HAY WA11..68 D2
Windsor Gv WGNE/HIN WN2..37 E5
Windsor Rd AIMK WN4.....61 E4
  GOL/RIS/CU WA3.....70 D1
  LEIGH WN7.....53 F5
  SKEL WN8.....17 E4
  WGNW/BIL/O WN5.....59 E1
Windsor St ATH M46.....53 F1
  WGN WN1.....3 F3
Windy Bank Av
  GOL/RIS/CU WA3.....71 F1
Windyhill Dr BOLS/LL BL3.....27 H2
Winfield Cl WGNNW/ST WN6..21 H5
Wingate Rd LHULT M38.....41 C4
Wingates Gv WHTN BL5.....25 C2
Wingates La WHTN BL5.....25 H1
Wingates Rd WHTN BL5.....25 H1
Wingates Sq WHTN BL5.....25 H2
Wingfield Cl WGNNW/ST WN6..21 H1
Winifred St WGNS/IIMK WN3..34 D2
Winmarleigh Gdns LEIGH WN7..64 D5
Winscar Rd WGNE/HIN WN2 ..36 A2
Winsford Cl RNFD/HAY WA11..68 C2
Winslow Rd BOLS/LL BL3.....36 B5
Winsmoor Dr AIMK WN4.....60 B4
Winstanley Pl WGNS/IIMK WN3..34 D2
Winstanley Rd AIMK WN4.....46 C4
  SKEL WN8.....17 E5
  WGNS/IIMK WN3.....46 D1
  WGNS/IIMK WN3.....58 A2
Winstanley St
  WGNS/IIMK WN3.....33 G2
Winster Dr WGNE/HIN WN2 ..49 E1
The Winsters SKEL WN8.....17 E4
Winterfield Dr BOLS/LL BL3...27 H2
Winterton Cl WHTN BL5.....26 B4
Winton Av WGNW/BIL/O WN5..33 E3
Winton Gn HOR/BR BL6.....15 E2
Winton Rd GOL/RIS/CU WA3..71 F4
Winward St BOLS/LL BL3 *.....27 H1
  WHTN BL5.....25 H4
Winwick La GOL/RIS/CU WA3..77 E2
Winwick Rd NEWLW WA12.....76 A3

Wirral Dr WGNS/IIMK WN3.....46 D1
Witham Cl WGNNW/ST WN6..10 A1
Witham Rd SKEL WN8.....16 C4
Withington Av
  GOL/RIS/CU WA3.....73 F5
Withington Dr TYLD M29.....54 B4
Withington Gra
  WGNE/HIN WN2.....23 G3
Withington La WGNE/HIN WN2..23 G3
Withins Rd RNFD/HAY WA11 ..68 B1
Withnell Cl WGNE/HIN WN2 ..21 C4
Witton Wy RNFD/HAY WA11 ..43 F4
Woburn Av LEIGH WN7.....51 F4
Woburn Cl RNFD/HAY WA11 ..68 C2
Wolford Dr TYLD M29.....54 B2
Wolfson Sq AIMK WN4.....60 D3
Wolmer St AIMK WN4.....60 D2
Wolsey Cl AIMK WN4.....60 D1
Wolver Cl LHULT M38 *.....41 G2
Wolverton SKEL WN8.....17 E4
Woodbrook Dr
  WGNS/IIMK WN3.....33 E4
Woodchurch WGN WN1.....3 J2
Woodcock Dr WGNE/HIN WN2..49 G1
Woodcote Gv AIMK WN4 *.....47 G5
Wood Cottage Cl WALK M28 ..41 E5
Woodcourt WGNS/IIMK WN3 ..34 A2
Woodcroft SKEL WN8.....17 E5
  WGNNW/ST WN6.....8 D4
Wooddagger Cl
  WGNE/HIN WN2.....36 C3
Woodedge AIMK WN4.....60 D3
Woodfield Crs AIMK WN4.....60 D3
Woodfield Dr WALK M28.....55 G5
Woodfield Gv FWTH BL4.....41 H2
Woodfield St WGNE/HIN WN2..23 F2
Woodford Cl GOL/RIS/CU WA3..71 E2
Woodford St WGNE/HIN WN2..36 D2
  WGNW/BIL/O WN5.....33 G2
Woodgarth LEIGH WN7 *.....64 B1
Woodgreen Cl WGNE/HIN WN2..36 A4
Woodhead Gv
  WGNS/IIMK WN3.....48 A1
Woodhouse Dr
  WGNNW/ST WN6.....21 F2
Woodhouse La
  WGNNW/ST WN6.....21 F2
Woodhouse St ATH M46.....53 E1
Woodhurst Dr
  WGNNW/ST WN6.....21 H5
Woodland Av NEWLW WA12 *..76 A1
  WGNE/HIN WN2.....37 E3
Woodland Dr AIMK WN4.....61 E1
  LEIGH WN7.....65 H4
Woodland Gv WGN WN1.....3 F1
Woodland Rd TYLD M29.....54 C2
Woodlands Av LEIGH WN7.....65 E5
  WGNS/IIMK WN3.....35 E2
Woodlands Dr ATH M46.....38 D5
  WGNE/HIN WN2.....20 A1
Woodlands Pk NEWLW WA12 *..61 F5
The Woodlands HOR/BR BL6..15 H2
  WGN WN1.....22 C2
Woodley Gv LEIGH WN7.....64 A4
Woodley Park Rd SKEL WN8 ..17 G1
Woodnook Rd WGNNW/ST WN6..8 D2
Woodrow SKEL WN8.....16 D5
Woodrush Rd
  WGNNW/ST WN6.....21 H5
Woodshaw Gv WALK M28.....55 H3
Woodside Av AIMK WN4.....47 H5
Woodside Cl SKEL WN8.....19 F5
Woodside Rd
  RNFD/HAY WA11.....43 F2
Woodside Vw ATH M46.....39 F3
Wood's La AIMK WN4.....61 F2
Wood Sorrel Wy
  GOL/RIS/CU WA3.....71 F1
Woods Rd WGNE/HIN WN2.....23 H1
Wood's St WGNS/IIMK WN3 ...34 B7
Woodstock Cl LEIGH WN7.....65 E5
Wood St ATH M46.....38 C4
  GOL/RIS/CU WA3.....54 A3
  TYLD M29.....54 A3
  WGNE/HIN WN1.....37 E5
  WGNS/IIMK WN3.....33 C1
  WGNW/BIL/O WN5.....33 C1
  WHTN BL5.....26 D3
Woodvale Av ATH M46.....38 C5
  WGNE/HIN WN2.....36 B5
Woodvale Dr
  GOL/RIS/CU WA3.....63 F5
Wood Vw WGNNW/ST WN6......9 F5
Woodville Rd
  WGNS/IIMK WN3.....35 E4
Woodwards Rd WHTN BL5.....37 H2
Woodyates St
  WGNW/BIL/O WN5.....33 C2
Woolden St WGNNW/ST WN6..9 G5
Wooler Gv WGNE/HIN WN2 ...50 A1
Woolston Dr TYLD M29.....54 B3

Woolston Rd RNFD/HAY WA11..68 A3
Woolton Cl AIMK WN4.....60 C1
Worcester Av
  GOL/RIS/CU WA3 *.....70 C1
  WGNE/HIN WN2.....36 C2
Wordsworth Av ATH M46.....39 E3
  FWTH BL4.....41 G1
  WGN WN1.....51 G4
  WGN WN1.....22 B2
  WGNW/BIL/O WN5.....32 A2
  WGNW/BIL/O WN5.....45 G2
Wordsworth Rd LHULT M38...41 F3
Worsbrough Av WALK M28.....55 H1
Worsley Av WALK M28.....55 F1
Worsley Cl
  WGNW/BIL/O WN5 *.....32 D3
Worsley Gn
  WGNW/BIL/O WN5.....32 C5
Worsley Gv WALK M28.....55 F1
Worsley Mesnes Dr
  WGNS/IIMK WN3.....33 H3
Worsley Rd BOLS/LL BL3.....27 H1
Worsley St GOL/RIS/CU WA3..70 B1
  WGNW/BIL/O WN5.....32 C3
Worsley Ter WGN WN1 *.....2 D3
Worthing Gv ATH M46.....38 C5
Worthington St
  WGNE/HIN WN2.....36 A2
Worthington Wy
  WGNS/IIMK WN3.....47 H1
Wotton Dr AIMK WN4.....61 G3
Wraxhall Crs LEIGH WN7.....51 C4
Wray St WGN WN1.....3 H5
Wrenbury Cl
  WGNW/BIL/O WN5.....32 C3
Wren Cl WGNW/BIL/O WN5.....20 C4
Wrenswood Dr WALK M28.....55 H3
Wrightington St WGN WN1......2 C2
Wright St AIMK WN4.....47 C5
  WGN WN1.....35 F5
  WGNE/HIN WN2.....49 C4
Wrigley Rd RNFD/HAY WA11..68 B3
Wrington Cl LEIGH WN7.....51 C4
Wyatt Cv AIMK WN4.....61 C3
Wycliffe Rd RNFD/HAY WA11..68 B2
Wycombe Dr TYLD M29.....54 A4
Wykeham Cl WGNS/IIMK WN3..35 E2
Wynard Av WGN WN1.....3 F5
Wyndham Av BOLS/LL BL3.....27 H1
Wynne St LHULT M38.....41 F3
  TYLD M29.....53 C2
Wynton Cl LEIGH WN7.....64 D4
Wyre Av WGNE/HIN WN2.....49 F1
Wyre Dr WALK M28.....55 C4
Wyrevale Gv AIMK WN4.....61 F3
Wythall Av LHULT M38.....41 C2

Y

Yarn Cft TYLD M29.....54 A4
Yarrow St WGNE/HIN WN2 .....35 A4
Yates Dr WALK M28.....41 F5
Yates Gv WGNNW/ST WN6.....21 G1
Yates St LEIGH WN7.....51 G4
  WGNS/IIMK WN3.....33 H1
Yeadon SKEL WN8.....17 C4
Yealand Gv WGNE/HIN WN2..36 D3
Yellow Brook Cl
  WGNE/HIN WN2.....12 D4
Yellow Lodge Dr WHTN BL5...26 C4
Yewbarrow Cl TYLD M29.....54 A4
Yewdale SKEL WN8.....17 F4
  WGNNW/ST WN6.....9 C4
Yewdale Av RNFD/HAY WA11..58 A5
Yewdale Crs WGN WN1.....22 A3
Yewdale Rd AIMK WN4.....47 H4
Yewdale WGNNW/ST WN6 .....21 C2
Yewtree Av ATH M46.....38 D4
Yew Tree Av NEWLW WA12....68 D5
Yew Tree Dr HOR/BR BL6.....15 C4
Yew Tree Wy
  GOL/RIS/CU WA3.....70 C2
York Av TYLD M29.....53 C1
York Chambers WGN WN1 *.....2 C3
York Rd AIMK WN4.....61 F4
  WGNE/HIN WN2.....36 C3
York Rd South AIMK WN4.....61 F4
Yorke St ATH M46.....39 E5
  GOL/RIS/CU WA3.....62 A2
  LEIGH WN7.....66 A2
Youd St LEIGH WN7.....64 D1
Young St LEIGH WN7.....66 B2
Yvonne Cl AIMK WN4.....61 C1

Index - featured places

Abbey Lakes Sports Centre
  WGNW/BIL/O WN5.....31 G1
Abraham Guest High School
  WGNW/BIL/O WN5.....32 B2
Abram Bryn Gates
  Primary School
  WGNE/HIN WN2.....49 E4
Abram CE Primary School
  WGNE/HIN WN2.....49 G1
Acorn Business Centre
  LEIGH WN7.....65 G2
Adlington CC
  CHLY/EC PR7.....7 F1
Alexander House
  Health Centre
  WGNE/HIN WN2.....35 G5

All Saints RC Primary School
  GOL/RIS/CU WA3.....70 C1
AMF Bowling
  WGNS/IIMK WN3.....2 B6
Appley Bridge All Saints CE
  Primary School
  WGNNW/ST WN6.....8 B1
Ashton Grange Industrial
  Estate AIMK WN4.....48 A5
Ashton-in-Makerfield
  Golf Club
  AIMK WN4.....60 B4
Ashton Leisure Centre
  AIMK WN4.....60 D2
Ashton Medical Centre
  AIMK WN4.....60 D1

Ashton Town AFC
  AIMK WN4.....61 G2
Ashurst Health Centre
  SKEL WN8.....17 G1
Aspull Clinic
  WGNE/HIN WN2.....12 D5
Aspull Holy Family RCP School
  WGNE/HIN WN2.....23 H1
Atherton Industrial Centre
  ATH M46.....39 E4
Atherton Public Baths
  ATH M46.....38 D5
Bag Lane Industrial Estate
  ATH M46.....38 D4
Beacon Country Park
  HOR/BR BL6.....18 C4

Beacon Park Public Golf Centre
  SKEL WN8.....18 B2
Beacon School
  SKEL WN8.....18 B5
Beaumont Hospital
  HOR/BR BL6.....15 G2
Bedford Hall Methodist Primary
  WGNE/HIN WN2.....23 G3
Bedford High School
  LEIGH WN7.....65 G3
Beech Hill Primary School
  WGNS/IIMK WN3.....21 H2
Bee Fold Medical Centre
  ATH M46.....52 C1
Bee Hive Industrial Estate
  HOR/BR BL6.....14 D5

Bel-Air Hotel
  WGN WN1.....22 B1
Belle Green Industrial Estate
  WGNE/HIN WN2.....23 F5
Bickershaw CE Primary School
  WGNE/HIN WN2.....50 C3
Billinge Chapel End Primary
  School WGNW/BIL/O WN5..58 D2
Billinge Clinic
  WGNW/BIL/O WN5.....58 D2
Billinge Hospital
  WGNW/BIL/O WN5.....45 G1
Birchley St Marys RC Primary
  School WGNW/BIL/O WN5..58 C2
Birleywood Health Centre
  SKEL WN8.....30 A2

Bishop Martin CE Primary
School *SKEL* WN8 ....30 A1
Bispham Hall Business Park
WGNW/BIL/O WN5 ....45 F1
Black Moss School
SKEL WN8 ....16 C3
Blackrod Church School
HOR/BR BL6 ....7 H5
Blackrod Primary School
HOR/BR BL6 ....13 F2
Bolton Golf Club
HOR/BR BL6 ....15 F2
Bolton Road Industrial Estate
WHTN BL5 ....26 A4
Bolton Running Track
HOR/BR BL6 ....14 B3
Bolton Sports Arena
HOR/BR BL6 ....14 B3
Bolton Wanderers FC (Reebok
Stadium)
HOR/BR BL6 ....14 C3
Boothstown Methodist School
WALK M28 ....55 E5
Borron Road Industrial Estate
NEWLW WA12 ....69 F5
Brackley Municipal Golf Club
LHULT M38 ....40 D2
Bradley Hall Trading Estate
WGNNW/ST WN6 ....5 F1
Bridgewater Primary School
LHULT M38 ....41 H4
Britannia Bridge Primary
School *WGNS/IIMK* WN5 ....34 D2
Brookfield High School
WGNE/HIN WN2 ....36 B4
Brookfields Primary School
SKEL WN8 ....16 C3
Brook Lodge Primary School
RNFD/HAY WA11 ....43 E3
Brook Mill Medical Centre
LEIGH WN7 ....65 F1
Byrchall High School
AIMK WN4 ....61 E5
Cansfield High School
AIMK WN4 ....60 D2
Carr Mill Junior School
RNFD/HAY WA11 ....58 B5
Chanters Industrial Estate
ATH M46 ....53 C1
Chowbent Primary School
ATH M46 ....39 F5
Christ Church Pennington CE
Primary School
LEIGH WN7 ....65 E2
Claypool Primary School
HOR/BR BL6 ....14 D1
Clegqs Lane Industrial Site
LHULT M38 ....41 G2
Clough Fold Primary School
SKEL WN8 ....17 H3
Cobbs Brow Primary School
SKEL WN8 ....17 F2
College Street Health Centre
LEIGH WN7 ....65 E1
Collier Brook Industrial Estate
ATH M46 ....38 D5
Comtech Business Park
WHTN BL5 ....25 H2
Concourse Shopping Centre
SKEL WN8 ....17 G4
Corpus Christi Primary School
RNFD/HAY WA11 ....43 E4
Crawford Village Primary
School *SKEL* WN8 ....30 B5
The Cricketer Sports Club
WGNS/IIMK WN3 ....34 A3
Cricket Street Business Centre
WGNW/ST WN6 ....21 H5
Crow Orchard Primary School
SKEL WN8 ....17 E3
Deane Leisure Centre
BOLS/LL BL3 ....27 G1
Deanery CE High School
WGN WN1 ....2 B4
The Deane School
BOLS/LL BL3 ....27 G1
Dean Wood Golf Club
SKEL WN8 ....19 F5
Delph Side Primary School
SKEL WN8 ....17 G5
De Vere Whites Hotel
HOR/BR BL6 ....14 C3
Diamond Business Park
RNFD/HAY WA11 ....56 C2
Dobson Park Industrial Estate
WGNE/HIN WN2 ....35 F2
Dodd Lane Industrial Estate
WHTN BL5 ....25 E1
Douglas Valley Business Park
WGN WN1 ....11 F5
Dukesgate Primary School
LHULT M38 ....41 F3
East Gillbrands Industrial
Estate *SKEL* WN8 ....29 F1
Eatock Primary School
WHTN BL5 ....37 H2
Ellenbrook Primary School
WALK M28 ....55 G4
Ellesmere Retail Park
WALK M28 ....41 H5
Ellesmere Shopping Centre
LHULT M38 ....55 F2
Elmers Green CP School
SKEL WN8 ....18 A4
Empress Industrial Estate
WGNE/HIN WN2 ....3 J6
English Martyrs RC Primary
School *RNFD/HAY* WA11 ....68 A2
Fairfield Hospital
RNFD/HAY WA11 ....57 F4
Fairlie CP School
SKEL WN8 ....30 A5
Fall Birch Hospital Lodge
HOR/BR BL6 ....15 F1
Farnworth Social Circle CC
FWTH BL4 ....41 H1

Firsdale Industrial Estate
LEIGH WN7 ....51 F5
Fishwicks Industrial Estate
RNFD/HAY WA11 ....68 C1
Foyer & Coops Business Centre
WGN WN1 ....2 B5
Fred Longworth High School
TYLD M29 ....53 F2
The Galleries Shopping Centre
WGN WN1 ....2 C4
Garrett Hall Primary School
TYLD M29 ....54 C4
Garswood Primary School
AIMK WN4 ....59 H2
Garswood United FC
AIMK WN4 ....59 G1
The Gates Primary School
WHTN BL5 ....26 A3
Gathurst Golf Club
WGNNW/ST WN6 ....9 E5
Gidlow Cemetery
WGNNW/ST WN6 ....10 D5
Gilded Hollins Primary School
LEIGH WN7 ....64 B5
Glazebury CE Primary School
GOL/RIS/CU WA3 ....73 H2
Glenburn High School
SKEL WN8 ....17 F5
Golborne Clinic
GOL/RIS/CU WA3 ....62 C5
Golborne CP School
GOL/RIS/CU WA3 ....70 B1
Golborne High School
GOL/RIS/CU WA3 ....62 D5
Grange Valley Primary School
RNFD/HAY WA11 ....68 A4
Grasmere Street Health Centre
LEIGH WN7 ....51 H5
Greenbank Industrial Estate
WGNE/HIN WN2 ....36 D5
Green Hall Primary School
AIMK WN4 ....39 G4
Haigh Hall Country Park
WGN WN1 ....12 A4
Haigh Hall Golf Complex
WGNE/HIN WN2 ....12 A4
Hallgate Bus Station
WGN WN1 ....2 C4
Hall Green Clinic
SKEL WN8 ....31 E1
Harrop Fold High School
WALK M28 ....55 C1
Hart Common Golf Club
WHTN BL5 ....37 E1
Haslemere Industrial Estate
WGNS/IIMK WN3 ....47 H3
Hawkley Brook Trading Estate
WGNS/IIMK WN3 ....47 F1
Hawkley Hall High School
WGNS/IIMK WN3 ....34 A5
Haydock CC
RNFD/HAY WA11 ....68 A2
Haydock Lane Industrial Estate
RNFD/HAY WA11 ....68 B1
Haydock Medical Centre
RNFD/HAY WA11 ....68 A3
Haydock Park Golf Club
NEWLW WA12 ....70 A4
Haydock Park Racecourse
NEWLW WA12 ....61 F5
Hazel Business Park
RNFD/HAY WA11 ....56 D2
Heathfield Primary School
BOLS/LL BL3 ....27 H3
Hesketh Fletcher CE High
School *ATH* M46 ....52 D1
Hewitt Business Park
RNFD/HAY WA11 ....31 H4
Higher Folds Primary School
LEIGH WN7 ....53 E4
Highfield CE Primary School
WGNS/IIMK WN3 ....32 D4
Highfield CC
WGNS/IIMK WN3 ....32 D4
Highlea Secondary School
WALK M28 ....55 E3
Hillside Health Centre
SKEL WN8 ....17 H4
Hilton Lane Primary School
WALK M28 ....41 F5
Hindley All Saints CEP School
WGNE/HIN WN2 ....36 B3
Hindley Business Centre
WGNE/HIN WN2 ....36 A3
Hindley Green Primary
School
WGNE/HIN WN2 ....51 E1
Hindley Hall Golf Club
WGNE/HIN WN2 ....24 A5
Hindley High School
WGNE/HIN WN2 ....36 C3
Hindley Leisure Centre
WGNE/HIN WN2 ....36 C4
Hindley Primary School
WGNE/HIN WN2 ....36 B3
Hindsford Primary School
ATH M46 ....53 F2
HM Prison
WGNE/HIN WN2 ....50 A1
Holden Road Trading Estate
LEIGH WN7 ....65 F1
Holland Business Park
BRSC L40 ....16 B1
Holland Moor Primary School
SKEL WN8 ....30 B1
Hollins Primary School
WGNE/HIN WN2 ....36 D3
Hollywood Bowl
HOR/BR BL6 ....14 C2
Holy Family RC Primary School
WALK M28 ....49 F2
Hope Special School
WGNE/HIN WN2 ....36 C3
Houghwood Golf Club
WGNW/BIL/O WN5 ....45 E4

Howe Bridge Crematorium
LEIGH WN7 ....52 A2
Howe Bridge Sports Centre
ATH M46 ....52 C2
Hulton Hospital
BOLS/LL BL3 ....27 H2
Ince CE Primary School
WGNE/HIN WN2 ....35 F1
Ince Clinic & Community Centre
WGNE/HIN WN2 ....35 F1
Innkeeper's Lodge Warrington
GOL/RIS/CU WA3 ....71 F3
International Swimming Pool
WGN WN1 ....2 D6
James Brindley Primary School
WALK M28 ....55 H2
John Street Medical Centre
GOL/RIS/CU WA3 ....70 B1
Kilhey Court Hotel
WGN WN1 ....6 B5
Kingsdown High School
WGNW/BIL/O WN5 ....32 D1
Kingshill School
TYLD M29 ....53 G3
Kirkfield Hotel
WGNE/HIN WN2 ....69 H5
Kirkless Industrial Estate
WGNE/HIN WN2 ....23 F3
Lamberhead Green Primary
School *WGNW/BIL/O* WN5 ....32 B1
Lamberhead Industrial Estate
WGNW/BIL/O WN5 ....32 B1
Landgate Industrial Estate
AIMK WN4 ....47 H3
Lathom High School
SKEL WN8 ....17 E2
Leigh Business Park
LEIGH WN7 ....65 G3
Leigh CC
LEIGH WN7 ....64 D4
Leigh CE Infant School
LEIGH WN7 ....65 E1
Leigh CE Junior School
LEIGH WN7 ....65 E1
Leigh Central Primary School
LEIGH WN7 ....65 E1
Leigh Centurions RLFC
LEIGH WN7 ....51 H5
Leigh County Court
LEIGH WN7 ....65 E1
Leigh FC
LEIGH WN7 ....51 H5
Leigh Golf Club
GOL/RIS/CU WA3 ....72 C5
Leigh Infirmary
LEIGH WN7 ....52 B4
Leigh Rangers ARLFC
LEIGH WN7 ....66 A2
Leigh RUFC
LEIGH WN7 ....64 D5
Little Digmoor Primary School
SKEL WN8 ....29 G2
Little Theatre
TYLD M29 ....53 G3
Lockett Business Park
RNFD/HAY WA11 ....61 F1
Longshoot Health Centre
WGN WN1 ....3 F3
Lostock Industrial Estate
HOR/BR BL6 ....14 D3
Lostock Primary School
HOR/BR BL6 ....15 H4
Low Hall Primary School
WGNE/HIN WN2 ....35 F5
Lowton Business Park
GOL/RIS/CU WA3 ....71 H1
Lowton High School
GOL/RIS/CU WA3 ....72 A1
Lowton J & I School
GOL/RIS/CU WA3 ....71 H2
Lowton St Marys CE Primary
School *GOL/RIS/CU* WA3 ....71 H1
Lowton West Primary School
GOL/RIS/CU WA3 ....70 D1
Lyme Community Primary
School *NEWLW* WA12 ....68 C5
Mabs Cross Primary School
WGN WN1 ....2 C2
Markgate Shopping Centre
WGNE/HIN WN2 ....2 C4
Market Hall
SKEL WN8 ....17 G4
WGN WN1 ....2 C5
Market Street Medical Centre
WGNE/HIN WN2 ....36 A2
Marsh Green CP School
WGNW/BIL/O WN5 ....21 E5
Marsh Green Health Centre
WGNW/BIL/O WN5 ....21 E4
Marston Bentley Industrial
Estate *WGNE/HIN* WN2 ....23 G3
Martland Mill Business Park
WGNW/BIL/O WN5 ....21 E3
Martland Mill Industrial Estate
WGNW/BIL/O WN5 ....20 D3
Marus Bridge Health Centre
WGNS/IIMK WN3 ....47 G1
Marus Bridge School
WGNS/IIMK WN3 ....47 F1
Mason Street Industrial
Estate
WGNS/IIMK WN3 ....2 A6
Mayflower Brewery
WGN WN1 ....2 D3
Maypole Industrial Estate
WGNE/HIN WN2 ....49 H4
Meadow Bank Primary School
ATH M46 ....38 D4
Mere Oaks School
WGN WN1 ....11 E5
Middlebrook Retail & Leisure
Park *HOR/BR* BL6 ....14 C2
Millbrook Business Centre
RNFD/HAY WA11 ....56 D3
Millbrook Primary School
WGNNW/ST WN6 ....9 G4

Millingford Industrial Estate
GOL/RIS/CU WA3 ....70 C1
Montrose School
WGNW/BIL/O WN5 ....33 E1
Moorside Primary School
SKEL WN8 ....30 B1
Mornington High School
WGNE/HIN WN2 ....36 C3
Moss Industrial Estate
LEIGH WN7 ....64 A5
Mossy Lea Primary School
WGNNW/ST WN6 ....4 A1
Newton Bank Preparatory
School *NEWLW* WA12 ....69 H5
Newton Health Clinic
NEWLW WA12 ....69 E5
Newton-le-Willows Community
High School *NEWLW* WA12 ....69 G4
Newton-le-Willows Sports Club
NEWLW WA12 ....69 F4
Newton Westpark Primary
School *LEIGH* WN7 ....51 F3
Nicol Mere School
AIMK WN4 ....60 D1
Norley Hall CC
WGNW/BIL/O WN5 ....32 C1
North Quarry Business Park
WGNW/ST WN6 ....8 C1
North Walkden Primary School
WALK M28 ....41 H3
Nugent House School
WGNW/BIL/O WN5 ....58 C2
Nye Bevan Swimming Pool
SKEL WN8 ....17 G4
Oakhill Trading Estate
LHULT M38 ....41 G3
Old Boston Trading Estate
RNFD/HAY WA11 ....68 D1
Orrell Clinic
WGNW/BIL/O WN5 ....31 H1
Orrell Newfold CP School
WGNW/BIL/O WN5 ....31 G5
Orrell RUFC
WGNW/BIL/O WN5 ....31 H3
Orrell Water Park
WGNW/BIL/O WN5 ....31 H4
Our Lady Immaculate RC
Primary School
AIMK WN4 ....47 F5
Our Lady of the Rosary RC
Primary School *LEIGH* WN7 ...64 A1
Our Lady Queen of Peace RC
High School *SKEL* WN8 ....17 E1
Our Lady RC Primary School
WGNE/HIN WN2 ....12 D5
Our Lady & St Lancashire
Martyrs RC Primary School
WALK M28 ....41 F5
Pagefield Industrial Estate
WGNW/BIL/O WN5 ....21 G4
Paragon Business Park
WGNE/HIN WN2 ....14 D2
Park Business Centre
WGNE/HIN WN2 ....36 A4
Park Industrial Estate
AIMK WN4 ....60 B3
Parklee Primary School
ATH M46 ....52 D1
Parochial CE Primary School
WHTN BL5 ....25 H5
Parsonage Retail Park
LEIGH WN7 ....51 H5
Peel Hall CP School
LHULT M38 ....41 E5
Pemberton Business Centre
WGNW/BIL/O WN5 ....33 E2
Pemberton Clinic
WGNW/BIL/O WN5 ....33 E2
Pemberton Primary School
WGNW/BIL/O WN5 ....32 D2
Pennington Flash Country
Park *LEIGH* WN7 ....64 B4
Pepper Mill Business Park
LEIGH WN7 ....2 E6
Pioneer Industrial Estate
WGNE/HIN WN2 ....33 F2
Platt Bridge Clinic
WGNE/HIN WN2 ....49 F1
Premier Lodge
AIMK WN4 ....61 E4
WGNW/ST WN6 ....9 G1
Prestwich Industrial Estate
ATH M46 ....38 C4
Prospect House Medical Centre
WGNE/HIN WN2 ....36 A3
Prospect Industrial Estate
WGNE/HIN WN2 ....36 A3
The Quadrangle Business
Centre *WGNE/HIN* WN2 ....37 E4
Quality Hotel
SKEL WN8 ....30 C3
Rainford CE Primary School
RNFD/HAY WA11 ....43 E5
Rainford Health Centre
RNFD/HAY WA11 ....43 F5
Rainford High Technology
College *RNFD/HAY* WA11 ......43 F3
Rainford Industrial Estate
RNFD/HAY WA11 ....43 E5
Rectory CE Primary School
NEWLW WA12 ....60 A1
Reebok Museum
HOR/BR BL6 ....14 C2
Regent Park Golf Course
HOR/BR BL6 ....15 G3
RL Hughes Primary School
AIMK WN4 ....60 D3
Robin Park Arena
WGNW/BIL/O WN5 ....21 G5
Robin Park Sports Centre
WGNW/BIL/O WN5 ....21 G5
Roby Mill CE Primary School
SKEL WN8 ....19 E2
Rose Bridge High School
WGN WN1 ....3 J4

Ross Business Centre
WGNW/BIL/O WN5 ....33 E3
Royal Albert Edward Infirmary
ATH M46 ....22 B3
Sacred Heart RC Primary
LEIGH WN7 ....64 D1
WGNE/HIN WN1 ....37 E5
WGNNW/ST WN6 ....21 G5
WHTN BL5 ....26 A4
St Aelreds RC Technology
College *NEWLW* WA12 ....69 C5
St Aidans CE Primary School
WGNW/BIL/O WN5 ....58 D1
St Aidans RC Primary School
WGNS/IIMK WN3 ....47 E1
St Ambrose Barlow RC Primary
School *TYLD* M29 ....66 D1
St Andrews CE Primary School
SKEL WN8 ....21 C3
WHTN BL5 ....27 H5
St Andrews Methodist
Primary School
WALK M28 ....41 G5
St Annes CE Primary School
LEIGH WN7 ....21 E2
St Benedicts RC Primary
School *WGNE/HIN* WN2 ....35 H2
St Bernadettes Catholic
Primary School
WGNNW/ST WN6 ....9 F4
St Catharines CE Primary
School *WGN* WN1 ....3 G5
St Catherines RC Primary
School *GOL/RIS/CU* WA3 ....71 F1
St Cuthberts RC Primary
School *WGNW/BIL/O* WN5 ....33 E2
St Davids CE Primary School
WGNE/HIN WN2 ....12 C3
St Edmund Arrowsmith RC
High School *AIMK* WN4 ....60 D4
St Edmunds Catholic Primary
School *SKEL* WN8 ....17 E4
St Edmunds RC Primary School
LHULT M38 ....41 G4
St Edwards Catholic Primary
School *WGNW/BIL/O* WN5 ....33 C1
St Gabriels RC Primary School
LEIGH WN7 ....53 F4
St Georges Central CE Primary
School
TYLD M29 ....53 H2
St Georges CE Primary School
ATH M46 ....38 C4
WGNW/BIL/O WN5 ....37 C1
St George's RC Secondary
School *WALK* M28 ....55 H1
St Helens Community College
NEWLW WA12 ....69 E5
St James CE Primary School
WGNS/IIMK WN3 ....33 G3
WHTN BL5 ....38 A3
St James Catholic Primary
School *WGNW/BIL/O* WN5 ....31 G4
St James Primary School
FWTH BL4 ....41 G1
RNFD/HAY WA11 ....68 B3
St James RC Primary School
WGN WN1 ....17 G1
St John Fisher Catholic High
School *WGNW/ST* WN6 ....21 G2
St John Rigby College
WGNW/BIL/O WN5 ....20 A3
St John Southworth RC J&I
School *AIMK* WN4 ....61 G2
St Johns CE Infant School
LEIGH WN7 ....52 A5
St Johns CE J & I School
WGNE/HIN WN2 ....23 E2
WGNW/BIL/O WN5 ....23 F5
St Johns CE Primary School
WGNW/BIL/O WN5 ....32 C2
St Johns Mosley Common CE
Primary School *WALK* M28 .....55 E5
St Johns RC Primary School
SKEL WN8 ....17 H4
St Josephs Catholic Primary
School *WGNNW/ST* WN6 ....4 A4
St Josephs RC Primary School
LEIGH WN7 ....65 F2
LHULT M38 ....41 F3
St Josephs RC School
HOR/BR BL6 ....14 D1
St Judes Catholic Primary
School *WGNS/IIMK* WN3 ....33 G3
St Lukes CE Primary School
GOL/RIS/CU WA3 ....71 F2
St Lukes RC Primary School
SKEL WN8 ....30 B2
St Marks RC Primary School
WGNNW/ST WN6 ....5 F5
St Marks Catholic Primary
School *SKEL* WN8 ....18 B5
St Marks CE Primary School
WGNW/BIL/O WN5 ....33 C1
St Mary CE Primary School
WGN WN1 ....27 C1
St Mary & Johns RC Primary
School *WGN* WN1 ....2 E3
St Marys Catholic Junior
School *NEWLW* WA12 ....69 C5
St Marys Catholic Primary
School *SKEL* WN8 ....69 F5
St Marys CE J & I School
WGNS/IIMK WN3 ....35 E4
St Marys RC High School
TYLD M29 ....66 D2
St Matthews RC Primary
School *AIMK* WN4 ....30 A1
St Michaels CE Primary Howe
Bridge School
ATH M46 ....52 C1
St Nathaniels CE Primary
School *WGN* WN1 ....35 G5
St Oswalds RC J & I School
AIMK WN4 ....61 E3

St Patricks RC Primary School
WGN WN1 ....3 F5
St Pauls CE Primary School
WGNS/IIMK WN3 ....33 G5
St Pauls Peel CE
Primary School
LHULT M38 ....41 E3
St Peters Catholic
High School
WGNW/BIL/O WN5 ....32 A1
St Peters CE Infant School
LEIGH WN7 ....64 B1
St Peters CE Junior School
LEIGH WN7 ....64 B1
St Peters CE Primary School
AIMK WN4 ....47 G5
WGNE/HIN WN2 ....35 H3
St Peter's CE Primary School
NEWLW WA12 ....69 G5
St Philips CE Primary School
ATH M46 ....39 F5
St Richards Catholic Primary
School *SKEL* WN8 ....16 B4
St Richards RC Primary School
ATH M46 ....38 D4
St Stephens CE Primary School
TYLD M29 ....54 A5
WGN WN1 ....3 G1
St Teresas Catholic Primary
School *SKEL* WN8 ....19 E4
St Thomas CE Primary School
AIMK WN4 ....61 F3
GOL/RIS/CU WA3 ....62 C5
LEIGH WN7 ....65 G2
WHTN BL5 ....26 C4
St Thomas More Catholic High
School *WGNW/BIL/O* WN5 ......33 G1
St Thomas the Martyr CE
Primary School *SKEL* WN8 ....31 E1
St Wilfrids CE Primary School
WGNW/ST WN6 ....10 C1
St Williams RC Primary School
WGNE/HIN WN2 ....3 K7
Sandy Lane Health Centre
SKEL WN8 ....16 C4
Scholes Shopping Precinct
WGN WN1 ....3 F4
Scot Lane End CE Primary
School *HOR/BR* BL6 ....13 F2

Scot Lane Industrial Estate
HOR/BR BL6 ....13 F4
Scot Lane Primary School
WGNW/BIL/O WN5 ....33 G1
Seven Brooks Medical Centre
ATH M46 ....39 E5
Shakerley CE Primary School
TYLD M29 ....53 H1
Shevington CP School
WGNNW/ST WN6 ....9 E4
Shevington Vale Primary
School *WGNNW/ST* WN6 ......8 D2
Skelmersdale College
(Northway Centre)
SKEL WN8 ....17 G4
Skelmersdale College
(Westbank Centre)
SKEL WN8 ....17 G5
Skelmersdale Park Primary
School *SKEL* WN8 ....16 D4
Skelmersdale Sports Centre
SKEL WN8 ....29 H1
Skelmersdale United FC
SKEL WN8 ....16 B5
South Lancashire Industrial
Estate *AIMK* WN4 ....48 A5
Southside Industrial Park
ATH M46 ....38 C4
Sovereign Business Park
WGN WN1 ....3 F7
Spinning Gate Shopping
Centre
LEIGH WN7 ....65 E1
Springbank Industrial Estate
WGNE/HIN WN2 ....35 G5
Spring View CC
WGNE/HIN WN2 ....3 F7
Standish Clinic
WGNNW/ST WN6 ....10 B2
Standish Community High
School *WGNNW/ST* WN6 ......4 D5
Standish Court Golf Club
WGNNW/ST WN6 ....10 C1
Standish CC
WGNNW/ST WN6 ....10 B2
Stone Cross Business Park
GOL/RIS/CU WA3 ....70 C2
Stone Hill Industrial Estate
FWTH BL4 ....41 H1

Summersales Industrial Estate
WGNS/IIMK WN3 ....32 C4
Tanfield Special School
WGNE/HIN WN2 ....36 C3
Three Sisters Racing Circuit
AIMK WN4 ....48 B4
Towngate Business Centre
LHULT M38 ....40 D3
Travel Inn
GOL/RIS/CU WA3 ....70 C2
HOR/BR BL6 ....15 E2
WGNS/IIMK WN3 ....47 G2
WGNW/BIL/O WN5 ....32 A1
Travelodge
RNFD/HAY WA11 ....68 B1
Trinity Primary School
SKEL WN8 ....16 D4
Tweed Street Industrial Estate
LEIGH WN7 ....65 G2
Twelve Apostles RC Primary
School *LEIGH* WN7 ....51 G3
Twiss Green Primary School
GOL/RIS/CU WA3 ....72 D5
Two Porches School
ATH M46 ....39 E5
Tyldesley Cemetery
TYLD M29 ....54 C3
Tyldesley Primary School
TYLD M29 ....54 A4
Tyldesley Swimming Pool
TYLD M29 ....53 F2
UGC Cinema
WGNW/BIL/O WN5 ....21 G5
Up Holland High School
WGNW/BIL/O WN5 ....31 F4
Victoria Industrial Estate
LEIGH WN7 ....51 H5
Victoria Trading Estate
WGNS/IIMK WN3 ....2 A6
VUE Cinema
HOR/BR BL6 ....14 C2
Warrington Road Industrial
Estate *WGNS/IIMK* WN3 ......33 F3
Washacre Primary School
WHTN BL5 ....38 A1
Waterside Trading Estate
LEIGH WN7 ....65 G2
West Gillbrands Industrial Estate
SKEL WN8 ....28 D1

Westhoughton CC
WHTN BL5 ....25 H5
Westhoughton Clinic
WHTN BL5 ....25 H5
Westhoughton Golf Club
WHTN BL5 ....25 G4
Westhoughton High School
WHTN BL5 ....26 A5
Westhoughton
Industrial Estate
WHTN BL5 ....25 H3
Westhoughton Primary School
WHTN BL5 ....26 A4
Westleigh CE (St Pauls)
Primary School
LEIGH WN7 ....51 H3
Westleigh CC
LEIGH WN7 ....64 C1
Westleigh High School
LEIGH WN7 ....51 G2
Westleigh Methodist Primary
School *LEIGH* WN7 ....51 G3
Westwood Cemetery
WGNS/IIMK WN3 ....34 C3
Wharton Primary School
LHULT M38 ....40 D2
Wheatlea Industrial Estate
WGNS/IIMK WN3 ....47 G3
Whelley Hospital
WGN WN1 ....3 G1
Whiteledge Centre
SKEL WN8 ....17 G5
The Wiend Centre
WGN WN1 ....2 D5
Wigan Athletic FC & Wigan
Warriors RLFC (The JJB
Stadium)
WGNS/IIMK WN3 ....21 F5
Wigan Borough Cemetery
WGNS/IIMK WN3 ....34 C3
Wigan Crematorium
WGNS/IIMK WN3 ....34 C4
Wigan Golf Club
CHLY/EC PR7 ....6 C5
Wigan & Leigh College
WGN WN1 ....2 B3
Wigan & Leigh College &
Community Sixth
Form College *LEIGH* WN7 ....64 D3

Wigan Little Theatre
WGN WN1 ....2 E4
Wigan Magistrates Court
WGN WN1 ....2 E6
Wigan Pier
WGNS/IIMK WN3 ....2 A7
Wigan RUFC
WGN WN1 ....11 G5
Willow Grove School
AIMK WN4 ....61 H1
Wingates Industrial Estate
WHTN BL5 ....25 G2
Winstanley College
WGNW/BIL/O WN5 ....31 H5
Winstanley Medical Centre
WGNS/IIMK WN3 ....33 E5
Winstanley Primary School
WGNS/IIMK WN3 ....46 D1
Woodfield Primary School
WGN WN1 ....22 B1
Wood Fold Primary School
WGNNW/ST WN6 ....10 A2
Woodlands Hospital
WALK M28 ....41 F4
Woodlands Industrial Estate
NEWLW WA12 ....69 F3
Worsley Business Park
TYLD M29 ....55 E3
Worsley Mesnes Primary
School *WGNS/IIMK* WN3 .....33 H4
Worsley Road Industrial Estate
FWTH BL4 ....41 H2
Worsley Trading Estate
LHULT M38 ....40 D3
Worthington Lakes Business
Park *WGN* WN1 ....11 F2
Wrightington Hospital
WGNNW/ST WN6 ....8 D1
Wrightington Hotel
WGNNW/ST WN6 ....4 A4
Yew Tree Trading Estate
RNFD/HAY WA11 ....68 A1

Acknowledgements

The Post Office is a registered trademark of Post Office Ltd. in the UK and other countries.

Schools address data provided by Education Direct.

Petrol station information supplied by Johnsons

One-way street data provided by © Tele Atlas N.V. Tele Atlas

Garden centre information provided by

Garden Centre Association  Britains best garden centres

Wyevale Garden Centres

The statement on the front cover of this atlas is sourced, selected and quoted from a reader comment and feedback form received in 2004

Notes

Notes

AA Street by Street   QUESTIONNAIRE

Dear Atlas User
Your comments, opinions and recommendations are very important to us.
So please help us to improve our street atlases by taking a few minutes
to complete this simple questionnaire.

You do not need a stamp (unless posted outside the UK). If you do not want to remove
this page from your street atlas, then photocopy it or write your answers on a plain sheet
of paper.

Send to: The Editor, AA Street by Street, FREEPOST SCE 4598,
Basingstoke RG21 4GY

ABOUT THE ATLAS...

Which city/town/county did you buy?

Are there any features of the atlas or mapping that you find particularly useful?

Is there anything we could have done better?

Why did you choose an AA Street by Street atlas?

Did it meet your expectations?

Exceeded ☐   **Met all** ☐   **Met most** ☐   **Fell below** ☐

Please give your reasons

Where did you buy it?

For what purpose? (please tick all applicable)

To use in your own local area ☐   To use on business or at work ☐

Visiting a strange place ☐   In the car ☐   On foot ☐

Other (please state)

LOCAL KNOWLEDGE...

Local knowledge is invaluable. Whilst every attempt has been made to make the information contained in this atlas as accurate as possible, should you notice any inaccuracies, please detail them below (if necessary, use a blank piece of paper) or e-mail us at *streetbystreet@theAA.com*

ABOUT YOU...

Name (Mr/Mrs/Ms)

Address

Postcode

Daytime tel no   **Mobile tel no**

E-mail address

Please only give us your e-mail address and mobile phone number if you wish to hear from us about other products and services from the AA and partners by e-mail or text or mms.

Which age group are you in?

Under 25 ☐   25-34 ☐   35-44 ☐   45-54 ☐   55-64 ☐   65+ ☐

Are you an AA member?   YES ☐   NO ☐

Do you have Internet access?   YES ☐   NO ☐

The information we hold about you will be used to provide the product(s) and service(s) requested and for identification, account administration, analysis, and fraud/loss prevention purposes. More details about how that information is used is in our Privacy Statement, which you will find under the heading "Personal information" in our Terms and Conditions and on our website. Copies are available from us by post, by contacting our Data Protection Manager at AA, Fanum House, Basing View, Hampshire, Basingstoke RG21 4EA.

We may want to contact you about other products and services provided by us or our partners but please tick the box if you DO NOT wish to hear about such products and services from us by mail or telephone. ☐

Thank you for taking the time to complete this questionnaire. Please send it to us as soon as possible, and remember, you do not need a stamp (unless posted outside the UK).   ML201z